Bluegrass Banjo For Dummies®

by Bill Evans

Bluegrass Banjo For Dummies®

Published by: **John Wiley & Sons, Inc.,** 111 River Street, Hoboken, NJ 07030-5774, www.wiley.com

Copyright © 2015 by John Wiley & Sons, Inc., Hoboken, New Jersey

Media and software compilation copyright © 2015 by John Wiley & Sons, Inc. All rights reserved.

Published simultaneously in Canada

No part of this publication may be reproduced, stored in a retrieval system or transmitted in any form or by any means, electronic, mechanical, photocopying, recording, scanning or otherwise, except as permitted under Sections 107 or 108 of the 1976 United States Copyright Act, without the prior written permission of the Publisher. Requests to the Publisher for permission should be addressed to the Permissions Department, John Wiley & Sons, Inc., 111 River Street, Hoboken, NJ 07030, (201) 748-6011, fax (201) 748-6008, or online at http://www.wiley.com/go/permissions.

Trademarks: Wiley, For Dummies, the Dummies Man logo, Dummies.com, Making Everything Easier, and related trade dress are trademarks or registered trademarks of John Wiley & Sons, Inc., and may not be used without written permission. All other trademarks are the property of their respective owners. John Wiley & Sons, Inc., is not associated with any product or vendor mentioned in this book.

LIMIT OF LIABILITY/DISCLAIMER OF WARRANTY: WHILE THE PUBLISHER AND AUTHOR HAVE USED THEIR BEST EFFORTS IN PREPARING THIS BOOK, THEY MAKE NO REPRESENTATIONS OR WARRANTIES WITH RESPECT TO THE ACCURACY OR COMPLETENESS OF THE CONTENTS OF THIS BOOK AND SPECIFICALLY DISCLAIM ANY IMPLIED WARRANTIES OF MERCHANTABILITY OR FITNESS FOR A PARTICULAR PURPOSE. NO WARRANTY MAY BE CREATED OR EXTENDED BY SALES REPRESENTATIVES OR WRITTEN SALES MATERIALS. THE ADVICE AND STRATEGIES CONTAINED HEREIN MAY NOT BE SUITABLE FOR YOUR SITUATION. YOU SHOULD CONSULT WITH A PROFESSIONAL WHERE APPROPRIATE. NEITHER THE PUBLISHER NOR THE AUTHOR SHALL BE LIABLE FOR DAMAGES ARISING HEREFROM.

For general information on our other products and services, please contact our Customer Care Department within the U.S. at 877-762-2974, outside the U.S. at 317-572-3993, or fax 317-572-4002. For technical support, please visit www.wiley.com/techsupport.

Wiley publishes in a variety of print and electronic formats and by print-on-demand. Some material included with standard print versions of this book may not be included in e-books or in print-on-demand. If this book refers to media such as a CD or DVD that is not included in the version you purchased, you may download this material at http://booksupport.wiley.com. For more information about Wiley products, visit www.wiley.com.

Library of Congress Control Number: 2014957115

ISBN 978-1-119-00430-1 (pbk); ISBN 978-1-119-00429-5 (ebk); ISBN 978-1-119-00426-4 (ebk)

Manufactured in the United States of America

C10011890_070119

Contents at a Glance

Table of Contents

Introduction

● ●

You may have first heard the magnificent sound of bluegrass banjo
40 years ago in a movie or on TV. Or maybe you just heard it for the
first time recently, with its fast and furious flurry of notes sending the latest
acoustic rock anthem or country hit into musical overdrive. Now, you just
can't get it out of your head. Nothing inspires the musical imagination like the
banjo, and once you're hooked, sooner or later, you have to do something
about it.

If you're ready to take it to the next step, you've come to the right place!
Whether you're 8 or 80, and especially if you have no prior musical experience, *Bluegrass Banjo For Dummies* will help you unlock the secrets of great
banjo picking in bluegrass style. Whether you're a total newbie or an experienced player looking for fresh ideas and new techniques, get ready to have
more fun playing banjo than you ever thought possible. With the help of
Bluegrass Banjo For Dummies, you can achieve your banjo dreams!

About This Book

Bluegrass Banjo For Dummies is a step-by-step, practical guide to playing the
five-string banjo in the world's most popular and widely heard style. From
the music of Earl Scruggs to Béla Fleck and Mumford & Sons, the brilliantly
fast fingerpicking techniques that define bluegrass banjo are heard today not
just in bluegrass, folk, and country music, but in everything from jazz and
classical to jam-band alt-rock styles.

Bluegrass Banjo For Dummies can take you wherever you want to go with
the five-string banjo, whether it's playing old favorites on your front porch,
holding your own in a bluegrass jam session, or exploring the advanced
techniques used by today's professionals. Along the way, you'll master a
truckload of well-loved bluegrass banjo tunes and master the skills needed to
sound great playing with others.

Haven't got a banjo yet? No worries! You'll soon know what to look for in a
quality bluegrass banjo and get the accessories you need to jumpstart your
picking. From playing your first chords, to getting started with picking and fretting patterns to mastering more advanced Scruggs, melodic, and single-string
techniques, it's all waiting for you right here in *Bluegrass Banjo For Dummies.*

People absorb knowledge in different ways, and you'll find a variety of resources within these pages and online to match the methods that work best for you. Be sure to check all these out as you work through this book:

- **Read step-by-step instructions.** If you're starting from scratch, rest assured that you'll find detailed explanations for the most important things you'll need to do in order to get started out right. No fingers, strings, or frets are left behind!

- **Look at the photos.** Finding comfortable hand positions, fretting chords, and working out melodic and single-string positions can be a challenge. Compare what you're doing with the photos to stay on the right track.

- **Listen to the audio tracks.** Developing and using good listening skills will considerably speed your banjo-playing progress. Head online to download files of every example presented in this book and listen to these tracks repeatedly to get the sound of each technique and tune in your head. Some examples even have guitar accompaniment and are designed for you to play along.

- **Consult the banjo tablature.** *Tablature* captures the sound of banjo music in a visual, written form, showing all the note-to-note details to help you more easily remember your fancy picking- and fretting-hand maneuvers. Banjo tablature is easy to understand, and you'll get rolling much more quickly by referring to it as needed as you work out tunes and techniques.

- **Watch the online videos.** Be sure to spend some time with the more than 35 online videos that demonstrate many of the most important ideas and songs presented in the book. You'll find clips on everything from finding comfortable hand positions to fretting chords and mastering roll patterns, and even a guide to changing strings.

With all these different ways of exploring the world of bluegrass banjo, you just can't go wrong. *Bluegrass Banjo For Dummies* is going to make a banjo player out of you, guaranteed! All you have to do is get started.

Speaking of which, there's no need to read this book cover to cover. It's designed for you to use as a complete bluegrass banjo reference, providing whatever information you need at a moment's notice. Check out the table of contents and feel free to jump right in with those chapters or sections that interest you most. If at any point you find that you're in over your head, all you have to do is flip back a few chapters for a review of more basic materials. The index at the back of the book is your destination for a comprehensive list of what's covered (or if you want to immediately find *all* the places in the book where I invoke the name of Earl Scruggs!).

I've saved some interesting information for the gray-shaded sidebars that you'll encounter throughout the book. Although these sidebars cover topics that are related to that chapter's content, you can save these for later, when you're taking a break between practice sessions.

When you encounter a web address that breaks across two lines in the print edition of this book and you're wanting to visit that site, just key in the web address exactly as it appears in the text as if the line break doesn't exist. You're in luck if you're reading *Bluegrass Banjo For Dummies* in an e-book format — all of you have to do is click the web address to be transported directly to that web page.

Icons Used in This Book

The following icons are found frequently throughout the margins of this book. They're designed to highlight specific information that's worthy of your extra attention:

This icon links you to online audio tracks and video clips demonstrating the tunes and techniques presented in the text. There's nothing that compares to actually hearing and seeing how it's done, so make listening and watching a central part of your practice experience by visiting www.dummies.com/go/bluegrassbanjo.

This icon points to fundamentally important knowledge that you'll use often in your banjo-playing adventures. It's stuff that's worth remembering!

Although banjo players love technical stuff, this icon points to information that isn't essential to your playing that you can revisit when you're ready.

This timesaving icon tips you off to shortcuts or practical strategies to reach your banjo goals more quickly and easily.

Proceed with caution when encountering this icon to avoid bigger problems down the road, such as unlearning bad practice habits or having to repair a damaged instrument or bruised ego.

Beyond the Book

You can head online for additional materials designed to maximize your banjo-playing adventures. Check out the Cheat Sheet at www.dummies.com/cheatsheet/bluegrassbanjo to review bluegrass roll patterns, melodic and single-string scales, and up-the-neck chord positions.

Build your repertoire of licks, discover playing strategies you can use at your next jam session, play chord progressions to ten instrumental favorites, and start to assemble your essential accessories. You'll find all this information and more waiting for you online at www.dummies.com/extras/bluegrassbanjo.

And best of all, every musical example in the book has an accompanying online audio track. In addition, there are more than 35 video clips demonstrating the most important concepts, techniques, and tunes presented in *Bluegrass Banjo For Dummies*. You can listen and watch online at www.dummies.com/go/bluegrassbanjo or download these files directly to your favorite portable device. You've got no excuses now that you can take these tunes and techniques with you wherever you and your banjo may go!

Where to Go from Here

I know you want to hit the ground running on your banjo journey, and *Bluegrass Banjo For Dummies* is designed for you to head straight to your favorite destinations in whatever order works best for you.

Here are a few recommendations on how to get started:

✔ If you're shopping for your first bluegrass banjo, pay a visit to Chapter 2, where you'll get acquainted with the parts of the banjo and find a complete buyer's guide.

✔ If you're playing music for the first time on your banjo, head over to Chapter 3 to get in tune and to fret your first chords.

✔ If you already know a few chords and want to begin working on authentic bluegrass picking styles, get your fingerpicks on and head over to Chapter 4.

✔ If you're interested in working on the playing techniques you'll use to play with other musicians in bluegrass jam sessions and in bands, check out Chapters 9 and 10.

✔ If you're a more experienced player and you want to explore progressive banjo styles, head to Chapters 11 and 12 and get to know melodic and single-string banjo styles.

Part I
Getting Started with Bluegrass Banjo

In this part . . .

✔ Discover what's unique about bluegrass banjo style.

✔ Select a great instrument and essential accessories that match your budget.

✔ Get in tune and become familiar with the musical ingredients of bluegrass songs.

✔ Make sense of chord diagrams and tablature, the written forms of banjo music, to deepen your understanding and speed your progress.

✔ Fit the fingerpicks on your picking hand and find your optimal picking-hand position to make playing easier and to get a great sound from your banjo.

✔ Change chords and play picking patterns to your first songs, getting comfortable with the chords you'll need for many other songs.

Chapter 1

Bluegrass Music and the Banjo

● ●

In This Chapter

▶ Becoming familiar with Scruggs, melodic, and single-string bluegrass banjo styles

▶ Discovering the African and early American roots of the banjo

▶ Finding jams, festivals, and music camps in your area

▶ Establishing great practice techniques from the beginning

● ●

In 1945, when the 21-year-old North Carolina banjo player Earl Scruggs stepped on stage on the Grand Ole Opry for the first time and began to play, no one could've imagined the worldwide musical phenomenon that was being launched at that moment. This was something new, a sound that was both complex and wild, redefining the musical potential of the five-string banjo for all who experienced it.

That banjo sound pulls in more people today than ever before. There are many ways to make music on the five-string banjo, but none has captivated so many musicians or is as versatile as the style that originated with Earl Scruggs. This way of playing is called three-finger, bluegrass, or Scruggs-style banjo, and it's a defining characteristic of bluegrass music. If it's bluegrass, it simply has to have a banjo played in this way.

Over the last several decades, banjo players have built upon Earl's contributions by developing new three-finger techniques (called melodic and single-string banjo) that allow musicians to more easily incorporate jazz, classical, world music, and even rock influences into bluegrass banjo style. From bebop to Bach, the kinds of music that can be played using the variety of the three-finger approaches available today are virtually unlimited.

In this chapter, you step back in time to survey the long and fascinating history of the instrument before exploring what's unique about bluegrass banjo style. I introduce you to the basic musical skills within these pages that will turn you into a great bluegrass banjo player.

Uncovering Banjo History

By the mid 20th century, the banjo had been in the Western Hemisphere for more than 300 years, arriving from West Africa first in the Caribbean and then by the 1750s in colonial America. By the mid 19th century, the banjo had become one of the most popular instruments in the United States, played by African Americans and Anglo Americans alike.

African banjo roots

Many kinds of banjolike instruments are played by West African musicians, ranging in size, number of strings, and playing methods. With the slave trade, thousands of African musicians were forcibly brought to the Western Hemisphere over several hundred years, bringing with them ideas about music making and instruments. What we know about the banjo in the Caribbean and in the United States comes from travelers' accounts of music making and drawings and paintings of early instruments. (For a classic study of African music in the New World, including early banjo music, check out Dena Epstein's landmark book *Sinful Tunes and Spirituals*.)

Modern banjos reflect the African influence in two very important ways

- ✔ **Banjo heads:** The unique sound of the banjo is largely determined by the skin or plastic *head* that acts as the top vibrating surface of the instrument. (Head to Chapter 2 for more on modern banjo parts.) This method of transmitting sound is found on banjos from all historical periods from both Africa and the United States and remains the primary tone-producing feature of the modern bluegrass banjo.

- ✔ **High-pitched drone strings:** The other defining characteristic of the banjo is the presence of a high-pitched *drone string* that's within easy reach of the picking-hand thumb, located next to the banjo's lowest-pitched string. A drone string provides the continuous note that you hear repeatedly in banjo music of all types. This unusual arrangement of strings has resulted in many of the unique playing techniques used on the banjo both in Africa and in the United States. All banjo players love to hear the ring of that high fifth string, even as this aspect of our playing sometimes mystifies those around us.

Figure 1-1 compares a modern-day West African banjo called an *ekonting* with a modern-day bluegrass instrument. Note that both instruments have skin or plastic heads for the top playing surface. It's easy to locate the short fifth string on a modern banjo — it's on the left side of the banjo neck, ending at the tuning peg that's located halfway up the banjo neck. The ekonting has only three strings, with its high-pitched drone string also located on the left side of the neck. The strings on this instrument are made from plastic fishing wire and there are no tuning pegs — you slide the knotted wire up and down the neck to change the pitch of a string!

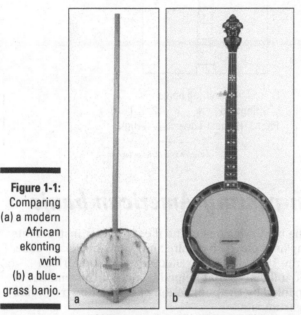

Figure 1-1:
Comparing (a) a modern African ekonting with (b) a bluegrass banjo.

(a) Photograph courtesy of Elderly Instruments; (b) Photograph by Anne Hamersky

Now compare the arrangement of banjo strings to the guitar, as shown in Figure 1-2. Whether it's Earl Scruggs's driving bluegrass, Pete Seeger's folk styles, or Béla Fleck's jazz-influenced original music, it's just not banjo music without this high-pitched fifth string (which, by the way, is almost always played with the picking-hand thumb).

In Chapter 5, I introduce you to *roll patterns,* which are the right-hand picking sequences that are the basis of three-finger banjo technique. These roll patterns are designed around the unique arrangement of banjo strings, as is also the case with *melodic-style banjo,* a way of playing scales on the banjo (see Chapter 11).

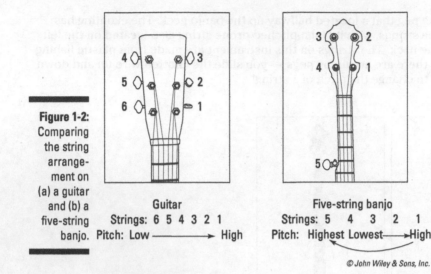

Figure 1-2: Comparing the string arrangement on (a) a guitar and (b) a five-string banjo.

Guitar
Strings: 6 5 4 3 2 1
Pitch: Low ——→ High

Five-string banjo
Strings: 5 4 3 2 1
Pitch: Highest Lowest ——→ High

© John Wiley & Sons, Inc.

19th- and 20th-century American banjo

By the mid 19th century, the banjo was one of the most popular instruments in the United States and England, played by white and black musicians alike. The *minstrel banjo style* of the 1840s to 1860s reflects continuing African and African-American banjo influences that helped launch the instrument to international fame, accompanied by the publication of the first instructional books and factory-made instruments.

By the 1860s, new ways of playing banjo were adopted from American guitar styles, leading to the virtuosic finger-picked ragtime-influenced music of the *classic banjo style* of the late 19th and early 20th centuries. Much of classic-style banjo music is played using a three-finger picking technique that's similar to bluegrass playing.

Five strings became the standard on the banjo by the 1850s, but frets were not commonplace on the instrument until the 1880s. To add volume and clarity, heads were attached more tightly with additional metal brackets, and tone rings and resonators were introduced by the early 20th century. Figure 1-3 compares a mid 19th-century minstrel banjo to an early 20th-century instrument.

When record company representatives and folklorists began to document the music of the rural South in the 1920s and 1930s, they uncovered a wealth of regional banjo styles. Radio created hillbilly banjo-playing stars, like Uncle Dave Macon and Molly O'Day, and recordings helped to spread influential playing styles all across the United States. This recorded legacy continues to influence banjo players today.

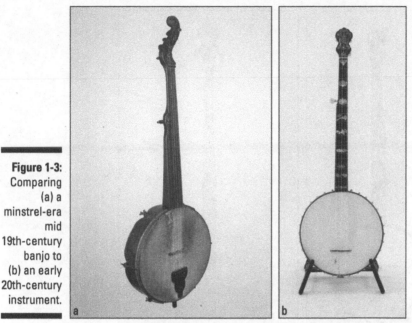

(a) Photograph courtesy of © Larry Marcus 2014; (b) Photograph by Anne Hamersky

Old-time banjo encompasses a wide range of banjo styles of Southern origin that includes *clawhammer* (also called *frailing*), as well as two- and three-finger picking styles. *Clawhammer banjo* is a very popular way of playing the banjo today, at home in old-time traditions all over the world, as well as used as accompaniment by singer-songwriters such as Sarah Jarosz and Gillian Welch.

The five-string banjo found other ways to national awareness in the mid 20th century. As young people discovered the power of folk songs played on the banjo, Pete Seeger popularized the banjo among urban audiences, playing music on a long-neck banjo. Pete's style was eclectic, drawing on old-time and popular music influences.

Figure 1-4 compares the kind of banjo typically used to play old-time music (in this case a handmade banjo by Chuck Lee) with a long-neck Pete Seeger Vega model instrument.

If you're interested in trying your hand at all the banjo styles mentioned in this section, check out my book *Banjo For Dummies*.

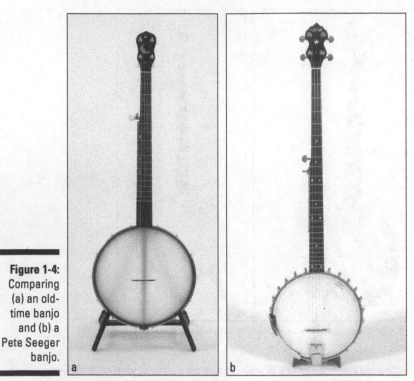

Figure 1-4:
Comparing
(a) an old-
time banjo
and (b) a
Pete Seeger
banjo.

a   b

(a) Photograph by Anne Hamersky; (b) Photograph courtesy of Elderly Instruments

Bluegrass Banjo Yesterday and Today

Thousands of new players became attracted to the sound of the banjo after hearing Earl Scruggs play, first with mandolin player Bill Monroe in the 1940s and then with longtime musical partner Lester Flatt from 1949 to 1968. As new musicians absorbed Earl's style, they contributed innovations of their own, which have greatly expanded the range of music that can be played on the banjo using bluegrass picking techniques.

Today, you hear the sound of bluegrass banjo not only from mainstream bands like Alison Krauss & Union Station (featuring the rock-solid banjo playing of Ron Block) and the Lonesome River Band (with Sammy Shelor), but also in jam bands like Leftover Salmon (with Andy Thorn) and the Infamous Stringdusters (with Chris Pandolfi) and in the acoustic/chamber/jazz fusion music of the Punch Brothers (featuring the amazing Noam Pikelny).

It's all about Earl

It's impossible to overestimate Earl Scruggs's contributions to the art of bluegrass banjo playing. Hundreds of thousands of players from all over the world took up the banjo in the 1950s and 1960s and became bluegrass musicians after hearing Scruggs play "Foggy Mountain Breakdown" and "The Ballad of Jed Clampett."

Utilizing a blazingly precise technique that allowed him to play faster than anyone thought possible on the banjo, Earl singlehandedly created an entire musical language that has been used by generations of players to create songs and accompany others in all kinds of musical contexts.

The genius of Earl's accomplishments is in how flexible his three-finger approach is in regard to creating different kinds of sounds on the banjo. Influential bluegrass players such as Sonny Osborne, J. D. Crowe, Bill Emerson and Jim Mills have emphasized different aspects of Earl's technique to create their own unique banjo styles that remain solidly connected to Earl's approach.

In Chapter 5, I explore Earl's basic vocabulary of picking-hand roll patterns. Chapter 7 presents many of his most essential licks, along with classic bluegrass songs arranged in Scruggs's style. Chapter 8 explores the inner workings of Earl's technique, providing insight into how you can create your own music using Scruggs style as your guide. Chapters 9 and 10 explore the techniques Earl devised for accompanying others in bluegrass bands.

Melodic and single-string styles

If there is one limitation to Scruggs-style banjo, it's the challenge of playing fast-moving melodies that move up and down a scale, as you hear in fiddle tunes, modern jazz, and classical music. Beginning in the 1950s, banjo players introduced new picking approaches to solve this technical problem.

Melodic banjo style

Melodic banjo enables you to play scales on the five-string banjo where you strike a different string with each consecutive note you play, as in Scruggs-style banjo. Bill Keith and Bobby Thompson came up with this idea independently of one another in the early 1960s. As members of Bill Monroe's band (the same band that Earl Scruggs played in back in the 1940s), blue-grass banjo players were dazzled by Keith's ability to play fiddle tunes like "Sailor's Hornpipe" and "Blackberry Blossom," capturing every note that the fiddle played.

Chapter 11 introduces you to melodic banjo playing both up and down the neck, presenting scale exercises and tunes in the keys of G, C, D, and A.

Single-string banjo style

Single-string banjo was first developed in the 1950s by bluegrass pioneers Eddie Adcock and Don Reno. Borrowing from lead guitar-playing techniques, single-string style allows you to play consecutive notes of a scale on the same string, using the thumb and fingers of the picking hand in alternation in a manner that's similar to how guitar and mandolin players use a flatpick.

The musical potential of this way of playing banjo took a huge leap forward in the 1980s with Béla Fleck's technical breakthroughs. As new innovators such as Noam Pikelny and Ryan Cavanaugh continue to open up the potential of this way of playing, the banjo is finding a more comfortable home in classical and jazz music.

Chapter 12 helps you blaze your own musical paths with single-string banjo, with exercises and tunes that will unlock the fingerboard both up and down your banjo neck.

Joining In: Jams, Festivals, and Camps

You already love the sound of bluegrass banjo, but you'll be hooked for the rest of your life as a banjo *player* when you connect to the worldwide community of other banjo players and bluegrass musicians who love the banjo as much as you do! Bluegrass banjo sounds best when played with others. Even as a beginner, you can jump right in to enjoy making music with others. Taking part in the jam sessions, festivals, and camps in your region with like-minded musical souls is the best way to fast-track your progress on the banjo.

Finding jams

Jam sessions are informal group gatherings of bluegrass musicians that are held in living rooms, community buildings, and public spaces, as well as at larger musical events. Most jams are public events in which all musicians are welcome. When you're comfortable tuning your banjo and playing a few chords with roll patterns in a steady rhythm (which you'll master after checking out Chapters 3, 4, and 5), you'll be right at home in a *slow jam,* which is a jam designed especially for beginners and often directed by a local bluegrass teacher. Your local music store or regional bluegrass music association is a great place to learn about jams in your area.

TIP

You can get the opportunity to play a song or two of your choice at a jam session. Do your part and arrive at the session with a couple of favorites that you can play without stopping. And playing slowly is fine — you get to set the tempo, because it's your tune! Don't forget to spend time internalizing the chord progression to your songs — you'll need to use accompaniment techniques to support the other musicians when it's their turn to take a solo.

Heading out to festivals

Bluegrass festivals are multiday, family-friendly events found all across North America where you bring your banjo and your camping gear and spend an entire weekend jamming in the campground and checking out your favorite bands on stage. Although larger festivals pack more of a punch in regard to the national talent, it's often the smaller, regional events that have better jamming scenes. *Bluegrass Unlimited* magazine (www.bluegrassmusic.com) publishes a comprehensive annual festival guide.

Here's a short list of some of my favorite festivals:

- **Bill Monroe Memorial Bean Blossom Bluegrass Festival,** Bean Blossom, Indiana (www.billmonroemusicpark.com)

- **Father's Day Bluegrass Festival,** sponsored by the California Bluegrass Association, Grass Valley, California (www.cbaontheweb.org)

- **Gettysburg Bluegrass Festival,** Gettysburg, Pennsylvania (www.gettysburgbluegrass.com)

- **Grey Fox Bluegrass Festival,** Oak Hill, New York (www.greyfoxbluegrass.com)

- **MerleFest,** Wilkesboro, North Carolina (www.merlefest.org)

- **Palatka Bluegrass Festival,** Palatka, Florida (www.adamsbluegrass.com)

- **Pickin' in the Pines Bluegrass & Acoustic Music Festival,** Flagstaff, Arizona (www.pickininthepines.org)

- **RockyGrass,** Lyons, Colorado (www.bluegrass.com/rockygrass)

- **Walnut Valley Festival,** Winfield, Kansas (www.wvfest.com)

- **Wide Open Bluegrass,** Raleigh, North Carolina (www.wideopenbluegrass.com)

- **Wintergrass Music Festival,** Bellevue, Washington (www.wintergrass.com)

Attending a music camp

Imagine spending a weekend or an entire week doing nothing but practicing banjo all day, taking small-group classes, hanging out with your banjo heroes, playing with others in jams and student concerts and getting very little sleep. That's the music camp experience!

Music camps provide a great way to take great leaps forward on the banjo in a short amount of time. There are two basic kinds of camps to consider. One is an all-banjo camp where the students are — you guessed it — all banjo players; the other kind of camp offers instruction in all the bluegrass instruments or a variety of music styles. Each type of camp has its own strengths. All-banjo camps usually have larger banjo teaching staffs, allowing you to study with a variety of master teachers. Bluegrass camps focus on ensemble playing, often culminating in a student concert in front of family and friends.

Although banjo camps welcome all experience levels, including real beginners, most folks who head to a music camp are lower intermediate to intermediate players. Be sure to choose a camp that matches your experience level, but don't talk yourself out of attending a camp because you don't think you're good enough to go. Most camp attendees have been studying the banjo for one to five years and are going for the same reasons you are: to enjoy the company of other banjo players, absorb a *lot* of knowledge in a short amount of time, and play as much as possible.

I typically teach at up to ten camps a year, and I love every one of them. Here's a list of my favorite events:

- ✔ **American Banjo Camp,** Nordland, Washington (www.americanbanjocamp.com)

- ✔ **Banjo Camp North,** Charlton, Massachusetts (www.banjocampnorth.com)

- ✔ **California Bluegrass Association Music Camp,** Grass Valley, California (www.cbamusiccamp.com)

- ✔ **Midwest Banjo Camp,** Olivet, Michigan (www.midwestbanjocamp.com)

- ✔ **NashCamp,** Nashville, Tennessee (www.nashcamp.com)

- ✔ **NimbleFingers,** Sorrento, British Columbia, Canada (www.nimblefingers.ca)

- ✔ **Sore Fingers Week,** Chipping Norton, England (www.sorefingers.co.uk)

- ✔ **Suwannee Banjo Camp,** Live Oak, Florida (www.suwanneebanjocamp.com)

- ✔ **The Swannanoa Gathering,** Asheville, North Carolina (www.swangathering.com)
- ✔ **Walker Creek Music Camp,** Petaluma, California (www.walkercreekmusiccamp.org)
- ✔ **Weiser Banjo Camp,** Weiser, Idaho (www.banjocontest.org)

Becoming a Bluegrass Banjo Player

As you work through the techniques, exercises, and tunes found in this book, keep the following guidelines in mind to speed your progress and prepare for playing music with others.

Knowing chords and keeping good time

Banjo players devote a lot of practice time to working up fancy solos from *banjo tablature* (the written form of banjo music I introduce you to in Chapter 3). However, when playing with other musicians in jam sessions, you'll call upon a different set of skills than what you might use at home when you're practicing.

It's important to know your chords well, keep good time, and follow the chord progressions of the songs that are being played, without stopping. And don't forget to keep your banjo in tune to the best of your ability at all times! The best way to get comfortable with these skills is to find a slow jam in your area where you can try these things out and simply go for it. Another option is to attend a regular jam and hang on the outside of the playing circle, picking up skills as you go by watching others and asking questions. You'll be right in the middle of things in no time!

Playing roll patterns

Bluegrass banjo is all about precision in the picking hand, which is the right hand for right-handed banjo players. (Left-handed players can use their left hands for picking if they have banjo necks made especially for left-handed playing.) *Roll patterns* are the picking-hand note sequences that are at the heart of bluegrass banjo style. Earl Scruggs advises new players to repeat each roll pattern 10,000 times until it becomes second nature. If I only have a few minutes to practice, I'll grab my banjo and play a few roll patterns, matching them to whatever chord enters my mind. Some day, I'll be up to 10,000 repetitions myself!

The songs and accompaniment patterns that you encounter in *Bluegrass Banjo For Dummies* are based on roll patterns (see Chapter 5). As with speaking a new language, when you're conversant with the language of roll patterns, you'll be speaking in banjo sentences rather than stumbling over each word (or note). Mind your rolls, and you'll become a better player much more quickly.

Playing in the band: Lead and backup

When you're playing a red-hot solo to a bluegrass banjo classic (like one of the songs you can tackle in this book!), you're playing *lead*. When you're supporting other musicians and trying to make them sound their best while they're showing off and playing their leads, you're playing *backup*.

When playing with others, you'll spend most of your time playing backup, either in support of another instrumentalist or a singer. Bluegrass banjo players have developed some great techniques and licks that are designed just for backup playing (which you'll discover in Chapters 9 and 10). Don't ignore these skills in your practice time.

Chapter 2

Finding the Perfect Bluegrass Banjo and Getting the Gear You Need

In This Chapter

▶ Becoming familiar with different kinds of banjos

▶ Discovering the parts of a bluegrass banjo

▶ Selecting a great banjo that's within your budget

▶ Acquiring essential gear to help you get started

Find a beautiful piece of wood and shape it into something that looks like a banjo neck. Take some more wood and press it into a hoop and, with whatever wood is left over, create a shallow bowl. Add assorted metal parts, some tuning pegs, and a bit of plastic, and throw a drum head on top of the pile. Fasten it all together with some nuts and bolts, add some strings, and you've got yourself the makings of a bluegrass banjo!

It's unlikely that such an odd collection of components could be turned into one of the most beloved instruments in the world, but what makes a great banjo is how all these parts are put together. Whether you're in the market for your first instrument or you already own a bluegrass banjo, this chapter is your destination for distinguishing among the different kinds of banjos out there, recognizing what goes into a good banjo, and selecting the best instrument for your budget and playing style. I also give you a look at some of the essential gear that will help you hit the ground picking.

Identifying Different Kinds of Banjos

Musicians have loved the bright, unmistakable sound of a banjo so much that various types of banjos have been created through the years to more effectively play different styles of music. Irish, Dixieland, and traditional jazz musicians typically use instruments with four strings, and there are even banjos with six strings that are played just like a guitar.

Bluegrass music is played on a five-string banjo. Although most of the banjos you'll find in a music store are just this kind, there are even different varieties of five-string instruments to choose from. It's important to get to know what's out there to select an instrument that's just right for playing bluegrass.

From a distance, all banjos look pretty much the same. Any kind of instrument with the word *banjo* attached to it is going to have the familiar round body shape that we've all come to love, with a stretched, white head as its top playing surface. But there are some differences among banjos; in the following sections, I explain.

Tenor banjos, plectrum banjos, six-string banjos, and mandolin-banjos

As you move in closer, you'll discover that banjos can have different numbers of strings and necks of varying lengths. *Tenor banjos* and *plectrum banjos,* which were the most popular kinds of banjos for much of the early 20th century, both have four strings. You can tell a plectrum from a tenor by the plectrum's longer neck (see Figure 2-1).

If you attach a guitar neck to a banjo body, you have a *six-string banjo* (also called a *guitar banjo*). Even mandolin players occasionally like to get in on the banjo excitement by attaching a mandolin neck to a banjo pot, resulting in a hybrid instrument that's been called a *mandolin-banjo, banjolin,* or *mando-banjo.* (Obviously, mandolin players have a hard time deciding upon names for their instruments!)

All these banjos are truly wonderful instruments, but they *aren't* five-string banjos! With their varying numbers of strings and different tunings, these other banjos are played using different techniques than those used by bluegrass musicians, and musicians consider them different instruments.

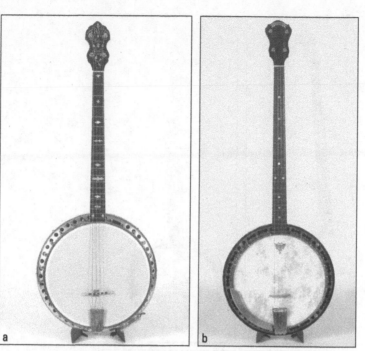

Figure 2-1:
A tenor banjo (left) and a plectrum banjo (right).

Photographs courtesy of Elderly Instruments

Five-string banjos: Open-back banjos and resonator banjos

The distinguishing characteristic of all five-string banjos is the short fifth string that's secured to the instrument with a tuning peg that's found almost halfway up the neck. That high-pitched fifth string is responsible for all kinds of great five-string banjo sounds, from old-time clawhammer to bluegrass and everything in between. If you'd like to try out a wide variety of historical and present-day five-string banjo styles, including clawhammer, check out my book *Banjo For Dummies*.

Five-string banjos come in two different varieties (see Figure 2-2):

✔ **Open-back banjos:** As its name implies, you can see the inside of the instrument from the rear of an open-back banjo. This is the kind of five-string banjo that was used by Pete Seeger and the Kingston Trio and is the preference for many old-time/clawhammer-style banjo players. Open-back banjos are generally quieter than resonator banjos, but with the proper adjustments, you can make an open-back banjo loudly crack. (Pay a visit to Chapter 13 for an introduction to the fine art of banjo setup.)

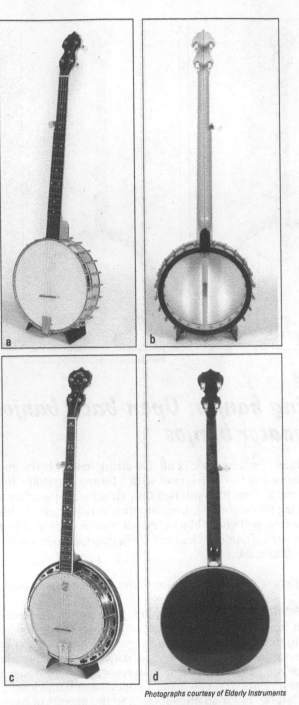

Figure 2-2: Comparing banjos: (a) open-back banjo, front; (b) open-back banjo, back; (c) resonator banjo, front; and (d) resonator banjo, back.

Photographs courtesy of Elderly Instruments

✔ **Resonator banjos:** A resonator banjo has a shallow, wooden, bowl-shaped addition that attaches to the back of the instrument. Resonators were first widely used on 1920s and 1930s Jazz Age tenor banjos and plectrum banjos to compete with the volume put out by a jazz band's horn section. The resonator projects the banjo sound out from the instrument and has, over time, become a distinguishing characteristic of the type of five-string banjo used to play bluegrass music.

Although players usually choose an open-back banjo or a resonator banjo based on the style of music that they want to play, you can play any kind of five-string banjo music on either type of banjo. Player preferences over time have determined these stylistic associations, but these are by no means hard-and-fast rules. It's much more important to jump in and start making music on whatever five-string banjo you have on hand. When you go to make your next purchase, you can consider whether you need an open-back or a resonator banjo based on the music you're playing and the kinds of sounds you most want to hear.

Recognizing a Great Bluegrass Banjo

Whether you're in the market for your first banjo or you want to understand more about how the parts of your instrument work, it's good to know your way around a bluegrass banjo. In this section, I fill you in on what all the parts do and which parts are crucial to banjo sound. You also come to know what goes into making a great banjo at various price levels, from an entry-level instrument to a professional one.

Today, there are better and more affordable choices in banjos than ever before. As you understand how a banjo works, you'll make a more informed choice when it's time to make your next purchase.

It's time to get to know what all that wood, metal, and plastic are designed to do. In the following sections, I explain everything that goes into a banjo, with special attention devoted to the differences between entry-level banjos and more expensive ones. If you have a banjo already in the house, grab it and locate these parts as you proceed through this section, comparing your instrument with what you see in Figure 2-3.

Surveying the banjo neck

The *neck* is the long piece of wood that attaches to the banjo body that guides the strings along the instrument's fretting surface (called the *fingerboard*). The neck holds the strings secure using *tuners,* four of which are located at the *peghead,* with the fifth string tuning peg located almost halfway up the neck.

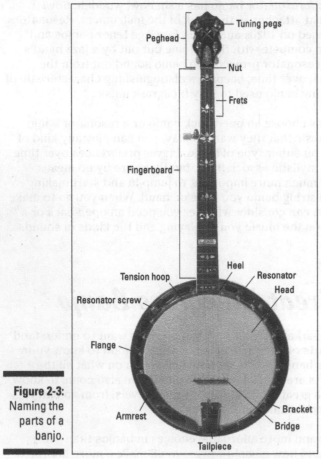

Figure 2-3:
Naming the parts of a banjo.

Peghead — Tuning pegs
Nut
Frets
Fingerboard
Tension hoop — Heel — Resonator
Resonator screw — Head
Flange
Armrest — Bracket
Bridge
Tailpiece

Photograph courtesy of Gruhn Guitars

Maple, mahogany, and walnut banjo necks

Bluegrass banjo necks are most commonly made of maple, mahogany, or walnut. The type of wood used for the neck usually matches the wood that's used for the surface of the *resonator* (the bowl-shaped piece of wood that's attached to the back of the banjo).

Banjo players and builders love to endlessly discuss the relative merits of each kind of wood. For an entry-level instrument, the type of wood used for the neck isn't as important as the banjo's general playability. However, with professional banjos, the type of wood can be an important distinguishing characteristic.

Generally speaking, a mahogany neck tends to gives a banjo a warmer sound, a maple neck is clearer and more bell-like, and a walnut neck lends the deepest tone.

Keep in mind that tone is the result of all the parts working together, and the neck is just one factor. The higher the quality of a banjo, the more the various parts are made to work together to create a great-sounding instrument.

Fingerboard and frets

The *fingerboard* is the piece of wood that's glued to the neck that holds the frets. *Frets* are the metal bars that are positioned horizontally to the direction of the strings at predetermined intervals along the fingerboard. When you place a finger behind a fret, you're shortening the string length and raising the pitch of the string. The great majority of bluegrass banjos have 22 frets, although lately some leading players are sporting fingerboard extensions, which add two higher frets — and two higher notes — to the total fingerboard length.

Figure 2-4 shows banjo hero Noam Pikelny's 24-fret fingerboard.

The pressure of a fretted string will very gradually wear down a fret after years of steady use. If you hear buzzing from the fretted notes on an older instrument, look to your frets as a potential source of the problem. A banjo repairperson can *dress* the frets by leveling out the fret surfaces, allowing a few more years of use before they have to be replaced.

Figure 2-4:
A 24-fret custom neck featuring a two-fret fingerboard extension.

Photograph courtesy of Noam Pikelny

Most fingerboards are made from rosewood or ebony but some entry-level banjos use the wood of the neck as the fingerboard. The majority of fingerboards are *flat,* but many players choose *radiused* fingerboards for their banjos. A radiused fingerboard is curved along its surface, requiring a radiused nut and bridge at either end of the banjo to keep the strings at a uniform height above the fingerboard. Figure 2-5 shows the differences.

Fans of radiused fingerboards point to the greater ease of playing contemporary banjo styles. Unfortunately, at this time, radiused fingerboards are options found only on more expensive instruments.

Tuners and Keith pegs

Tuners are the geared pegs that catch the strings at the neck end of the banjo and hold the strings in tune. The quality of the tuner usually correlates with the price of the banjo, but luckily, most all banjos have tuners that do the job well. Tuners do occasionally fail, but they're usually easy to replace with just a wrench.

A *geared fifth-string peg* makes tuning a lot easier and is worth swapping out for if you have an entry-level banjo without one.

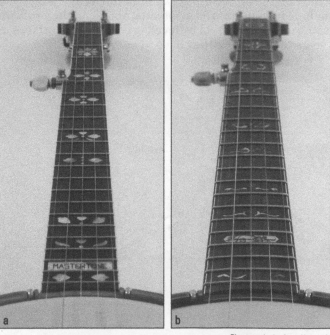

Figure 2-5: Comparing fingerboards: (a) flat and (b) radiused.

Photographs by Anne Hamersky

Keith D-tuners are deluxe tuners that allow you to control the up-and-down movement of the pegs to move precisely from one pitch to another. If you're in love with Earl Scruggs's "tuner" tunes like "Flint Hill Special" and "Randy Lynn Rag," Keith pegs should move to the top of your wish list. Banjo players most often install Keith pegs on the second and third strings.

Nut

The *nut* is the white slotted piece of plastic, ivory, or bone that keeps the strings in place at the peghead end of the fretboard and directs the strings to the tuning pegs. Like frets, the string notches in the nut can wear down over time, leading to buzzing on the open strings. Nuts can be reslotted or replaced by a qualified repairperson.

Truss rod

When steel strings came into wider use in the early 20th century, instrument builders needed to find ways to strengthen necks to withstand the greater pressure exerted by these new strings. The truss rod consists of one or two adjustable metal rods that run underneath the fingerboard, starting at the peghead and extending to the 14th fret; it maintains the neck at a consistent angle under the pressure of the strings. The truss rod is usually adjusted with a nut driver or Allen wrench at the peghead end.

A plastic or pearl truss rod cover on the peghead is the giveaway that your instrument has a truss rod. Chapter 13 shows you how you can set this adjustment yourself.

Knowing what's in the pot

The body of the banjo is called the *pot*. Think of the pot as the engine that drives the sound of your instrument. Most of the major tone-producing ingredients are found in the banjo pot, and the quality of these components has a direct relationship on how good your instrument sounds. Let's get under the hood to take a look at rims, tone rings, heads, resonators, and more.

Figure 2-6 reviews the main ingredients of the pot and shows you how these parts fit together.

Rim

The *rim* (sometimes called the *shell*) is the organic foundation of banjo sound. Assembled from laminated strips or blocks of maple, or occasionally mahogany, the rim supports the *tone ring* or *tension hoop* and *flange* and is a crucial part of the tone-producing mechanism of the banjo. It's essential to use a quality piece of wood for this part of the banjo; many builders brag about using older "hard rock" maple from northern forests or even wood that has spent some years underwater for their rims. Three-ply rims are standard on many professional-grade instruments, indicating that the rim is assembled from three concentric blocks of maple, pressed and glued together into a ring shape. The top of the rim is machined to match the tone ring, which is precisely fitted to its top.

Tone ring

The *tone ring* is the most discussed — and debated — element of bluegrass banjo sound. Banjos can sound great with no tone ring at all, and some banjos utilize a brass *tension hoop* in place of a ring. Most banjo players agree that the volume and brilliance associated with the characteristic sound of bluegrass banjo is in large part the result of the tone ring.

Tone rings come in two types: *flathead* and *arch-top*. The flathead ring creates a larger vibrating surface for the head and generally lends the banjo a deeper sound than the arch-top ring. Most players choose flathead tone rings for their banjos, but if you're in love with the bright, piercing tone of Ralph Stanley's banjo playing, the arch-top ring is just the ticket for you.

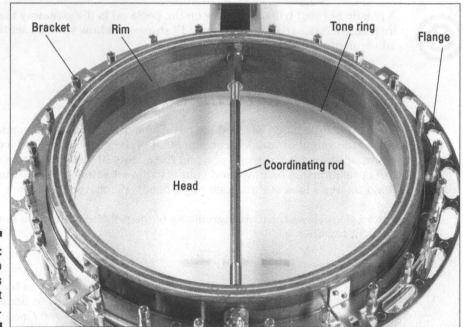

Figure 2-6:
The banjo pot and its component parts.

Photograph by Anne Hamersky

Liquid metal alloys are poured into a mold, and after cooling, the ring is machined to fit securely onto the rim. As with the rim, a higher-quality banjo should come equipped with a well-made tone ring. In the last two decades, a cottage industry has sprung up around the manufacture of tone rings using the same or similar metal formulas as used by Gibson on their prized banjos from the 1930s. These "prewar formula" rings are found on many professional-grade instruments today. However, because there was no single formula used in the 1930s, many varieties of prewar rings are available, and each ring does indeed sound just a bit different on a quality banjo.

Bluegrass banjo players sometimes swap out both the rim and tone ring on their instruments, replacing them with higher-quality parts or parts that will change the sound of their banjos. It's in the nature of the instrument and its players to experiment in this way, but these kinds of changes are usually only worth making on a professional-grade instrument.

Head

The *head* is the stretched plastic or (more rarely) skin membrane that is the top vibrating surface of the banjo. The head is stretched tightly across the top of the tone ring (or the rim if there is no tone ring) and held in place by the *stretcher band* and tightened via *brackets*. Heads dramatically affect banjo sound. (Find out more by heading over to the setup tips in Chapter 13.)

Bridge

The *bridge* conveys the vibrations of the string to the head and is another important element in the chain of banjo tone creation. Traditionally, bridges range from ⅝ inch to ¾ inch in height and are made from maple with an ebony cap. One of the quickest and easiest ways to change the sound of an entry-level banjo is to replace the factory bridge with a quality, handmade bridge. Chapter 13 helps you with this task.

Tailpiece

The *tailpiece* holds the strings at the pot end of the banjo and comes in several different styles. Check out the setup guide in Chapter 13 to find out more about how the tailpiece affects your banjo's tone and how it's adjusted.

Flange

The *flange* is the circular piece of metal that is fitted around the rim that provides a platform to mount the *resonator*. It also holds the bottom of the *brackets*.

Resonator

The *resonator* adds volume to your banjo and directs the sound you're making straight away from you and right into the ears of your adoring fans. Like the rim, a resonator is made from three layers of laminated wood, most often in some combination of maple and poplar, with a thin veneer of fancy maple, mahogany, or walnut on the back and sides that matches the wood of the neck. Some professional banjos have resonators with a single-piece carved back, like a fine guitar or mandolin.

Shopping for a banjo

Now that you know a bit more about the features of a great bluegrass banjo, you're ready to start your search for your next instrument.

You can find good choices at every price level, but keep in mind that the best choice for a first instrument may be one that's borrowed from a friend. If your banjo budget is severely limited, just about any banjo is better than no banjo at all to get you started. If it's got five strings that stay in tune, you're able to fret the strings, and the head isn't broken, then you're in business (at least for a little while).

Start playing on whatever is handy now and keep on the lookout for your next banjo using the following guidelines.

Sorting through beginner's choices

If you have your heart set on playing bluegrass music on the banjo, you'll want to find a banjo with a resonator. For around $400, you'll have your choice of quality entry-level banjos from respected companies like Deering, Gold Tone, Morgan Monroe, Recording King, and Saga. Don't worry if these banjos are comparatively plain in appearance — it's more important at this price level to find a banjo with good playability and solid construction.

You'll notice a big step up in sound if you can spend a bit more for a banjo with both a resonator and a tone ring. This will increase the price tag to around $700 or $800 for a new instrument, but because you'll be heard more effectively in a jam session, you might hold on to a banjo like this for a bit longer.

The best place to begin your search for your first banjo is at the music store in your area that specializes in acoustic instruments, not at one of those superstores where the walls are lined with hundreds of electric guitars and amps. Don't forget to also check out national acoustic retail outlets like Banjo.com (www.banjo.com) and Elderly Instruments (www.elderly.com) and the classified listings at banjo-friendly websites like Banjo Hangout (www.banjohangout.org) for more great deals. A used beginner's banjo can be a great way to go, but make sure it first gets the stamp of approval (with a guarantee) from the acoustic store's banjo specialist or from your banjo teacher.

Taking the next step up: Midpriced banjos

Expect to lay out $1,000 to $2,000 for the next step up in banjo features. At this price level, you're looking for an instrument with both a resonator and a tone ring that has higher-quality parts, better fit and finish, and decorative inlay patterns on the neck.

Many of the banjos in this price category stick closely to the classic design features of the celebrated 1930s Gibson Mastertone banjos and because they're foreign-assembled, they're more affordable. There are good options in this price range, but the key is to purchase one of these instruments from an acoustic specialty store that will provide an initial setup along with a guarantee. Check out Gold Star, Gold Tone, Recording King, and the U.S.-made Deering banjos as you explore what's available in this price category.

Getting a keeper: Professional banjos

Many of the finest new banjos being made today come from small shops of one to four craftspeople. You'll spend anywhere from $2,500 to $5,000 or more for these professional-grade instruments. If you're interested in customizing your banjo with a radiused fingerboard or fingerboard extension, or with a particular kind of tone ring or resonator wood, or even if you want an image of your dog as a 12th-fret inlay, a small shop or individual craftsperson is the way to go.

Each small shop typically specializes in a particular kind of high-end banjo. Some builders, like Ronnie Bales, Steve Huber, Frank Neat, Robin Smith, and Warren Yates, take pride in creating very close replicas of those prized old Gibson flathead banjos. Other builders, like Tom Nechville and Geoff Stelling, have patented unique pot designs that produce a different banjo tone from the Gibson model, while Jaroslav Prucha from the Czech Republic blends new and traditional banjo-building ideas. In the last decade, the Deering Banjo Company has emerged as the largest banjo maker in the world, with a wide variety of models to match most any budget and musical preference.

 If you're in the market for an instrument you'll play forever, it's a good idea not to rush into your purchase. Try out as many different instruments as you can with a visit to your closest acoustic music specialty shop or check out all kinds of banjos by heading to a bluegrass festival or banjo camp. Most banjo players are more than happy to talk *at great length* about every aspect of their instruments and will often let you test-drive their personal banjos, sometimes at your own risk. (The first time I met banjo great Sonny Osborne, he handed me his priceless old Gibson Granada across the record table and firmly said to me, "Now play me something."). Don't hesitate to seek out advice from more experienced players about their preferences.

Here are a few more celebrated builders to check out when choosing a professional banjo: American Made, Bishline, Hopkins, Huss & Dalton, Ome, Osborne Chief, Romero, Wildwood, and Williams.

 Gibson set the standard for bluegrass banjos with the models it manufactured in the 1920s and 1930s. The company came back strong in the late 1980s through the 2000s, making fine banjos again before stopping production in the early 2010s. A used Gibson banjo from this "reissue" era can be a great professional option, so don't pass over these instruments in your search for a quality banjo.

Taking It with You: Essential Gear

You could fill an entire music room with all the banjo accessories that are out there these days. However, you can get by just fine with a few items that you'll actually use every time you head out the door to play at your next jam session. Check out this short list to begin filling your personal banjo space with these fundamental accessories. Figure 2-7 shows you all these items.

Cases and gig bags

Unless you're really into that riding-the-rails-hobo thing that's all the rage these days, you'll want to use a case or gig bag to take your banjo with you the next time you hop a train or head out the door to play. Most entry-level banjos come with soft gig bags that provide adequate enough protection, but the more you have invested in your banjo, the more you'll want a good case.

Many intermediate-level banjos come with a wood-framed hard-shell case that's covered in vinyl; these are just fine for day-to-day use. If you're heading to the airport or loading your banjo into a touring van filled with suitcases, guitars, mandolins, and leisure suits, you may want to graduate to a carbon fiber or fiberglass flight case. These cases provide the ultimate protection at a steep price of up to $1,000, but they should last a lifetime.

Gig bags have the advantage of being lighter in weight than a hard-shell case and most have backpack-style straps that keep both hands banjo-free. Go for the heaviest padding you can find if you choose this route. Of special interest are cases that combine some of the best features of both gig bags and hard-shell cases. Check out the Continental Banjo Series from Reunion Blues (www.reunionblues.com) for the best of these new hybrid cases.

Figure 2-7: Gathering together essential accessories: (a) a gig bag and case and (b) a strap, capo, and tuner.

Photographs by Anne Hamersky

Gig bags usually take up less space than hard-shell and flight cases, which can be crucial as you attempt to carry your banjo onboard a puddle-jumper jet with tiny overhead compartments. However, no gig bag offers as much protection as a flight case, which is my usual choice when flying.

More than likely, you already have either a case or a gig bag that came with your banjo. Take a moment to check the fit of the banjo to your case by gently rocking the case back and forth with the banjo inside. Does the banjo move inside the case? Damage occurs most frequently when the banjo is jarred inside the case itself. Take some old T-shirts and wrap them around the empty space between the case and the banjo to create a warm, snug fit to secure your banjo. Your banjo will be safer, and you'll have some extra shirts available for those hot and humid summer festivals.

Strap

Much of the time you make music with others, you'll play standing up, and a banjo strap is absolutely necessary for these situations. Many players also use a strap to balance the weight of their instruments when sitting and practicing at home.

You can easily mistake a guitar strap for a banjo strap, so if you're making a new purchase, be sure to spring for an actual banjo strap (no matter what the electric guitar salesperson swears will work, dude).

I recommend attaching the strap to a bracket that's below the banjo neck. Pass the strap above your left shoulder and then underneath your right arm to attach to another bracket on the other side of your banjo below the tailpiece. You're now ready to take a stand with your banjo.

Capo

You may rarely use one at home, but you'll need a capo to keep up with the singers, mandolin players, and fiddlers at your next jam session. A *capo* is an adjustable clamp that you place behind a fret that raises the pitch of all four strings at once. With the capo, you can easily play in a new key using the chords and licks that are familiar to you in the key of G. Most banjo capos are designed to work for the first through the fourth frets with wider models available for the fifth fret and higher.

Instrumentals that are popular with mandolin players and fiddlers are often played in the keys of A or D. Bluegrass singers will choose the key that best suits their vocal range, with women choosing different keys than men. You'll need a capo in all these situations, so never leave it behind when you're heading out to play with others.

When using your capo to head into a new key, you also need to raise the pitch of the fifth string the same number of frets. Most banjo players install *spikes* on their banjo fingerboards to facilitate this change. Think of spikes as a capo for just the fifth string. It's worth having spikes installed even on a beginner's banjo because you'll need to raise that fifth string without breaking it the moment a tune gets called in a jam in the key of A, B♭, or B.

Tuner

You can't live without this accessory! Banjo players are often maligned by other bluegrass musicians in regard to their ability to get and keep their instruments in tune. Your best defense against such unfounded allegations is to regularly use a peghead-mounted electronic tuner. No tuner can replace your ear for fine-tuning adjustments, but if you're new to the tuning game, your tuner will help you develop your ear as you match a visual reading to what you're hearing.

Tuners start at $15, so there's no excuse not to have one in your case. Keep a couple extra batteries on hand, and you'll always be in good tune.

Chapter 3

Hitting the Ground Running: Tuning, Reading Music, and Making Chords

In This Chapter

▶ Tuning the banjo in open G tuning

▶ Interpreting chord diagrams and reading banjo tablature

▶ Understanding chord progressions and bluegrass song forms

▶ Access the audio tracks and video clips at www.dummies.com/go/bluegrassbanjo

If the five-string banjo is the first musical instrument you've ever played, you've made a great choice! You're about to have more fun than you ever thought possible with the bluegrass licks, techniques, and tunes that are found throughout this book. Before you can say "Dueling Banjos," you'll be making music that will surprise even your most skeptical friends and loved ones.

If you're a total newbie to both the banjo and playing music of any kind, this chapter helps you tackle the techniques, licks, and tunes that appear throughout this book. I introduce just enough musical concepts and terminology for you to become an expert at getting — and keeping — your banjo in tune. I also introduce you to the ways that rhythm and melody work with bluegrass songs. Along the way, you decipher the written language of banjo music as expressed through chord diagrams and banjo tablature.

The original bluegrass banjo masters — J. D. Crowe, Sonny Osborne, Don Reno, Earl Scruggs, and Ralph Stanley — learned almost exclusively by ear, while subsequent generations have become great players by using written resources, as well as by listening and watching others play. This chapter helps you discover your own learning style and move quickly into the banjo fast lane.

Tuning In

In order to preserve family harmony and to be welcome in any jam session, you need to be able to get your banjo in tune. Whether you're practicing at home or taking your banjo out to play with others, consider keeping your banjo in tune your contribution to world peace. In this section, I explain the different ways to keep your banjo in tune, whether you're using a clip-on tuner, tuning the banjo to itself, or tuning to another instrument.

Tuning is not a talent that you're born with, but it's a skill that becomes easier the more you do it. With a bit of experience and knowing what to listen for, you'll be able to hear even small differences when comparing the *pitches* (musical frequencies) of two strings. Be patient as you train your ears and don't hesitate to ask for help when playing with others. Everyone wants you to be in tune just as much as, if not more than, you do!

Getting into G tuning

Many different tunings are used for various kinds of banjo music, but for bluegrass banjo, the vast majority of the music you play uses *open G tuning*. Open G tuning indicates that the banjo is tuned to the notes that, together, sound a G-major chord when the strings are unfretted (or *open*). This is great news for the tuning afflicted, because it's easier to get comfortable tuning to a sweet-sounding, open chord.

String numbers and open G tuning

Musicians distinguish one musical pitch (or *note*) from another by assigning letter names to each pitch (see Appendix A for a complete inventory of all the musical note names and where they can be found on the banjo fingerboard). Banjo players also assign number names to each of their strings. The fifth string is the shortest and highest-pitched string on your banjo. With the banjo in your lap, the fifth string is the string that's the closest as you're looking down on the instrument (and just to avoid any confusion it's the "top" string when you're looking across at another banjo player's instrument). When you've located the fifth string, it's easy to assign numbers to the remaining strings. Keep in mind that the third string is right in the middle — this will come in handy when you begin to read banjo tablature.

Here are the pitches you'll need for open G tuning (listen to Audio Track 1 to hear me play these same notes on my banjo):

- **Fifth string:** G (one octave above third-string G)
- **Fourth string:** D
- **Third string:** G
- **Second string:** B
- **First string:** D (one octave above fourth-string D)

Octaves and major and minor chords

There are two D notes and two G notes in open G tuning, but these string pairs are not tuned to exactly the same pitch. In open G tuning, the fifth string is tuned one octave higher than the third-string G, and the first string is tuned one octave higher than the fourth-string D. When you play a note that is one octave above another note, the higher note is one-half the frequency of the lower note. Our ears hear these as equivalent notes, even though we can also hear that one is higher than the other.

The G, B, and D notes used in open G tuning on the banjo are also the three notes that make up the G-major chord. The chords used to play songs in blue-grass music are either *major* or *minor chords*. For hundreds of years, musicians and listeners have described a major chord as having a bright or happy quality and a minor chord as projecting an introspective or somber mood.

Bluegrass musicians love the irony of singing songs with depressing lyrics about unrequited love, murder, floods, and missing the now-abandoned log cabin where you and your dog were born using cheerful melodies with bright-sounding major chords. Minor chords can nevertheless crop up in songs using otherwise major chords, like the striking E-minor chord in the banjo classic "Foggy Mountain Breakdown"; some beautiful songs, like "Wayfaring Stranger," use mostly minor chords throughout.

Check out Appendix A for an exhaustive supply of all types of banjo chords. Turn to Chapters 9 and 10 for how to use major and minor chords up and down the neck to accompany others.

Tuning made easy with an electronic tuner

Life got incredibly easier for all five-string banjo players — and for those within earshot — with the invention of the clip-on electronic tuner. This inexpensive device is found attached to the pegheads of most bluegrass instruments at every jam session and even on stage.

Tuners come in a variety of shapes and sizes, but they all work in a similar way, as long as you purchase one that's made to attach directly to the peghead (rather than a standalone model that you place on a desktop or music stand or use as an app on a digital device). Here's a step-by-step guide on how to break in your new tuner:

1. **Attach the tuner to the end of the peghead and turn it on.**

   Make sure the tuner is set to "A = 440" so that its calibration will match other musicians' tuners. It's easy to mistake the power switch for the calibration button, and sooner or later you'll need to make this adjustment, consulting the instructions that came with your tuner.

2. **Lightly pick the third string and give the tuner a moment to display a consistent readout.**

   If you're close to being in tune, a G should appear on your tuner's readout. Tuners use lighted bars, needles, or strobes to indicate pitch. In Figure 3-1, for instance, the tuner is indicating that the G pitch is just a bit sharp, as the lighted indicator is slightly to the right of center.

Figure 3-1:
This clip-on tuner's readout indicates that the G note is just a bit sharp.

Photograph courtesy of Elderly Instruments

3. **Bring the string to tune following the direction of the tuner's readout.**

   When a string is higher in pitch than what's desired, the string is *sharp*. When a string is lower in pitch than it should be, it's *flat*. Each tuner indicates whether a string is sharp or flat in slightly different ways. As you turn your tuning peg to either raise or lower the string to the desired pitch, watch the readout on the tuner change. Your string will be in tune when the needle or lighted bars point straight up to the desired pitch.

4. **If your string is sharp, tune it below the desired pitch and then tune up.**

   This tip from the pros will keep the string in tune longer.

Tuners sometimes seem to have minds of their own. If your tuner suddenly sits down on the job and refuses to give you a sensible reading, try shifting the tuner to a new spot on your peghead. Also, a fresh battery will make a world of difference to keep your tuner running right. And you'll be able to see the tuner readout more clearly when you're playing around a campfire at a 2 a.m. jam session.

Tuning the banjo using relative tuning

In the days before electronic tuners, humans used only their ears to bravely tune their banjos. Whatever advances in tuning technology lie ahead, your ears will still always be your most accurate tuners. For those occasions when a tuner isn't handy or when you need to get in tune with another instrument, you'll call upon relative tuning to get your banjo ready to go.

Tuning the banjo to itself

Relative tuning can be done with or without a close family member present. With *relative tuning,* you use one of your open strings or the strings of another instrument as a reference point to get your banjo in tune. Here's how to do it, using the lowest-pitched fourth string as a guide:

1. **Fret the fourth string at the fifth fret, pick the note, and compare with the sound of the open third string.**

   For most banjos, you'll turn the third-string peg clockwise to raise the pitch. When the third string is tune, it should match an electronic tuner's G note. You'll now use this string to tune your second string.

2. **Play the third string at the fourth fret and tune the open second string to this pitch.**

   This time, you'll turn the second-string peg counterclockwise to raise the pitch. When the second string is in tune, your tuner should indicate a B note. It's now time to use this string to tune your first string.

3. **Play the second string at the third fret to tune the first string open.**

   Like the second string, you'll turn the first string by tuning the peg counterclockwise to raise the pitch. When the first string is in tune, it should read as a D note on your tuner. You now will fret the first string in order to tune your fifth string.

4. **Play the first string at the fifth fret to tune the fifth string open.**

   As you're looking at the fifth-string peg from above, you'll turn it counterclockwise to raise this string, which reads as a G note on your tuner.

You can start this process using any open string as a guide, and many players will first tune their open third string before tuning the rest of their instrument. In this case, you then use the open third string as a reference point to tune the lower-pitched fourth string by fretting it at the fifth fret.

Figure 3-2 shows the pitches of the banjo's open strings and reviews these relative tuning steps.

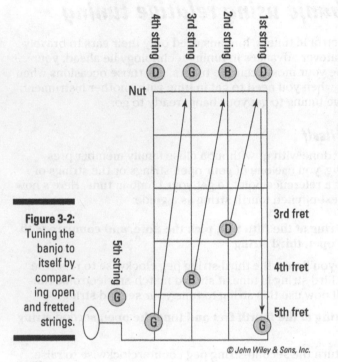

Figure 3-2:
Tuning the banjo to itself by comparing open and fretted strings.

© John Wiley & Sons, Inc.

To become a tuning wizard, check out Video Clip 1, where I show you how to tune your banjo using either relative tuning or an electronic tuner.

Tuning to another instrument

You can also use a reference note from another instrument, such as a dobro, guitar, fiddle, or mandolin, to get your banjo in tune. In this case, you're tuning one of your strings to match the same pitch on another instrument. You can then tune the rest of your strings using the relative-tuning methods outlined in the preceding section.

Here's a summary of the easiest ways to get your banjo in tune in this way:

- ✔ **Dobro:** The open fourth, third, second, and first strings on the dobro match these same open strings on your banjo (D, G, B, and D).

- ✔ **Guitar:** The open fourth, third, and second strings on the guitar match exactly the fourth, third, and second strings on your banjo. They're D, G, and B notes on both instruments.

- ✔ **Fiddle or mandolin:** The lowest string on these instruments (a G note) matches the open third string on your banjo, and the third string matches your open first string (a D note).

After you've tuned your banjo using either an electronic tuner or another instrument as a guide, it's a great idea to touch up the tuning once more by listening to each string and using your ears to identify any problem strings. At this point in the process, only very small adjustments should be needed. Try comparing the octaves at the fifth and third and fourth and first strings. Also try playing the first and fifth strings. If your banjo is in tune, these string pairs should all sound good when played together.

Reading Chord Diagrams and Tablature

Nothing replaces your ears and the time you spend with the banjo in your hands to train your fingers and brain to become a great banjo player, but chord diagrams and banjo tablature are useful tools that make the job of remembering where your fingers are supposed to go a lot easier. You'll master the techniques and tunes in this book more quickly if you become adept at using both tools.

Chord diagrams indicate the fretting-hand fingers used to form chords, while *banjo tablature* is the banjo player's equivalent of sheet music, showing all the moves that the picking and fretting hands make in the course of playing a particular song, along with the duration of each note played.

Forming chords using chord diagrams

Chords provide the framework for the songs you play on the banjo and are also the foundation for what you play with the fretting hand when accompanying others. *Chord diagrams* visually reproduce your banjo fingerboard, showing you the location of the fretting fingers on your strings and frets. Take a look at Figure 3-3 to check out the chord diagram for the C chord.

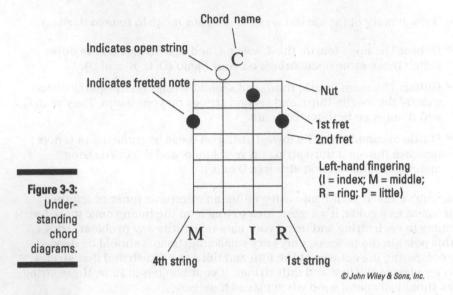

Chord name

Indicates open string

Indicates fretted note

Nut

1st fret

2nd fret

Left-hand fingering
(I = index; M = middle;
R = ring; P = little)

4th string   1st string

M   I   R

Figure 3-3:
Understanding chord diagrams.

© John Wiley & Sons, Inc.

If you turn your banjo around so that the instrument is facing you, that's how your strings and frets are represented in a chord diagram. Here are some tips for remembering how to read chord diagrams:

- The vertical lines match the strings of your instrument, with the fourth string on the far left and the first string on the far right.

- The top horizontal line corresponds to the banjo nut, with the next horizontal line below it the first fret, the next line below that the second fret, and so on.

- The circles represent fretted positions, indicating both strings and frets.

- Fretting-finger indications are indicated either below the chord diagram box, as shown here, or within the circles themselves. The following letters are used to indicate which fretting-hand finger is used:

  - I: Index finger

  - M: Middle finger

  - R: Ring finger

  - P: Pinky finger

  - T: Thumb

For the C chord, use your fretting-hand middle finger to fret the fourth string at the second fret. The third string is open. The second string is fretted at the first fret with the index finger, and the first string is fretted with the ring finger.

Now check out these chord diagrams for the G, D7, F, and D-major chords (see Figure 3-4).

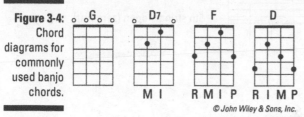

Figure 3-4:
Chord diagrams for commonly used banjo chords.

© John Wiley & Sons, Inc.

TIP

Chord diagrams can also be used to show how to fret up-the-neck chords where you need to fret the fifth string. In this case, the chord diagram adds an extra vertical line to the left, which represents this string. Check out Figure 3-5 to view a chord diagram for a D7 chord at the 12th fret.

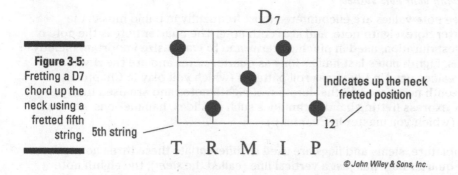

Figure 3-5:
Fretting a D7 chord up the neck using a fretted fifth string.

© John Wiley & Sons, Inc.

Understanding banjo tablature

Banjo tablature looks a lot like regular music with one big difference: In banjo tablature, the horizontal lines represent your five banjo strings, not a musical staff as in conventional music. The first string of your banjo is represented by the top line of tablature; the fifth string, by the bottom line.

Locating melody notes in tab

Instead of musical notes filling the lines and the spaces as in regular music, numbers are placed on the lines of banjo tablature, indicating what string is picked and whether that string is fretted (with "0" indicating an open string). Check out Figure 3-6 to see how this aspect of tablature works.

Figure 3-6:
Playing strings with open and fretted notes.

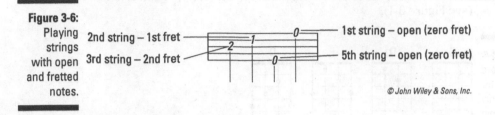

© *John Wiley & Sons, Inc.*

Getting the rhythm in tab

In addition to expressing melody, banjo tablature also conveys all the rhythmic aspects you need to play a song successfully. Rhythm can be the trickiest aspect of banjo tab to understand. Don't forget to consult the audio tracks and video clips at www.dummies.com/go/bluegrassbanjo to grasp the sound of each exercise and song in addition to consulting the tab.

Knowing your note values

Three note values are encountered most frequently in banjo music: the quarter note, eighth note, and sixteenth note. The quarter note is the note of longest duration, used in pinch patterns and to emphasize important melody notes. Eighth notes last half as long as quarter notes and are the rhythmic values used in bluegrass roll patterns (which you play in Chapter 5). Sixteenth notes are half the duration of eighth notes and are used to rhythmically express fretting-hand techniques such as slides, hammer-ons, and pulloffs (which you master in Chapter 6).

In tablature, stems and flags are used to differentiate these three note values. The quarter note has just a vertical line (called the *stem*); the eighth note has a stem and one beam or flag; and the sixteenth note has a stem and two beams or flags. Take a look at Tab 3-1 to see these differences.

Understanding time signatures

Time signatures convey how many beats are used to organize the rhythm of each song. Most bluegrass banjo music is played in a time signature of either 4/4 or 3/4. Time signatures are typically written with one number on top of another, like a fraction without the line, and are located in the tab at the very beginning of a song.

The top number indicates how many beats are in a cycle, and the bottom number represents the note value that equals one beat. A 4/4 time signature indicates a recurring rhythmic cycle of four beats where a quarter note equals one beat, while a 3/4 time signature points to a recurring cycle of three beats.

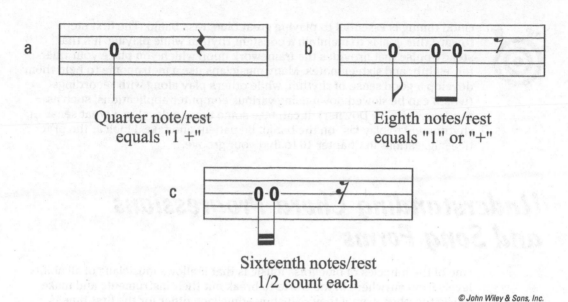

© John Wiley & Sons, Inc.

Tab 3-1: Reading quarter, eighth, and sixteenth notes in banjo tab.

A *measure* is the representation in tablature of this recurring cycle of beats. One measure is separated from another by a vertical line running through the tab staff. Each measure is equal in regard to the number of beats contained in each one and with the possible number of note combinations you can use to fill that measure.

The count for a 4/4 time signature is "one-two-three-four," creating a recurring cycle of four beats. A quarter note occupies the space between one number (or beat) and the next; it takes two eighth notes to fill this same amount of musical space. Four sixteenth notes are needed to occupy the same amount of musical space as one quarter note. The short rhythmic exercise in Tab 3-2 (Audio Track 2) reveals these differences.

© John Wiley & Sons, Inc.

Tab 3-2: Mixing quarter, eighth, and sixteenth notes.

Good timing is essential to playing great bluegrass banjo. The first step toward this goal is to maintain a constant rhythm while playing. It's that steady pulse that provides the framework upon which you place your quarter, eighth, and sixteen notes. Many musicians use a metronome to help them develop a good sense of rhythm, while others play along with recordings (which can be slowed down using various computer applications, such as the Amazing Slow Downer). It can take some time to develop a great sense of rhythm *and* to play fast on the banjo. Be patient and take a look at the practice suggestions in Chapter 16 to find your groove.

Understanding Chord Progressions and Song Forms

One of the miracles of bluegrass music is that it allows musicians of all ability levels from anywhere in the world to break out their instruments and make music together, even if they're just meeting each other for the first time. A shared repertoire of vocal songs and instrumentals helps make this possible. As you gain confidence playing with others, you also pick up the skills that allow you to quickly grasp and play along on new songs, sometimes on the fly.

Chord progressions are the road map that musicians follow to play a song together. Getting introduced to some of the common song forms used in bluegrass music will help you more quickly understand new songs as you hear them. To close this chapter on music fundamentals, it's time to take a look at how banjo players use their knowledge of chord progressions and song forms to become better players.

Reading the road map: Chord progressions

A *chord progression* is defined as the chords that are used to accompany a song, the order in which the chords are played, and how long each chord lasts before you move on to play the following one in the song. When you're comfortable with a few basic playing techniques, you can play along with all kinds of different songs, changing chords to match each song's unique progression. (Check out Chapter 4 to start using roll patterns to play along with chord progressions.)

Many bluegrass songs use just three chords. In the key of G, these chords are G, C, and D or D7. Musicians often describe the chord progression of a song using numbers or Roman numerals, indicating I, IV, and V (or 1, 4, and 5) in place of the G, C, and D7 chords.

I, IV, and V refer to the chords built on the first, fourth, and fifth notes of the major scale that corresponds to the *key* of a song. In the key of G, the G, C, and D notes are the first, fourth, and fifth notes of a G-major scale, and the chords built upon each of these notes are major chords. In the key of D, D, G, and A are the first, fourth, and fifth notes of the D-major scale. The D-, G-, and A-major chords are the chords you'll use most when playing a bluegrass song in this key.

Thinking of songs in terms of what's sometimes called the *number system* allows you to understand the chord structure of a song independent from its key. This can come in handy when using a capo or when playing a song in a different key to match the range of a singer.

Hearing bluegrass song forms

Bluegrass songs tend to sound alike because they use similar chord progressions and song forms. This is actually a good thing because it's what allows musicians to quickly pick up new songs in jam sessions. In this section, I take a look at a few of the most frequently encountered song forms in bluegrass.

Verse song form

Many bluegrass songs, like "Little Maggie," "Man of Constant Sorrow," and "Pretty Polly," use a song form that consists of a verse that's repeated over and over again until the song is finished. When you take a banjo solo on this kind of song, you follow the same chord progression and melody as when the singer is singing.

Verse/chorus song form

Other bluegrass songs consist of a verse, that's often sung by a lead singer, followed by a chorus sung in three-part harmony. Some songs, like "Will the Circle Be Unbroken," "Salty Dog Blues," and "Roll in My Sweet Baby's Arms," use the same chord progression for the chorus as for the verse. Other songs, like "Old Home Place," "Jesse James," and "Cabin in Caroline," use a different chord progression and melody for the chorus. When taking a banjo solo on a verse/chorus song form, you almost always follow the chord progression and melody of the verse.

Fiddle-tune song form

There's a special category of bluegrass instrumentals called *fiddle tunes* and this very large repertoire of instrumentals provides a very rich source of jam-session songs. Most fiddle tunes follow an AABB song form in which two contrasting sections, each with its own melody and chord progression, are played twice.

In a jam session, you'll hear vocal songs performed in a wide variety of keys based on the singer's vocal range. However, instrumentals are usually key specific. Don't forget your capo when you head out to play — you'll use it in both situations!

Chapter 4

Fretting and Picking

. . . .

In This Chapter

▶ Finding comfortable fretting- and picking-hand positions

▶ Trying out your first chords

▶ Fitting and using fingerpicks

▶ Playing the pinch pattern to accompany songs

▶ Access the audio tracks and video clips at www.dummies.com/go/bluegrassbanjo

. . . .

There's a lot to think about when you're playing bluegrass banjo: You've got chords to form, licks to play, and lots of notes to pick as fast as humanly possible. You'll be able to do all these things and a whole lot more if you develop great playing technique at the outset of your banjo explorations.

In this chapter, you discover the best ways to fret and pick by finding hand positions that are just right for you. You form your first chords, get comfortable with fingerpicks, and play your first songs using authentic bluegrass techniques. This is really the moment you've been waiting for: It's time to become a real bluegrass banjo player!

Fretting and Forming Chords

When you press the tip of a finger just behind one of the frets on your banjo fingerboard to find a new pitch to play, that's *fretting*. You use fretting techniques to make chords, find melody notes, and create cool effects that just can't be managed on the open strings of your banjo.

Every time you take your banjo out to play, you're going to need to fret one or more strings to play a song (unless your total repertoire consists of "Taps," which frankly, won't land you very many gigs). When you fret chords on the banjo, you'll use more than one finger to fret different strings at the same time. Because you'll be fretting pretty much all the time, it just makes sense to discover the most efficient and comfortable hand position to put all this energy to good use.

Finding a comfortable hand position

The key to finding the perfect fretting-hand position is to relax. Given our perfectionist tendencies, I know that this can be a difficult thing for banjo players to do. With a little deep breathing and awareness of what your hand is doing, you'll soon find your fretting groove. Check out these tips for easy fretting:

- ✔ **Practice relaxation, from your shoulder to your fretting hand.** Your hand will naturally find its best position if your arm is relaxed. As you release tension from your shoulder and elbow, your hand will move forward over the banjo fingerboard. This puts your fingers in better position to fret your favorite chords and licks.

- ✔ **Practice while wearing a banjo strap.** Many banjos are heavier at the headstock end of the instrument, where the tuners are located. Don't let your fretting hand support the weight of the neck or try to balance your banjo. That's the job of a properly fitted instrument strap.

- ✔ **Place your thumb on the upper half of the back of the neck (see Figure 4-1a).** As you fret individual notes and chords, position your hand almost perpendicular to the neck, as if you're reaching out to shake someone's hand. Keep the pad of your thumb touching the neck as you're fretting — try not to rotate onto the left side of your thumb because this will move your hand out of position.

- ✔ **Keep the palm away from the banjo neck (see Figure 4-1b).** The goal is to bring your fingers out in front of the fingerboard as much as possible to make fretting a lot easier. This step and the previous one will do just that! If you're positioning your fretting hand from the pad of your thumb, more than likely you won't be grabbing the neck with the palm of your hand. If you're accustomed to supporting the neck with the palm, you'll want to unlearn this habit by adopting this position.

- ✔ **Press the tips of fretting fingers just behind the fret (see Figure 4-1c).** Use your fingertips to make contact with the strings and position your fretting fingers just behind the frets. Try experimenting with the amount of downward pressure you exert as you form chords. You may be surprised at how little work it takes to get a great sound once your hand is in a good position.

✔ **Angle your fretting fingers so that they don't block any open strings.**
You'll often have an open string adjacent to a string you're fretting, as
in the C chord where the third string remains unfretted. Using those
fingertips as you form chords should minimize your fretting footprint
and allow those open strings to ring clearly.

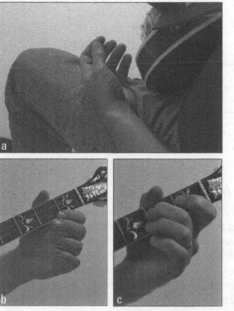

Figure 4-1:
Finding your
optimal fret-
ting hand
position:
(a) Placing
your thumb
on the neck,
(b) keeping
your palm
away from
the neck,
and (c) fret-
ting with the
tips of your
fingers.

Photographs by Anne Hamersky

Check out Video Clip 2 to review these fretting position tips. If you're ready
for more challenging left-hand maneuvers such as slides, hammer-ons,
pull-offs and bends, head over to Chapter 6 and jump in!

Fretting G, D7, C, and Em chords

Whether you're playing around a campfire jam session or improvising a
blazing solo at your next festival gig, chords are at the foundation of everything you do as a banjo player. A *chord progression* names the chords used in
a song, lets you know the order of these chords, and also lets you know how
long they last. It's the road map that everyone follows to play together, even
if they've never heard the song before the moment it begins.

The great news is that you only have to get familiar with a few chords to play a *lot* of different bluegrass songs. Start with the four chords in this section — G, D7, C, and Em (see Figure 4-2) — and then introduce yourself to new chords as you need them in the songs that you're playing (and check out Chapter 10 for some fancy up-the-neck chords). You'll soon be the master of your chord universe, especially with the help of all the chords listed in Appendix A of this book.

Figure 4-2:
Chord dia-
grams for
the G, D7, C,
and Em
chords.

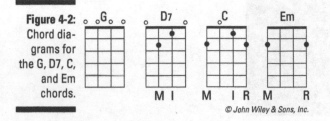

© John Wiley & Sons, Inc.

The G chord: *When you fret nothing at all*

In so many ways, banjo players have it much better than our guitar- and mandolin-playing brothers and sisters. We're louder, we play more notes, we have flashier instruments, and we usually get more applause than they do. We also can play the single most important chord we need in all of blue-grass music by fretting absolutely nothing at all. Amazing, isn't it? All right, we do need to be in G tuning to perform this unfretted feat, but you know how to tune your banjo already, right? (If not, head back to Chapter 3 for a refresher course.)

You'll soon use lots of flashy techniques that require you to be fretting one or more strings while playing a G chord. Chapter 6 covers them all: slides, hammer-ons, pull-offs, and chokes. They all go along with the G chord and will make it sound even cooler.

The D7 chord: *It takes two*

There are more than a few songs out there that just use two chords, the G and the D7 chords. Place your middle finger just behind the second fret of the third string and your index finger behind the first fret of the second string and you're in business (see Figure 4-3).

The C chord: *You can make it with three*

There are thousands of country, folk, bluegrass, and blues songs that use three chords and the C, G, and D7 chords together allow you to play just about all of them. When you've mastered the C chord, you'll be ready to cry in your beer as you're blowin' in the wind while buildin' that cabin home on the hill before your baby's done left you.

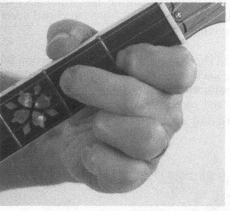

Figure 4-3:
Matching fretting fingers to strings for the D7 chord.

Photograph by Anne Hamersky

To fret the C chord, use your index finger to fret the second string at the first fret, just as you did for the D7 chord. In addition, you'll fret the fourth string at the second fret with your middle finger and your ring finger will fret the second fret of the first string. Make sure that your index and middle fingers aren't touching the third string, which remains open for the C chord (see Figure 4-4).

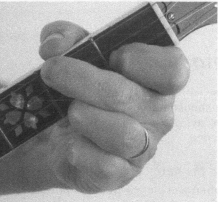

Figure 4-4:
Matching fretting fingers to strings for the C chord.

Photograph by Anne Hamersky

The Em chord: When it's time to get all emotional

The Em (pronounced "E minor") chord is the somewhat mysterious chord you hear in songs such as "Foggy Mountain Breakdown," "Blackberry Blossom," and "Cherokee Shuffle." Minor chords are characterized as having a melancholy sound when you hear them alone, but when it's used in a song with G, D, and C7 chords, like "Wagon Wheel," the Em chord adds an element of complexity that draws in your listeners.

To fret the Em chord, put all three of your fingers into position for the C chord (see the preceding section). Now, lift up your index finger to reveal the open second string. That's the Em chord. Your middle finger should be fretting the fourth string at the second fret and your ring finger the first string at the second fret. The third and second strings remain open for the Em chord (see Figure 4-5).

Figure 4-5:
Matching fretting fingers to strings for the Em chord.

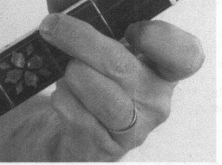

Photograph by Anne Hamersky

Strumming along

You'll want to get so familiar with chords that it seems as if your fretting fingers go where they need to almost automatically. You can make this happen by strumming along to your favorite songs, following the chord progressions and changing chords as needed.

Moving from one chord to the next

Keeping a steady rhythm when you play any song on the banjo means not slowing down as you change chords. Check out these tips for faster fretting:

✔ **Keep your fretting fingers pointed toward the fingerboard, as close to the open strings as possible.** You'll be much more accurate if your fingers don't have to move very far to touch the strings when it's time to fret a chord.

✔ **When you lift fretting fingers to play open strings, keep the fingers close and pointed toward the fingerboard.** You can breathe a sigh of relief when it's time to lift off of a chord, but keep those fretting fingers at the ready — you'll need them again very soon, guaranteed!

✔ **When it's time to move to a new chord, try to fret all the strings needed for that chord at the same time.** This skill may take a bit of effort, especially as you go to fret the C chord. Try moving slowly back and forth from whatever chord you're perfecting back to the open G chord to keep those fretting fingers in line.

Strumming your first songs

It's a lot more fun to familiarize yourself with chords by playing real songs where you'll actually use them. Don't worry about putting your fingerpicks on right now — you'll take care of that in the following sections of this chapter. For now, you'll sound great brushing downward across all five strings with a downward motion of your thumb in a steady rhythm, as you concentrate on changing chords.

PLAY THIS!
▶

In the following two examples, each downward strum is indicated by a slash mark and you play two strums per measure. Occasionally, well-known songs will have the same chord progression — that's the case with the song in Tab 4-1 (Audio Track 3).

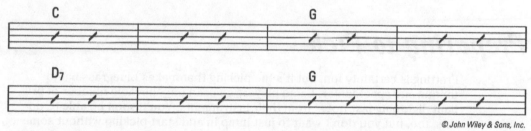

© John Wiley & Sons, Inc.

Tab 4-1: Strumming along to "This Land"-type chord progression using G, C, and D7 chords.

Bluegrass musicians love to sing and play "Little Darling Pal of Mine," and this song has the same chord progression as the very well-known "This Land Is Your Land." How are these songs different? The melodies and lyrics, of course, as well as the titles. (Which reminds me of the ever-popular bluegrass joke, "How can you tell one bluegrass song from another? The titles.")

PLAY THIS! ▶ After wrapping your fingers around "Little Darling," check out the song in Tab 4-2 (Audio Track 4). You're now adding the Em chord to the G, C, and D7 chords to play a progression that's reminiscent of the nouveau acoustic favorite "Wagon Wheel."

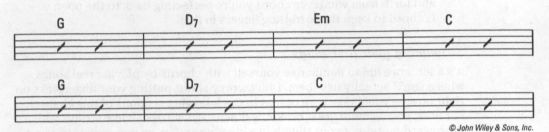

© John Wiley & Sons, Inc.

Tab 4-2: Strumming along to "Wagon Wheel"–type chord progression using G, C, D7, and Em chords.

You'll master these chord progressions much faster if you first listen to the audio tracks. When you're moving smoothly from one chord to the next, keeping a steady rhythm with your strums, try playing along with me.

Preparing to Pick

Fretting is certainly fun, but it's the picking that makes bluegrass banjo unique and spectacular. Banjo players coax an unbelievable number of brilliant, lightning-fast notes from their instruments. You'll soon be able to do this, too, but you don't want to just jump in and start picking without some guidelines to get you started.

It may sound like banjo players use all five fingers of their hands to play the many notes they play, but we actually just use our thumbs, index fingers, and middle fingers to create such a glorious racket. Bluegrass banjo style is also called *three-finger style* for this very reason. In this section, you begin to get the most out of your picking hand as you discover how fingerpicks and the proper hand position can help you find that authentic bluegrass banjo sound.

Selecting and fitting picks

Fingerpicks are an essential part of playing banjo in bluegrass style. You'll play louder, faster, and with more accuracy and power with fingerpicks turbocharging your thumb, index finger, and middle finger. You'll also hear a clearer, brighter tone from your instrument with the fingerpicks adding a percussive shimmer to the banjo's natural-born twang.

It can sometimes take a little while to get used to playing with fingerpicks, especially if you've already spent some time using just your bare fingers. They may feel bulky at first, but most players get accustomed to fingerpicks very quickly, often after just a few minutes of use. Don't delay this transition — your picking fingers will soon thank you for it!

You'll find myriad choices of fingerpicks waiting for you at your favorite local music store. Before you pick out your picks, it's a good idea to know what's available and how picks differ from one another.

Tweaking the thumbpick

Thumbpicks consist of a flat striking surface, or *blade*, which moves across the strings, and a *band* that attaches the pick around your thumb. The blade and band are usually shaped from one piece of molded plastic or folded metal, but many players today are choosing sophisticated (and more expensive) thumbpicks with polymer blades riveted to metal bands, such as the BlueChip pick (`www.bluechippick.net`).

Thumbpicks are often sized in small, medium, and large, according to the size of the band (in which case you look for an *S, M,* or *L* stamped somewhere on the pick), and blades also differ in length, shape and thickness. Make sure you choose a thumbpick with a snug fit — you don't want the pick moving on your thumb as you play. You'll choose the blade type based on what sounds best, feels right to your thumb, and best matches the band fit.

Many players settle on a medium blade length and thickness and will choose from brand names such as Acri, BlueChip, Dunlop, Ernie Ball, Fred Kelly, Golden Gate, National, and ProPik, among many others. Check out Figure 4-6 to take a look at some of these choices.

Figuring out the fingerpicks

Bluegrass banjo players prefer metal fingerpicks (instead of plastic) to get the pinpoint attack and crisp tone needed for bluegrass playing. Like the thumbpick, fingerpicks also consist of a blade that strikes the strings and a band that keeps the pick wrapped around your fingers.

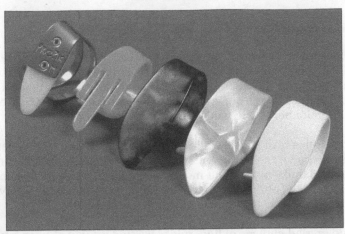

Figure 4-6:
Comparing plastic, metal, and polymer thumbpicks.

Photograph courtesy of Elderly Instruments

Fingerpicks come in a variety of sizes and shapes. Some fingerpicks fit larger hands well, and some fingerpicks are stiffer, providing more resistance and a different tone. Some fingerpicks have flat blades, while others are curved. All these differences can affect how the picks feel on your fingers and the sounds you produce when you play. Look for Acri, Bob Perry, Dunlop, National, Perfect Touch, ProPik, Sammy Shelor, and Showcase 41 fingerpicks, among other good choices, and check out Figure 4-7 to view some of the many different sizes and shapes of fingerpicks you can add to your collection.

Figure 4-7:
Comparing types of fingerpicks.

Photograph by Anne Hamersky

It's in the nature of bluegrass banjo players to try almost every kind of thumbpick and fingerpick that's available to find just the right fit and sound for their ever-changing tastes. There's nothing wrong with this! What works for you will change over time, and it's always fun to try out new picks and other banjo gadgets. Don't forget that all your purchases will make for great conversation starters at your next jam session.

If you're buying local, you'll be able to try on picks right in the store. If you're just starting out, I recommend taking home a pair of whatever picks they have in stock, as long as the picks aren't so big that they're falling off of your fingers. After you've gotten used to your first set of picks, you can check out online acoustic specialty stores for other pick options when you're feeling ready.

Putting on the picks

Fit the thumbpick with the blade side facing inward toward your other fingers. For the best playing angle, try positioning the pick between your first joint and the end of your thumb.

Place the fingerpicks on your picking-hand index and middle fingers with the blade side of the pick facing toward the palm of your hand, opposite your fingernails.

Many players prefer a curved fingerpick blade that fits more snugly against the end of the finger, but you may need to bend the blade of the pick to get this shape. Gradually push and pull on the pick until you find the desired angle. Figure 4-8 shows how the fingerpicks should look when properly shaped and positioned.

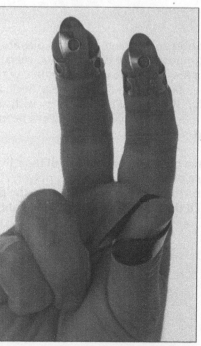

Figure 4-8:
Proper positioning of the thumbpick and fingerpicks.

Photograph by Anne Hamersky

Video Clip 3 reviews these steps and shows you how to get the best and most comfortable fit from your new thumbpick and fingerpicks.

Finding a great picking-hand position

I really want you to become a great bluegrass banjo player, and it's time to relate the single most important recommendation in this entire book to help get you there. Are you ready? Here it is:

The key to great playing is to find a comfortable picking-hand position that allows you to play with relaxation and ease while producing a beautiful, full tone with enough volume to peel the paint off of your neighbor's RV.

Bluegrass banjo is all about precision and power in the picking hand, and successful playing begins with how you position the hand to strike notes with the thumb, index finger, and middle finger. Read on to experience a method that I've developed over 40 years of teaching that has helped thousands of players achieve their banjo dreams. After you carefully follow the steps in this very important section, all you'll need is some paint to make amends with that neighbor.

Playing with relaxation

You may think that with all the notes that bluegrass banjo players typically are called upon to play, you're supposed to be extremely *un*-relaxed to play well. However, if you check out a few YouTube videos of some of the most well-known players of all time — folks like J. D. Crowe, Béla Fleck, Don Reno, and Earl Scruggs — you'll find that the best of the best play with an uncanny naturalness and relaxation, as if playing the banjo has always been the easiest thing in the world for them to do.

Although many great players have been playing almost all their lives, you, too, can discover this same sense of ease, even as a new player. Finding your comfort zone begins with relaxing the entire arm that will do the picking, from shoulder to fingertips. You'll then position your picking hand on the banjo head to get ready to play.

Proceed through the following steps to see how this works and watch Video Clip 4 to watch me demonstrate this process:

1. **While seated upright in a chair without arms, relax your picking arm completely, releasing all tension (see Figure 4-9a).**

   Try shaking out your hand a few times and feel the weight of your arm as it extends toward the floor.

2. **Send a wave of relaxation from the shoulder of the picking arm, down through your elbow and wrist to the ends of your fingers.**

   Hold this posture for a few moments and then try relaxing down a few more notches by allowing additional tension to escape from your arm in successive steps. You'll be surprised at how much more relaxed your arm can become through this mental repetition.

3. **When you feel just about as relaxed as you've ever been, lift your arm and place your hand on your thigh, with your palm facing upward (see Figure 4-9b).**

   As your hand remains relaxed, your fingers should be curved inward, as if you were loosely holding a ball. Remember this shape and the feeling of your hand at this moment. This is the position you want to maintain when you place your picking hand on the banjo head.

4. **Move your forearm to the armrest of your banjo and position the picking hand such that the palm and fingers face the banjo head and strings (see Figure 4-9c).**

   As you keep your elbow relaxed in toward your banjo, your hand will be above the strings and your wrist should be arched.

5. **Slide your forearm along the armrest until your ring finger and pinky finger make contact with the banjo head just below the first string and to the left of the bridge as you look down on your picking hand (see Figure 4-9d).**

   These anchor fingers provide a point of reference so that the fingers know where they are in relation to the strings.

A good playing position results from keeping your arm relaxed and positioning the picking fingers so that it's easy for them to reach the strings. Your ring finger and pinky finger should be making contact with the head but not touching the bridge. Remember to keep your wrist arched for the best results.

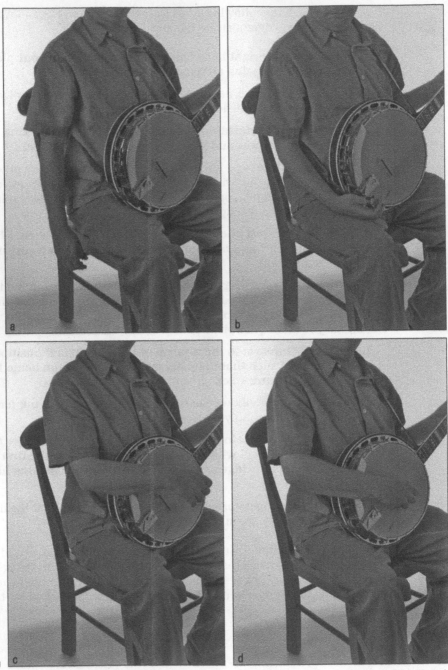

Figure 4-9:
Using relaxation techniques to position the picking hand.

Photographs by Anne Hamersky

Striking the strings

It's time for your picking fingers to meet the strings. In this section, I show you how you can continue to use relaxation techniques to bring out the strongest sound from your thumb, index finger, and middle finger.

Picking with the thumb

The thumb is the most active of the three fingers in bluegrass banjo, commonly playing the fifth through the second strings and sometimes even the first string, moving down and across to strike each string. The thumb adds drive and volume to your playing, and many picking patterns begin with a thumb note. When you're in the groove, you're "puttin' the thumb to it," which is a very good thing when you play bluegrass banjo.

With your wrist arched, use the blade of your thumbpick to meet the strings with a sweeping motion from the joint that's closest to your hand. The thumb should make contact by moving across the strings rather than having to move down and then up again. (If this is happening to you, check to see if you have enough wrist arch to get the sweeping motion you need.)

Picking with the index finger and middle finger

The index finger most often plays the second and third strings, and the middle finger plays the first string in bluegrass banjo. With the wrist arched, use your first joint (the one that's closest to your hand) to make contact by moving directly across the strings toward your palm without any sideways finger motion. After your finger has moved through a string, there's no need to purposely sweep it back out. Just relax, and the finger will return to its ready position on its own.

You'll get much more volume and power from your index finger and middle finger by moving primarily from the first joint of these fingers. How exactly do you do this? Well, you've probably already moved your fingers in this way before. Have you ever had to scratch a mosquito bite? If you're really needing to scratch that kind of itch, you'll be using the first joint of your fingers and that's the exact same motion you'll use when striking banjo strings with these fingers.

Anchoring the picking hand

You've probably noticed by now that your ring finger and pinky finger aren't allowed to wear picks and don't even get to strike the strings in bluegrass banjo. However, they're still important position players on your picking-finger team. By anchoring your hand on the banjo head, these fingers establish a stable and consistent picking-hand position. Your picking fingers know exactly where they are at all times in relation to your banjo strings, thanks to the support of your trusted anchor fingers.

Many new players have a difficult time at first keeping both fingers touching the banjo head to support the picking hand. They find that when the middle finger plays the first string, the ring finger just naturally wants to lift off and move together with the other finger. If you're arching your wrist and picking from the first joint of your index finger and middle finger, you'll find it easier to keep both fingers down. Figure 4-10 shows how your picking hand looks with one and two fingers of support.

Although several great professional players anchor their hands with only the pinky finger, the great majority of banjo players have found a way to use both the ring finger and pinky finger to support the picking hand. A trick that's worked for many of my students is to spend a few weeks anchoring with just the ring finger touching the banjo head, training it to remain steady and independent of the middle finger. When your ring finger is cooperating, it's a relatively easy task to plant the pinky finger to give further support.

If you've made the effort and you're still having trouble keeping both fingers down, you have the green light to play with only the pinky anchoring your hand. Getting a good sound and playing with relaxation should be your primary goals as you discover your optimal picking-hand position. If it feels comfortable and sounds right, you're on the road to finding what works best for you.

Figure 4-10:
Anchoring
the picking
hand with
(a) the ring
finger and
pinky finger
gives more
stability
than using
(b) just the
pinky alone.

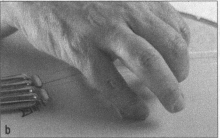

Photographs by Anne Hamersky

Picking with Patterns: The Pinch

You've found a comfortable picking-hand position and you've got your thumbpicks and fingerpicks on your fingers. You're ready to finally play! In this section, you try out the *pinch pattern,* a basic technique that you can use to follow chord progressions and play songs with others. Although it's relatively simple compared to what you'll encounter in subsequent chapters, the pinch pattern is a bona-fide, honest-to-goodness, real bluegrass banjo picking technique. It's time to take the first step on your bluegrass banjo journey!

Playing pinches

Here's your complete guide to playing the pinch pattern:

1. **Play the third string with your thumb.**

2. **Play the fifth, second, and first strings with your thumb, index finger, and middle finger.**

3. **Play the fourth string with your thumb.**

4. **Repeat Step 2.**

The pinch pattern derives its name from the motion your fingers make in Steps 2 and 4 to play the three strings together.

Check out Audio Track 5 and Video Clip 5 to experience this important bluegrass picking-hand technique. Tab 4-3 shows the pinch pattern in banjo tab for the G, C, D7, and Em chords.

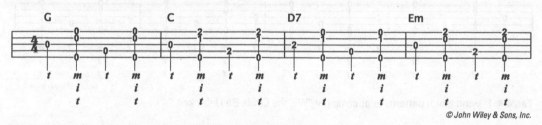

© John Wiley & Sons, Inc.

Tab 4-3: Playing the pinch pattern for the G, C, D7, and Em chords.

Trying out the pinch pattern

The pinch pattern allows you to hit the ground quickly and make some great music with others without a lot of fuss (or practice!). Try playing the pinch pattern for two bluegrass standards, "Will the Circle Be Unbroken" (Tab 4-4; Audio Track 6) and "Long Journey Home" (Tab 4-5; Audio Track 7).

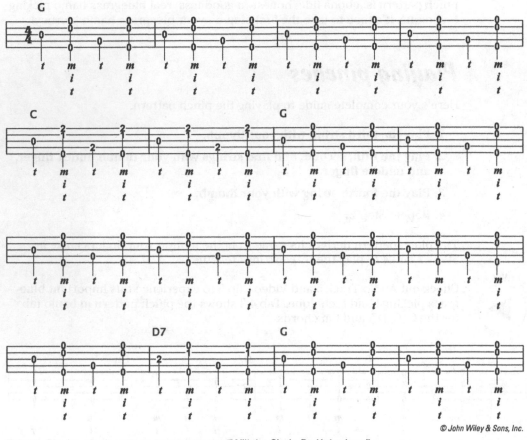

© John Wiley & Sons, Inc.

Tab 4-4: Playing pinch patterns to accompany "Will the Circle Be Unbroken."

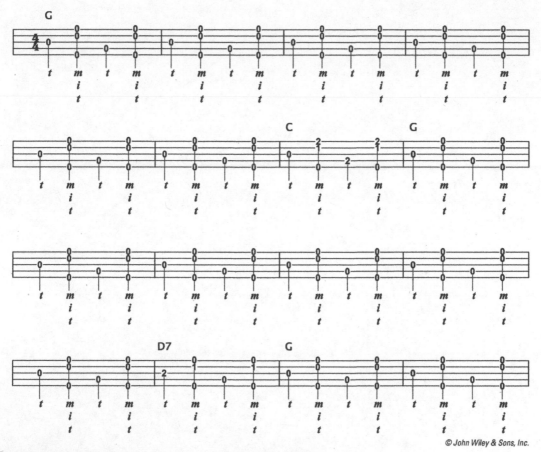

Tab 4-5: Playing pinch patterns to accompany "Long Journey Home."

Part II

Let's Roll! Scruggs-Style Banjo Essentials

Photograph by Anne Hamersky

Find essential bluegrass banjo intros and endings in a free article at
www.dummies.com/extras/bluegrassbanjo.

In this part . . .

✔ Get acquainted with ten essential picking patterns and discover how to create variations to match the chords you play in songs.

✔ Add fretting-hand techniques (slides, hammer-ons, pull-offs, and bends) to give your playing an authentic bluegrass banjo sound.

✔ Play dozens of great bluegrass banjo licks and classic banjo instrumentals arranged for new players.

✔ Find and match melodies to bluegrass playing techniques to create your own banjo music in bluegrass style.

✔ Use licks to enhance your playing and venture up the neck to create solos.

Chapter 5

Picking Techniques: Roll Patterns

In This Chapter

▶ Getting familiar with bluegrass banjo roll patterns

▶ Creating variations on roll patterns

▶ Using roll patterns to accompany bluegrass songs

▶ Access the audio tracks and video clips at www.dummies.com/go/bluegrassbanjo

*B*luegrass banjo players fit a *lot* of rapidly played notes into tight musical spaces. It's one of the things we love most about the instrument, and it's now time to unravel the mystery of how this amazing musical feat is accomplished. In this chapter, you pick up the picking skills that will help you become a bona-fide bluegrass banjo picker. Get out your banjo, get your thumbpick and fingerpicks on, and get ready to embark on the five-string ride of a lifetime!

Playing Roll Patterns

It's that stream of fast, cascading fingerpicked notes that grabs the ear and fires the musical imagination and causes us to fall in love with the sound of bluegrass banjo. *Roll patterns* are the repeated sequences of strings picked by the thumb, index finger, and middle finger that make all this banjo virtuosity possible. It's the essential and unique characteristic of bluegrass banjo style.

The great news is that the basic roll patterns are not difficult to play. With practice and a bit of time, you'll soon work up to the picking speeds you associate with your favorite banjo heroes. The first step is to get to know these rolls like the back of your hand, or, in this case, like your picking-hand finger.

Understanding how roll patterns work

Roll patterns are the basic building blocks of bluegrass banjo style. Banjo players utilize these picking-hand sequences not only to create melodies and play solos but also to accompany singers and other instrumental soloists in a bluegrass band. (If you already know the basic rolls, you may want to head over to Chapter 8 to experience how rolls are used to create solos; also be sure to check out Chapters 9 and 10 to experience how rolls are used to accompany others in bluegrass bands.)

Whether you're the featured performer or supporting others in a jam session or band, when you play roll patterns, you're doing what banjo players are expected to do: Play as many notes as possible! It's up to you to play these patterns as cleanly as you can and in good rhythm, and that's where repetition and practice come in.

What roll patterns have in common

To ease your mastery of bluegrass roll patterns, keep in mind that all rolls share the following characteristics:

✔ **Roll patterns are picked by a different finger with each successive note.** This is the key to the flowing, cascading sound of bluegrass banjo. This characteristic also allows you to play rolls *fast,* and what could be better than that?

✔ **Roll patterns move to a different string with each successive note that you pick.** Just as you play each note with a different finger, you also strike a different string with each successive note you pick. Each roll has a unique picking-hand and string sequence.

✔ **Roll patterns are usually made up of eight notes.** Each note is equal to every other in duration and an eight-note roll fills up one complete measure of musical space. This characteristic allows you to easily use rolls as accompaniment to songs, as you can mix and match rolls to the song's chord progression.

✔ **Roll patterns are played in 4/4 time.** The rhythm that matches each roll pattern is counted out as "one plus two plus three plus four plus." If you're counting evenly and picking a roll note each time you say (or think of) a number, then chances are great that you're playing in good rhythm.

✔ **Roll patterns are used to create songs and to accompany others.** Other musicians have to practice those tedious major, minor, and (for you jazz buffs) demented scales, but banjo players can hit the ground running if equipped with just one or two roll patterns in their picking arsenal. The greatest bluegrass songs of all time are built from roll patterns. Playing roll patterns is also the best way to sound great when playing with others in jam sessions and in bands.

Which fingers pick which strings

The picking-hand thumb is the most active of the three fingers in bluegrass banjo. You use the thumb to play the fifth, fourth, third, and second strings for most all roll patterns. Later on, you even use your thumb to play the first string when playing single-string style, so it's a good idea to burn those banjo-picking calories now and give your thumb a good workout.

You use the picking-hand index finger to play the third or second strings, and you pick the first string with your middle finger, as needed, for the majority of roll patterns. It's important to be comfortable with a good picking-hand position before jumping in to play any music on the five-string banjo, so feel free to head back to Chapter 4 if you need a review of how to find your most comfortable playing position.

It's now time to get down to some real picking by getting acquainted with the most important roll patterns used in bluegrass banjo. Remember to play each roll slowly at first and try to match your sound to what you hear me play on the matching audio and video tracks.

Don't forget that repetition is the key to success, *especially* with roll patterns. Today's greatest banjo players have perfected these rolls by repeating them thousands of times, but just about everyone can play these patterns pretty smoothly — if slowly — after only a few minutes of trying them out. Try to pick each note clearly and with some force, because you'll need to turn up your banjo-picking volume when playing in a band. If you can memorize the unique sound of each roll as you play it, then you soon won't have to rely on the banjo tablature. This is a good thing — it's considered bad form to take banjo tab with you into a jam session!

The forward-reverse roll

The forward-reverse roll is probably the most user-friendly of all bluegrass banjo roll patterns. It's a versatile roll that is used in many playing situations and it just feels good to play. Your picking-hand fingers will like it!

Here's a step-by-step guide to learning your first bluegrass roll pattern. Using the guidelines in Chapter 4, fit the picks on your fingers, place your right hand in position, and try out the following sequence of notes:

1. **Pick the third string with your thumb.**
2. **Pick the second string with your index finger.**
3. **Pick the first string with your middle finger.**

4. **Pick the fifth string with your thumb.**

   Now it's time to reverse the flow of right-hand notes.

5. **Pick the first string with your middle finger.**

6. **Pick the second string with your index finger.**

7. **Pick the third string with your thumb.**

8. **Pick the first string with your middle finger.**

Tab 5-1 (Audio Track 8) shows what the forward-reverse roll looks like in banjo tablature. Be sure to take a look at Video Clip 6 to see me demonstrate the forward-reverse roll with G, C, and D7 chords

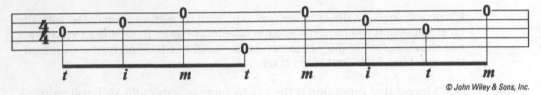

© John Wiley & Sons, Inc.

Tab 5-1: The forward-reverse roll.

The quickest way to master these roll patterns is to repeat them over and over again until they become automatic. To avoid driving your loved ones any crazier than they may already be, try changing chords at the beginning of each new roll pattern to add some spice to your practice sessions. Using the chords that you already know, you can make up a chord progression of your own or you can follow the chord progression to a real bluegrass song.

Playing roll patterns in this way is also a great way to accompany others. Tab 5-2 (Audio Track 9) is what the forward-reverse roll would sound like when used to accompany the bluegrass classic "Nine Pound Hammer"; Tab 5-3 (Audio Track 10) is what it sounds like when used to accompany the classic "Little Maggie."

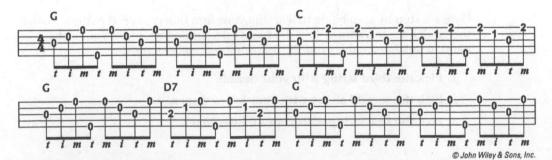

© John Wiley & Sons, Inc.

Tab 5-2: The forward-reverse roll with "Nine Pound Hammer."

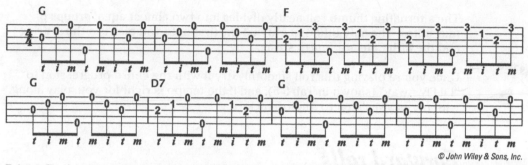

© John Wiley & Sons, Inc.

Tab 5-3: The forward-reverse roll with "Little Maggie."

The alternating thumb roll

The alternating thumb roll is the first thing I'd think to play if I were taking a leisurely stroll down a country road on a spring morning with my banjo in hand. Sometimes called the *thumb-in-and-out roll*, the easygoing sway of the alternating thumb roll is at the heart of classic songs like "Cripple Creek" and "I'll Fly Away." As its name implies, every other note is a thumb note. Here's a step-by-step guide:

1. **Pick the third string with your thumb.**

2. **Pick the second string with your index finger.**

3. **Pick the fifth string with your thumb.**

4. **Pick the first string with your middle finger.**

5. **Pick the fourth string with your thumb.**

6. **Pick the second string with your index finger.**

7. **Pick the fifth string with your thumb.**

8. **Pick the first string with your middle finger.**

Tab 5-4 (Audio Track 11, Video Clip 7) shows the alternating thumb roll in banjo tab.

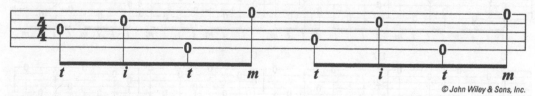

© John Wiley & Sons, Inc.

Tab 5-4: The alternating thumb roll.

The alternating thumb roll neatly divides into two almost equal groups of four notes. The only difference is that the first note you pick is a third string and the fifth note is a fourth string.

Once you're playing this roll smoothly, try it with the chord progression to "I'll Fly Away" (shown in Tab 5-5), and if the tempo is right for you, play along with me as you listen to Audio Track 12.

Forward rolls

Have you ever sat behind the wheel of one of those big old John Deere farm machines and driven it straight across a field, steering a perfectly straight line from one end to the other on a hot summer afternoon? Well, no, I haven't done that either, but this is what I sometimes think about when I'm playing forward rolls on songs like "Fireball Mail" and "Will the Circle Be Unbroken." Forward rolls put the drive and power into the sound of bluegrass banjo. You simply can't have cornfield cred without knowing your forward rolls backward and, yes, forward.

Forward rolls come in several varieties, with different sequences of picking-hand fingers. However, at some point in every eight-note forward roll, you pick two thumb–index–middle sequences that provide the propulsion needed for forward roll liftoff.

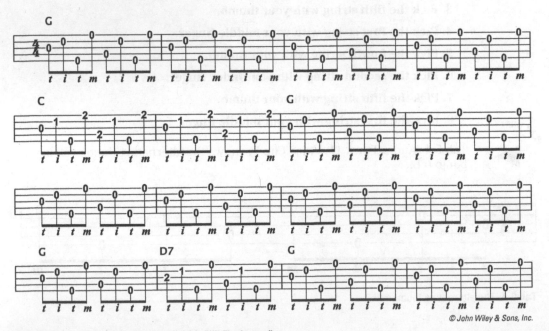

© John Wiley & Sons, Inc.

Tab 5-5: The alternating thumb roll with "I'll Fly Away."

Let's get started by trying out a couple of straightforward examples that emphasize the T–I–M-ness that's at the heart of the forward roll:

✔ **Forward roll 1 (see Tab 5-6; Audio Track 13)**

   • Picking-hand finger sequence: T–I–M–T–I–M–T–M

   • String sequence: 3–2–1–3–2–1–3–1

✔ **Forward roll 2 (see Tab 5-6; Audio Track 13):** All roll patterns sound better with the fifth string added, so now try this different string sequence, using the same picking-hand sequence as in forward roll 1:

   • New string sequence: 3–2–1–5–2–1–5–1

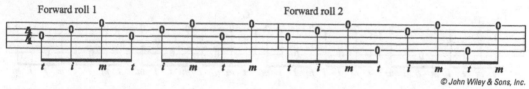

© John Wiley & Sons, Inc.

Tab 5-6: Forward rolls 1 and 2.

Forward rolls 1 and 2 begin with two three-note groupings of T–I–M and conclude with one two-note grouping of T–M. This sequence gives you the eight notes needed to fill a measure. You can create new forward rolls by changing the order of these two- and three-note groupings:

✔ **Forward roll 3 (see Tab 5-7; Audio Track 13):** Try taking the two-note group that was at the end of forward rolls 1 and 2 and move these notes to the beginning of a new forward roll. Then follow those first two notes with the two three-note T–I–M groupings. Here's an especially powerful sequence of strings and picking-hand fingers using this way of playing a forward roll:

   • Picking-hand finger sequence: T–M–T–I–M–T–I–M

   • String sequence: 3–1–5–3–1–5–3–1

✔ **Forward roll 4 (see Tab 5-7; Audio Track 13):** Try a new string sequence that still uses the same picking-hand sequence:

   • String sequence: 2–1–5–2–1–5–2–1

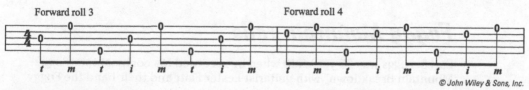

© John Wiley & Sons, Inc.

Tab 5-7: Forward rolls 3 and 4.

Forward roll 4 sounds great when fretting a C chord because you're now picking two of the three strings that you're fretting.

Forward rolls are fantastic choices to use to accompany songs because they create rhythmic drive. Try forward rolls 3 and 4 for "Will the Circle Be Unbroken," moving from roll 3 for the G and D7 chords to roll 4 for the C chord (see Tab 5-8; Audio Track 14).

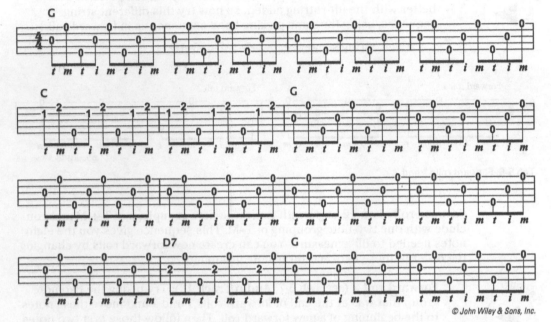

© John Wiley & Sons, Inc.

Tab 5-8: Forward rolls with "Will the Circle Be Unbroken."

It's a great idea to begin your forward rolls with the picking-hand thumb whenever possible. The act of using the thumb, instead of the index finger, for the first beat of a measure will help you to feel the downbeat of each new measure more powerfully. Because chord changes commonly occur on downbeats, you're also helping yourself remember the chord progression when moving your thumb to play that first note of a new chord. *Putting the thumb to it,* as they say down in North Carolina, is one of Earl Scruggs's most important innovations, which is reason enough to try it!

Foggy Mountain rolls

Earl Scruggs was 25 years old when he recorded his composition "Foggy Mountain Breakdown" with guitarist Lester Flatt and their band the Foggy

Mountain Boys in December 1949. This recording is probably the most important song in the history of bluegrass banjo, and the key to playing it like Earl is to get to know your Foggy Mountain rolls.

There are two kinds of Foggy Mountain rolls. It's a good idea to get familiar with both variations because then you can use one or the other depending upon which roll sounds best and feels the most comfortable.

✔ **Foggy Mountain roll 1:** Here's a step-by-step guide:

- Pick the second string with your index finger.

- Pick the first string with your middle finger.

- Pick the second string with your thumb.

- Pick the first string with your middle finger.

- Pick the fifth string with your thumb.

- Pick the second string with your index finger.

- Pick the first string with your middle finger.

- Pick the fifth string with your thumb.

The key to playing the Foggy Mountain roll with power and speed is to begin the roll with the picking-hand index finger playing the second string followed by the thumb (instead of the index finger) striking the next second string you play in this roll. Take note that this roll ends with the thumb, which requires you to begin a new Foggy Mountain roll with the index finger.

✔ **Foggy Mountain roll 2:** This version of the Foggy Mountain roll is exactly the same as roll 1, except you now leave out the second note. The first note of roll 2 is a quarter note that takes up the space of two eighth notes. (If you're suddenly feeling dizzy at the mention of these musical terms, head back to Chapter 3 for an explanation of quarter and eighth notes, measures, and all things related to rhythm.) You're playing seven instead of eight notes, but keep in mind that you're still filling the same amount of musical space usually occupied by eight notes.

Here's a step-by-step explanation:

- Pick the second string with your index finger.

- Pick nothing, allowing the second string to ring.

- Pick the second string with your thumb.

- Pick the first string with your middle finger.

- Pick the fifth string with your thumb.

- Pick the second string with your index finger.
- Pick the first string with your middle finger.
- Pick the fifth string with your thumb.

Tab 5-9 (Audio Track 15) shows what both Foggy Mountain rolls look like in banjo tab.

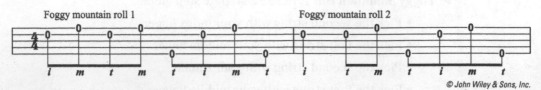

© John Wiley & Sons, Inc.

Tab 5-9: Foggy Mountain rolls 1 and 2.

It's a lot more fun practicing rolls using the chord progressions to real songs. Try the Foggy Mountain roll with the bluegrass classic "Long Journey Home" (Tab 5-10), and play along with Audio Track 16 after you've worked up a bit of speed. You can use roll 1 or 2 or mix and match as you play through the chord progression.

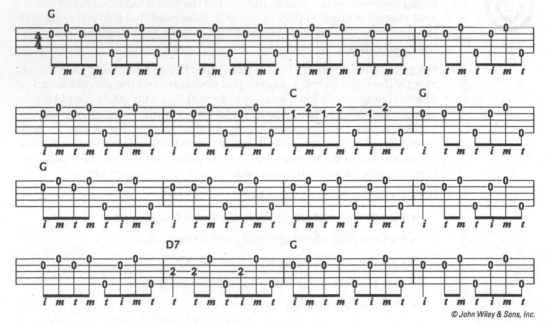

© John Wiley & Sons, Inc.

Tab 5-10: "Long Journey Home" with Foggy Mountain rolls.

The lick roll

The *lick roll* has nothing to do with rock-'n'-roll banjo posturing, but it's the roll pattern that is used to play just about everyone's favorite lick. A *lick* is a musical phrase that you can use in many different songs; the lick that goes with this particular roll is used perhaps more than any other in bluegrass banjo. Getting familiar with the right-hand sequence will speed your progress when you add the fretting hand (and if you can't wait to dip your fingers into an entire bucketful of great licks, head over to Chapter 7).

The lick roll combines the first four notes of a forward roll with the last four notes of a forward-reverse roll. When you start using this roll in songs, you'll discover that it's frequently used when you need a fourth-string melody note at the end of a measure:

> Picking-hand sequence: T–M–T–I–M–I–T–M
>
> String sequence: 3–1–5–3–1–3–4–1

Tab 5-11 (Audio Track 17) shows what the lick roll looks in banjo tab.

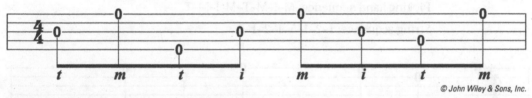

© John Wiley & Sons, Inc.

Tab 5-11: The lick roll.

Most players find that the trickiest part of the lick roll comes mid-measure, when you give the picking-hand index finger a real workout as you reverse direction in the note sequence. Don't sweat it! Just breathe deeply and repeat the roll slowly, playing each note as clearly as you can to give your fingers and your brain the opportunity to get accustomed to this new pattern.

Other rolls you'll need

The various combinations of picking and string sequences that you can create on the banjo is virtually infinite, although some are easier to play than others. You probably won't use the following rolls as much as the basic rolls presented earlier in this chapter, but they're all fun to play and you may end up needing them sooner than you think!

Backward roll

This roll (shown in Tab 5-12; Audio Track 17) is used in the classic Earl Scruggs tunes "Home Sweet Home" and "Ground Speed."

Picking-hand sequence: M–I–T–M–I–T–M–I

String sequence: 1–2–5–1–2–5–1–2

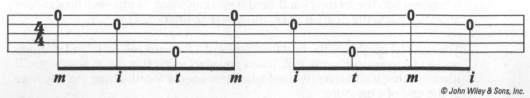

© John Wiley & Sons, Inc.

Tab 5-12: Backward roll.

Middle leading/Osborne roll

This roll pattern (shown in Tab 5-13; Audio Track 17) was first used by banjo great Sonny Osborne (who is no relation to Ozzy, just in case you were wondering):

Picking-hand sequence: M–I–M–T–M–I–M–T

String sequence: 1–2–1–5–1–2–1–5

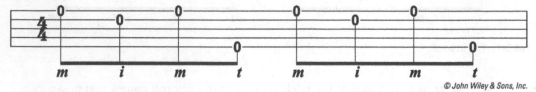

© John Wiley & Sons, Inc.

Tab 5-13: Middle leading/Osborne roll.

Index leading

Bill Keith uses the roll shown in Tab 5-14 (Audio Track 17) to create some memorable licks.

Picking-hand sequence: I–T–I–M–I–T–I–M

String sequence: 2–3–2–1–2–3–2–1

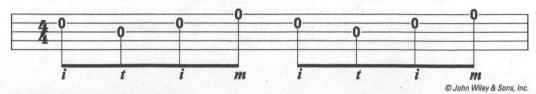

© John Wiley & Sons, Inc.

Tab 5-14: Index leading roll.

Dixie Breakdown roll

Banjo pioneer Don Reno created this new roll (shown in Tab 5-15; Audio Track 17) to use in this breathtaking tune. This roll requires a *lot* of repetition to work up to Don's speedy tempos.

Picking-hand sequence: T–I–M–I–T–I–M–I

String sequence: 3–2–1–2–3–2–1–2

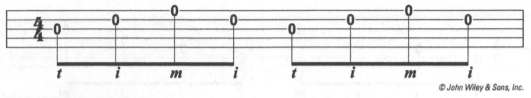

© John Wiley & Sons, Inc.

Tab 5-15: Dixie Breakdown roll.

Playing it straight or playing with bounce

Some banjo players play roll patterns very evenly, with each of the eight notes taking up the same amount of musical space. Other players will add a bit of a lilt to their roll patterns. Bluegrass players use the term *bounce* to refer to this approach. In this case, the roll notes that fall on the 1, 2, 3, and 4 beats last just a bit longer than the notes that fall on the + beats, which occur between the numbered beats.

Banjo players lean toward one or the other way of playing based on what they hear others play and what sounds best for each song. Some hardcore banjo purists insist on playing the notes of the rolls very evenly, and this is indeed the bluegrass way when you're playing something fast or going for a driving rhythm using forward rolls. However, slower songs or tunes with a Celtic feel can sound pleasing to the ear with a bit of banjo bounce, especially when using alternating thumb rolls.

Béla Fleck and Ralph Stanley tend to play straight roll notes while melodic innovator Bill Keith adds a bit of bounce to much of his playing. On Flatt & Scruggs's classic instrumental "Shucking the Corn," which is played *very* fast, Earl Scruggs employs just a *tiny* bit of bounce on the alternating thumb rolls he uses in the first few measures, but then he moves to very straight, driving forward rolls for the subsequent measures. Great music can be created by playing it straight, bouncing it, or mixing the two approaches!

My advice is to first drill roll patterns by playing the notes as straight as you can in order to build your picking-finger strength and to help develop your overall sense of rhythm. After the rolls have become second nature, you can try adding a bit of bounce to any song that you think sounds better with it. When playing with other musicians, try to match the rhythm that others are playing to make the group sound its best.

Arpeggio roll

There are times when you need to play across all four banjo strings, but what's the most efficient way to do this when you only have picks on your thumb and two fingers? Play this roll (shown in Tab 5-16; Audio Track 17) to uncover the answer!

Picking-hand sequence: T–I–T–M–T–I–T–M

String sequence: 4–3–2–1–4–3–2–1

© John Wiley & Sons, Inc.

Tab 5-16: Arpeggio roll.

Using Roll Patterns in Songs

As you work through the songs in this book, take note of the different ways that roll patterns are used to create melodies. The artistry of bluegrass banjo playing involves choosing the best rolls and licks to express the melody and emotion you're feeling at that moment.

The first step toward this level of mastery is to be comfortable with the basic versions of as many roll patterns as possible, mixing and matching them in ways that sound good for the song you're playing. The next step is to then experiment with variations of these rolls that even more effectively match your song's chords and melodies. Chapter 8 provides an in-depth look at how you can create your own solos in bluegrass style.

In this section, you send your playing into overdrive by unlocking the secret of how to create dozens of variations based on the roll patterns you already know. Your playing is about to take a huge leap forward, so get your picks on and let's go!

Creating your own roll variations

Roll patterns are defined by the sequence of picking fingers (thumb, index finger, or middle finger) along with the specific strings that you play (first to the fifth strings). When you're comfortable with the standard versions of the basic rolls (as outlined in the previous sections of this chapter), you can create authentically bluegrass-sounding variations by using the same order of picking fingers to play different strings.

Using the forward-reverse roll as an example, the order of picking fingers for this roll is T–I–M–T–M–I–T–M and the standard string sequence is 3–2–1–5–1–2–3–1. By moving the third-string/thumb and second-string/index notes down a string when needed, you can play variations that draw attention to these lower strings.

Check out Tab 5-17 (Audio Track 18) to see how this process works. The standard version of the forward-reverse roll is presented in the first measure, followed by a few easy-to-play variations.

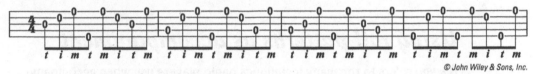

© John Wiley & Sons, Inc.

Tab 5-17: Forward-reverse roll with variations.

The variations that you can play for each roll are going to be different, depending upon the order of picking fingers. Now try out some of the many different ways you can play the alternating thumb roll (see Tab 5-18; Audio Track 19), forward roll (see Tab 5-19; Audio Track 20), Foggy Mountain roll (see Tab 5-20; Audio Track 21), and lick roll (see Tab 5-21; Audio Track 22). Next, try coming up with new rolls of your own!

© John Wiley & Sons, Inc.

Tab 5-18: Alternating thumb roll with variations.

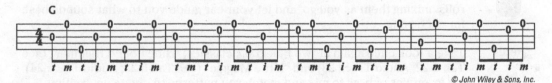

© John Wiley & Sons, Inc.

Tab 5-19: Forward roll with variations.

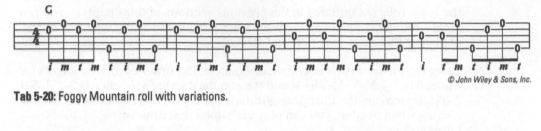

© John Wiley & Sons, Inc.

Tab 5-20: Foggy Mountain roll with variations.

© John Wiley & Sons, Inc.

Tab 5-21: Lick roll with variations.

Using roll patterns as accompaniment

Backup refers to the many techniques banjo players use when accompanying other musicians in a bluegrass jam session or band. The brilliant, steady stream of notes that roll patterns provide is one of the best things you can play in this support role, and it's also the banjo's unique contribution to the bluegrass sound. So, roll away to your heart's content, but not so loudly as to drown anyone out, please!

When you're playing backup, your goal is to make everyone around you sound their best. All the basic rolls take up one measure of musical space and can be played interchangeably as you follow a song's chord progression. As long as you're playing in good rhythm, you really can't go wrong — all rolls are well designed to fill up the available musical spaces in a distinctively bluegrass way. When fretting chords, it's a good idea to choose roll patterns that feature the strings you're fretting, but if you're only comfortable with just one or two rolls right now, it's fine to play these over and over again.

The more roll patterns and variations that you're comfortable playing from memory, the more variety you'll bring to your backup playing. Although forward rolls provide the most drive, it's a great idea to try using a variety of rolls, mixing them as you go, and let your ear guide you to what sounds best for each song.

Take a look once again at two bluegrass classics, "Nine Pound Hammer" (see Tab 5-22; Audio Track 23) and "Little Maggie" (see Tab 5-23; Audio Track 24) for examples of how to mix and match roll patterns to create an exciting-sounding backup. Pay special attention to the roll variations used for the C and F chords in these examples.

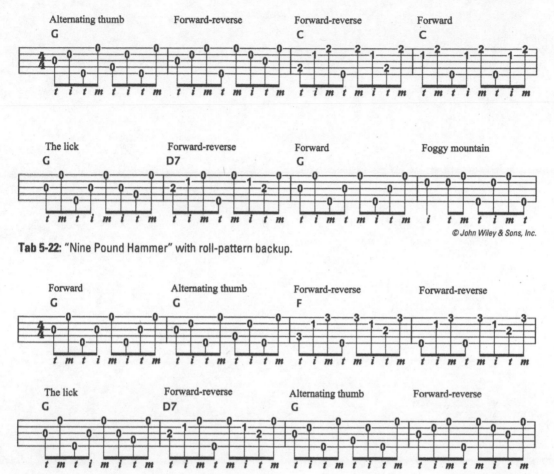

Tab 5-22: "Nine Pound Hammer" with roll-pattern backup.

Tab 5-23: "Little Maggie" with roll-pattern backup.

Chapter 6

Fretting Techniques and Putting the Hands Together

In This Chapter

▶ Adding expression to your playing with fretting-hand techniques

▶ Playing slides, hammer-ons, pull-offs, and chokes

▶ Integrating fretting-hand techniques with roll patterns

▶ Access the audio tracks and video clips at www.dummies.com/go/bluegrassbanjo

The picking hand deserves credit for a lot of the flash in bluegrass banjo, but the fretting hand has big responsibilities, too. Not only do you form chords with the fretting hand, but you can also use fretting techniques to add musical expression and coherence to your playing. And yes, it is possible to get emotional *and* be coherent on the banjo at the same time!

Slides, hammer-ons, pull-offs, and chokes (or bends) are the fretting techniques that banjo players call upon to make roll patterns and chords come alive. In this chapter, you discover the correct way to perform all these fancy moves. When you then combine techniques with the picking and fretting hands, you're using all the ingredients you need to play in an authentic bluegrass style (for a review of bluegrass roll patterns, see Chapter 5).

Although the fretting hand can't compete with the sheer number of notes that the picking hand can play at a moment's notice, when you create or embellish notes with the fretting hand, those around you will sit up and take notice. Because you can never have too much soulful expression in your playing, it's time to check out everything that the fretting hand does to make bluegrass banjo sound great.

Heading into the Slide

When you create a new note on your banjo by moving a finger up or down the fingerboard on the same string from one fretted position to another, you're playing a *slide*. Slides create continuity and give a smoothness to your playing, allowing you to connect one note to the next in a flowing way that's similar to how great bluegrass vocalists add feeling and expression to their singing.

Some of the most exciting moments in bluegrass banjo history have been created with slides. Who can forget the amazing 3rd- to 20th-fret second-string slide that Earl Scruggs plays at the beginning of his second solo on the January 1957 recording of "Shuckin' the Corn"? Or Earl's booming, low fourth-string slide that serves the introduction to the song "Hot Corn, Cold Corn," as he played it in Carnegie Hall on December 8, 1962? Okay, I bet that you probably haven't heard either of these songs yet, but I promise that the sound of a great slide is something you'll never forget after you experience it!

Luckily, most slides don't require you to leap tall fretboards in a single bound. Most of the time, you can get by just fine with slides that move from one to three frets' distance on your fingerboard.

It's entirely possible to play slides that move from a higher fret to a lower fret, but you'll almost always prefer slides that travel from a lower to a higher fret (giving you the sound of a note moving from a lower to a higher pitch).

In the following sections, you get comfortable playing the slides that banjo players like to use the most in bluegrass style. Then you integrate these slides with roll patterns to build a basic bluegrass banjo vocabulary to create licks and phrases that you can use in all kinds of songs. Get out your banjo and put on your fingerpicks because it's time to feel the power of the slide!

Slipping into third-string slides

The third string, second- to third-fret slide is one of the main attractions of the banjo classic "Cripple Creek" and is a great place to begin your sliding adventures. Here's a step-by-step guide:

1. **Fret the third string at the second fret with the middle finger of your fretting hand.**

2. **Pick the third string with the picking-hand thumb.**

3. **Move the fretting finger up one fret, from the second to the third fret.**

   It's important to keep the pressure down with your fretting finger to sound the new note as you slide.

4. **After you've arrived at your destination, continue to apply pressure with your fretting finger to allow the new note you've just created to continue to ring.**

Check out Audio Track 25 and Video Clip 8 to see and hear the sound of this slide; then take a look at Tab 6-1 to see how it appears in banjo tablature. You'll see two notes (the second and third frets of the third string) connected to one another with a *slur*. The slur indicates the beginning and end of your slide. The *s* below these notes lets you know that you'll be using a slide to connect the two notes. Pick the third string, sounding the second-fret note, and then move your finger to the third fret. You'll need to maintain the fretting pressure on the string to hear the new note you've just created with your slide.

© John Wiley & Sons, Inc.

Tab 6-1: Playing third-string slides from the second to the third fret.

You use the same techniques to play slides anywhere on your banjo, so when you learn how to do this in one or two places on a couple of strings, it's easy to apply these maneuvers whenever and wherever you need them.

Playing third-string slides with the alternating thumb roll

Banjo players don't live by fretting techniques alone! When you get comfortable with the slide (along with all the other fretting techniques covered in this chapter), you want to use it while simultaneously picking bluegrass roll patterns. Don't be surprised if a huge grin lights up your face when you combine these fretting- and picking-hand techniques. You're capturing the real bluegrass sound when you play in this way, and you should notice a big difference in the quality of your playing after you've mastered these skills.

When you add the third-string slide to the alternating thumb roll, you're playing a lick that just about every banjo player uses in the second half of "Cripple Creek" (see Tab 6-2; Audio Track 25).

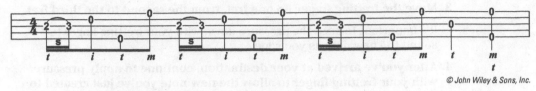

© John Wiley & Sons, Inc.

Tab 6-2: Playing third-string slides with the alternating thumb roll.

Every now and then, banjo tablature isn't able to completely capture the nuances of how a lick or phrase is supposed to be played. In Tab 6-2, the tab seems to indicate that the slide is to be completed before you pick the second string. However, you'll sound better if you stretch out the timing of the third-string slide just a bit so that it leads directly into the second-string open note that follows it, without an interruption in sound. Think of the slide as a flowing movement from the third string, second fret up toward the second string open, and you'll start to get the idea. There's no way to write this in tab exactly the way it's supposed to sound, so this is a case where listening and watching really come in handy.

It's difficult for adults to undertake different tasks with each hand simultaneously, but that's exactly what you're being asked to do when you combine roll patterns with fretting techniques. The secret to sounding great is to keep an even, steady rhythm in your picking hand (just as I hope you did when you were drilling roll patterns by themselves as exercises in Chapter 5). Think of the slide and the other fretting techniques in this chapter as embellishments that are added to, but don't alter, your picking-hand rhythm. When you play the exercises in this chapter in this way, the sound of great bluegrass banjo playing will begin to flow effortlessly from both hands.

Playing third-string slides with the forward roll

Now try adding one additional fret to your third-string slide, moving from the second to the fourth fret with your fretting-hand middle finger. Note that when you play the slide in this way, your arrival note should be the same pitch as your open second string (if not, check your banjo tuning!). Play Tab 6-3 (Audio Track 26) to hear the difference.

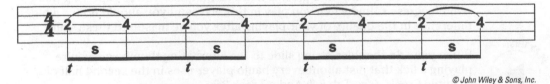

© John Wiley & Sons, Inc.

Tab 6-3: Playing third-string slides from the second to the fourth fret.

This third-string slide sounds great with a forward roll. Take note of how the phrase in Tab 6-4 (Audio Track 26) really draws attention to the sound of the open second-string B notes in the roll.

© John Wiley & Sons, Inc.

Tab 6-4: Playing third-string slides with the forward roll.

Playing third-string slides with the lick roll

The third-string slide takes center stage in the most frequently played lick in all of bluegrass banjo. When you add this slide to the lick roll, you're well on your way to mastering an essential banjo phrase that you can use in almost every song you'll play (and you'll be the coolest banjo kid on your block after you dive into this and all the other great licks in Chapter 7).

Take a look at Tab 6-5 and give a listen to Audio Track 26 to hear this slide incorporated into the lick roll.

© John Wiley & Sons, Inc.

Tab 6-5: Playing a third-string slide with the lick roll.

The 2–3 and 2–4 slides on the third string are interchangeable. Feel free to use one or the other with any roll pattern according to the sound you want to hear at that moment. When you slide to the third fret, you'll hear a more blues-oriented sound, while the fourth-fret slide draws attention to the B pitch that is shared with the open second string.

Blasting into fourth- and first-string slides

The fourth string is the lowest in pitch, as well as the heaviest and thickest of all your banjo strings. For these reasons, it's the perfect string for playing booming, swooping slides that lend some heavyweight authority to your playing.

Fourth-string slides are most often played up to the fifth-fret G note, which is the same pitch as your open third string. Because many bluegrass songs (such as "Will the Circle Be Unbroken" and "Fireball Mail") begin with a G note on the first main beat, it's great to have a few sliding fourth-string phrases ready to call up from memory as you kick off your next great bluegrass banjo solo.

Here's a step-by-step guide to the most frequently played fourth-string slide:

1. **Fret the fourth string at the second fret with the middle finger of your fretting hand.**

2. **Pick the fourth string with your picking-hand thumb.**

3. **Slide the fretting finger up three frets, from the second to the fifth fret.**

   Because your fourth string is a heavier-gauge string than your third string, don't be surprised if it takes a little more pressure to get a great sound from your fourth string.

4. **Keep the fretting pressure on to let the fifth-fret note ring.**

Try playing Tab 6-6 (Audio Track 27) to feel the power of the fourth-string slide. View Video Clip 8 to see how you can play the most frequently used slides on the third, fourth, and first strings.

© John Wiley & Sons, Inc.

Tab 6-6: Playing fourth-string slides.

Playing fourth-string slides with the forward roll

Banjo players use slides to embellish and draw attention to important melody notes. The fourth-string slide to the fifth fret emphasizes the G note, and you can reinforce that melody note even further by including the G note in your roll patterns. Check out Tab 6-7 and Audio Track 27 to hear how this is done for the forward roll.

© John Wiley & Sons, Inc.

Tab 6-7: Playing fourth-string slides with the forward roll.

Playing "potatoes" using fourth-string slides

Bluegrass musicians often kick off instrumentals with an introduction that communicates how fast the song is going to be played and lets the other players know that the tune is beginning. Musicians call these kickoff patterns "potatoes," and Tab 6-8 and Audio Track 27 present the most frequently played banjo introductory lick, using a fourth-string slide that travels from the fourth to the fifth frets.

© John Wiley & Sons, Inc.

Tab 6-8: Playing potatoes with the fourth-string slide.

Playing first-string slides

Any slide that you play on the fourth string you can also play on the first string, because both strings are tuned to D pitches. "Cripple Creek" and "Fireball Mail" are just two banjo classics where you'll need a first string, second- to fifth-fret slide, as shown in Tab 6-9 (Audio Track 28). Don't forget to use the middle finger to pick the first string.

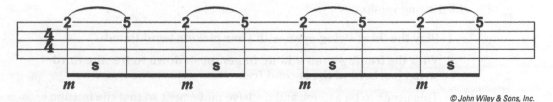

© John Wiley & Sons, Inc.

Tab 6-9: Playing first-string slides.

Bringing Down the Hammer-on

As its name implies, a *hammer-on* is played on the banjo when you fret a string you've just picked, using enough pressure to create a new note with the downward force of the fretting finger. A well-played hammer-on should sound a new note that's almost as loud as the picked note that immediately preceded it.

In the same way that you use a hammer to drive a nail, your fretting finger needs to meet the string with some force to create a great-sounding hammer-on. Your goal is to make the note you're creating with the fretting finger really crack! "Cumberland Gap" and "Foggy Mountain Breakdown" are two of bluegrass banjo's greatest hits that prominently feature hammer-ons, but you'll use this fretting-hand technique every time you pick up the banjo and play.

There are two kinds of hammer-ons that you'll get acquainted with in this section. An *open-string hammer-on* is played after picking an unfretted string while a *fretted hammer-on* moves from one fretted string to another higher fret on that same string.

You'll then combine hammer-ons with roll patterns, adding to the basic set of techniques you'll soon use to play and create great-sounding songs in bluegrass style. Just as with the slides, when you've mastered the skills you need to play hammer-ons, you can use them anywhere you need them on your banjo fingerboard.

Playing open-string hammer-ons

It's time to put the hammer down to master the most frequently played hammer-ons in all of bluegrass banjo, where you'll move from an open string to the second fret on the third and fourth strings. Here's how to play the third-string version:

1. **Play the third string open with your picking-hand thumb.**

2. **With the fretting-hand middle finger, push down to fret the third string just behind the second fret.**

   This needs to be a quick and decisive movement so that the fretting finger doesn't mute the sound of the third string as it comes into contact with the string.

To play a fourth-string hammer-on, just shift everything over one string and that's all there is to it!

 Use the tips of your fretting fingers to fret the strings more accurately and with the force you need in order to make your hammer-ons really rock. For most hammer-ons, you'll call upon your middle finger to do the heavy lifting, but don't be alarmed if you find that it takes different amounts of pressure on each string to make your hammer-ons sound their best.

Tab 6-10 and Audio Track 29 show how you play hammer-ons on both the third and fourth strings, and Video Clip 9 explains each step in detail and even gives you a few more examples to try out. In banjo tab, a hammer-on is indicated by the letter *h*.

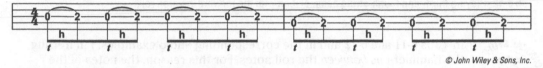

© John Wiley & Sons, Inc.

Tab 6-10: Playing third- and fourth-string hammer-ons.

Playing third- and fourth-string hammer-ons with the alternating thumb roll

Just as you did with slides, the best way to get started integrating hammer-ons with bluegrass roll patterns is to begin with the alternating thumb roll. Remember to keep the rhythm of your roll patterns constant as you hammer-on with your middle finger on the third and fourth strings.

Take a look at Tab 6-11 and give a listen to Audio Track 30 to hear the combination of third- and fourth-string hammer-ons with this roll. You'll soon play licks like these in "Cripple Creek" and many other songs.

It's much easier to tackle an entire song when you're already confident playing individual phrases like these by themselves, so don't hesitate to repeat each phrase in this chapter over and over again until it becomes second nature.

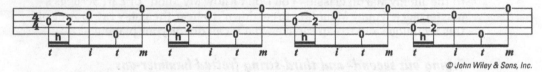

© John Wiley & Sons, Inc.

Tab 6-11: Playing third- and fourth-string hammer-ons with the alternating thumb roll.

Playing the fourth-string hammer-on with the forward-reverse roll

Now check out the fourth-string hammer-on with the forward-reverse roll. In Tab 6-12 (Audio Track 30), you insert the hammer-on into a complete eight-note roll pattern in the first measure. The second measure combines the hammer-on with the first four notes of the forward-reverse roll and a pinch pattern to give you a lick you'll soon use to play the banjo favorite "Cumberland Gap."

Tab 6-12: Playing third- and fourth-string hammer-ons with the forward-reverse roll.

In Tabs 6-11 and 6-12 and in the corresponding audio examples, I'm fretting the hammer-ons *between* the roll notes. For this reason, the notes of the hammer-on are written as sixteenth notes, with two beams, in the tablature. As you increase your speed, you may want to play the hammer-on at the exact same time as you pick the next note in the roll, which is what Earl Scruggs did when he played "Cumberland Gap" up to speed. Either approach will work as long as you're keeping a steady, consistent rhythm in your picking hand as you play roll patterns.

Playing fretted hammer-ons

The *fretted hammer-on* is only just a bit more complicated than the open-string variety. With a fretted hammer-on, you pick a fretted note first, rather than an open string, and you then call upon the services of a second fretting-hand finger to create the hammer-on. When you complete a fretted hammer-on, you'll be fretting the same string on two different frets with two different fingers.

Some of the most intense and exciting musical moments in bluegrass banjo history are the result of fretted hammer-ons! Check out J. D. Crowe's solo to the Jimmy Martin classic "You Don't Know My Mind" or Earl Scruggs's masterpiece "Foggy Mountain Breakdown" to hear the gutsy raw power of this technique and to experience what it can do for your playing!

Trying out second- and third-string fretted hammer-ons

Here's a step-by-step guide to the all-time classic second-string hammer-on that has inspired thousands to play bluegrass banjo:

1. **Fret the second string at the second fret with the fretting-hand index finger (see Figure 6-1a).**

2. **Pick the second string with the picking-hand index finger or thumb — your choice!**

3. **While continuing to fret the second fret, hammer-on with the middle finger behind the third fret.**

4. **Let this note ring while you continue to fret the second and third frets with both your index and middle fingers (see Figure 6-1b).**

5. **Now repeat!**

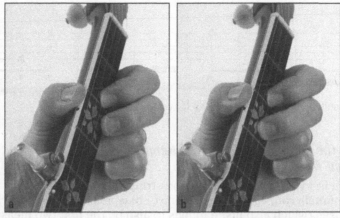

Figure 6-1: The position of (a) the fretting-hand fingers before playing fretted hammer-on and (b) the fingers after playing hammer-on.

Photographs by Anne Hamersky

TIP

Fretted hammer-ons frequently travel in groups of two, which is why you want to continue fretting the second fret after you've completed the hammer-on. When you lift the middle finger to play another fretted hammer-on, your index finger will already be in position and ready to go.

PLAY THIS!

You'll also want to try this fretted hammer-on using the third string, fretting from the second to the third fret. Tab 6-13 and Audio Track 31 will keep your fingers busy as you try out both hammer-ons. Note that you alternate picking these strings with your index finger and thumb in this example.

© *John Wiley & Sons, Inc.*

Tab 6-13: Playing second- and third-string hammer-ons.

Playing the second-string fretted hammer-on with the forward roll

The second-string fretted hammer-on embellishes the D note, which is also the same pitch as your open first string. When you're *really* serious about emphasizing your D notes, the forward roll is just what's needed for the occasion.

The following phrase is often used to kick off a song like "Sitting on Top of the World," or "On and On," where the first main-beat melody note is — you guessed it — a D! If you're familiar with the sound of bluegrass banjo style, you'll recognize this phrase. It's now time for you to dive into Tab 6-14 (Audio Track 31) to experience this for yourself!

© John Wiley & Sons, Inc.

Tab 6-14: Playing the second-string hammer-on with the forward roll.

Playing the second-string fretted hammer-on with the Foggy Mountain roll

When you fret two consecutive second-string hammer-ons while playing the Foggy Mountain roll, you're playing one of bluegrass banjo's most recognizable phrases (which also just happens to also be the first two measures of Earl Scruggs's classic "Foggy Mountain Breakdown"). Tab 6-15 (Audio Track 31) reveals this phrase in all its glory.

© John Wiley & Sons, Inc.

Tab 6-15: Playing second-string hammer-ons with the Foggy Mountain roll.

To facilitate playing Tab 6-15 with speed and power, don't forget to use your picking-hand index finger to start the roll but then strike the next second string (at beat two) with your thumb. The alternation of your index and thumb fingers will allow you to play the roll faster and the thumb will provide more punch in an unexpected place to add interest to this phrase. It'll also make you sound more like Earl Scruggs, which is reason enough for me!

Perfecting the Pull-off

A *pull-off* is created when your finger snaps a string that it's already fretting to sound a new note, either on an open string or at another fretted note. You move across the string with your fretting finger to sound the pull-off, tugging at the string with either an upward or a downward motion to pluck the new note.

Unless you're into banging on your banjo head as if it were a drum (which doesn't seem like a good idea for a variety of reasons), the *pull-off* is the most percussive technique you can play on the instrument. That makes it one of the most fun things you can do on the banjo as well. Like the slide and the hammer-on, you'll find all kinds of ingenious places to use pull-offs in every song you play. "Cripple Creek," "John Henry," and "Flint Hill Special" are just a few of the banjo favorites that pack a more powerful punch with pull-offs.

In this section, you experience the joys of pulling off using open- and fretted-string techniques and combine these pull-offs with roll patterns to wrap your fingers around more great-sounding authentic bluegrass banjo phrases.

Playing open-string pull-offs

Because many open-string pull-offs are played on the first string, this is the logical place to launch your pull-off explorations. Here's a step-by-step guide to making your journey a smooth one:

1. **Fret the first string at the second fret with the fretting-hand middle finger.**

2. **Play the first string with the middle finger of your picking hand.**

   Remember that in roll-based playing, whenever you need to play the first string, you almost always use your middle finger to pick the string.

3. **Pull away from the first string with your fretting finger, snapping it to fully sound the open first string.**

You can also play pull-offs from the second fret to the open string on the third and fourth strings. Tab 6-16 (Audio Track 32) gets you playing on all three strings. You'll have a much easier time playing pull-offs after you see how it's done, so don't forget to check out Video Clip 10 for a complete guide to all of the pull-offs covered in this section

© John Wiley & Sons, Inc.

Tab 6-16: Playing pull-offs on the first, second, and fourth strings.

The first string is situated close to the edge of the fingerboard, making it easy to get a tremendously powerful snap to your first-string pull-offs when you pull down, away from your banjo neck (as shown in Figure 6-2). When playing a third- or fourth-string pull-off, you have the choice of moving either up or down with the fretting finger. Most players quickly figure out which direction gives them the best sound and feels the most comfortable. Try both ways and go with what works best for you.

Figure 6-2:
Playing a first-string pull-off: (a) fretting at the second fret and (b) pulling down with the finger to play the pull-off.

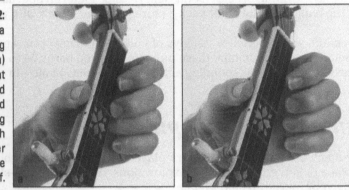

Photographs by Anne Hamersky

When you combine pull-offs with roll patterns, you want to position the pull-offs in between the notes of the roll, just as you played with the hammer-on. To emphasize this rhythmic approach, the tabs in this section will use sixteenth notes for the pull-offs.

Now try playing third- and fourth-string pull-offs with the alternating thumb roll. Tab 6-17 (Audio Track 32) shows you how it's done.

© John Wiley & Sons, Inc.

Tab 6-17: Playing the alternating thumb roll with third- and fourth-string pull-offs.

Playing fretted pull-offs

The *fretted pull-off* is another essential technique that defines the bluegrass banjo style. With this fretting-hand move, you'll be pulling off from one fret-ted note to another. It sounds a bit tricky, but the secret to success is to fret the same string with two different fretting fingers before you begin.

Here's a step-by-step guide for the most important of these pull-offs, a third-string pull-off that moves from the third to the second fret (and don't forget to watch Video Clip 10 to see how it's done).

1. **Fret the third string in two places at the same time, with the index finger at the second fret and the middle finger at the third fret (see Figure 6-3a).**

2. **Strike the third string with your picking-hand thumb.**

3. **Just after picking this string, pull across it with your fretting-hand middle finger while keeping the index finger in place at the second fret (see Figure 6-3b).**

   Your middle finger needs to move across the third string to create the pull-off as well as up to avoid hitting an adjacent string.

4. **Keep pressure down with your index finger on the second fret to sustain the new note.**

Figure 6-3:
Playing a third-string pull-off: (a) positioning the fretting-hand fingers and (b) pulling off with the middle finger.

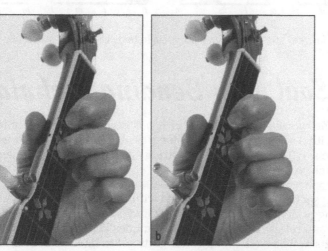

Photographs by Anne Hamersky

Playing fretted pull-offs with the alternating thumb roll

It's time to start mixing fretting techniques as you incorporate them into roll patterns. This alternating thumb roll phrase uses both slides and fretted pull-offs and pops up in a number of classic bluegrass songs such as "Doing My Time" and "Shuckin' the Corn" (Tab 6-18; Audio Track 33).

© John Wiley & Sons, Inc.

Tab 6-18: Playing the alternating thumb roll with third-string fretted pull-offs and slides.

Playing fretted pull-offs with the forward-reverse roll

This essential forward-reverse roll phrase combines a third-string slide with a fretted pull-off and is heard in many bluegrass songs. Keep your pull-offs nice and crunchy — you really want the string to snap as you pull across with your middle finger. Tab 6-19 (Audio Track 33) shows you how it's done.

© John Wiley & Sons, Inc.

Tab 6-19: Playing the forward-reverse roll with third-string fretted pull-offs and slides.

Adding Soul with Bending Techniques

Whether you call them *chokes* or *bends*, string-bending techniques can leave you with a serious case of the bluegrass banjo blues (which is a good thing by the way!). When you push a string against your banjo fingerboard to raise its pitch, you're playing a *choke*.

In this section, you get acquainted with the classic bending techniques used in "Foggy Mountain Breakdown." Then you move on to explore some of the bend-and-release and pre-bend techniques kept secret by blues and rock guitarists. Who says those guitar gods get to have all the fun? Move over Eric and B. B. and let the banjo players show you how it's done!

Playing the choke

The choke that you'll play most often in bluegrass banjo is on the second string at the tenth fret. Here's a step-by-step guide:

1. **Fret the second string at the tenth fret with the index or middle finger of your fretting hand — or both!**

Earl Scruggs used his index finger to play most chokes (see Figure 6-4a), while banjo great Ron Block uses both his index and middle fingers for more control, with the index finger fretting the ninth fret and the middle finger fretting the tenth fret on the second string.

2. **Pick the second string with either the thumb or index finger of your picking hand.**

3. **Push the second string up toward the third string to bend the string.**

Remember to keep the fretting pressure down so that you're experiencing the choke as one continuous sound. Don't be surprised if you find yourself bending the second string so far that you're also pushing the third string out of the way as well (as shown in Figure 6-4b).

4. **Return the second string back to its normal position by releasing the tension of the fretting finger.**

If you keep your finger in contact with the string as it returns to its original position, you'll be ready to follow one great-sounding choke with another (which is always a good thing!).

Figure 6-4: (a) Getting ready to play a second-string, tenth-fret choke; (b) bending the string to raise its pitch.

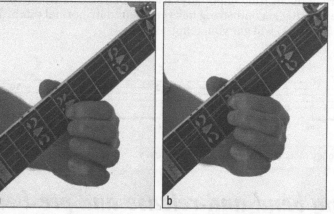

Photographs by Anne Hamersky

Check out Tab 6-20 (Audio Track 34) to try bending the second string for yourself. Take a look at Video Clip 11 to see me demonstrate the different kinds of chokes covered in this section.

The more you bend the string, the higher the pitch you hear. Try bending the string to raise the pitch the equivalent of one fret, and then try bending some more to raise the string two frets in pitch. Tab 6-20 uses the word *full* to indicate a choke that bends the strings in this manner.

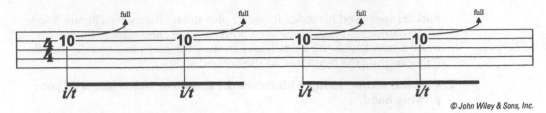

© John Wiley & Sons, Inc.

Tab 6-20: Playing the second-string, tenth-fret choke.

String and pitch bending techniques on the guitar, banjo, and harmonica represent musicians' attempts to capture the emotion of the human voice. You, too, can bring expression to your chokes by experimenting with how much and how quickly you bend the string. There's no one right way to play a choke because you're playing what you're feeling at that moment. If you're feeling it, you're playing it right!

When you combine the second-string choke with the Foggy Mountain roll, you're playing one of the most exciting phrases in all of bluegrass banjo. As you start to integrate chokes into this roll pattern, be careful to release the pressure of the fretting finger after each choke so that when you pick the string again, the second string has returned to its normal pitch. Tab 6-21 (Audio Track 34) will get you going.

© John Wiley & Sons, Inc.

Tab 6-21: Playing the Foggy Mountain roll with tenth-fret chokes.

Using bend-and-release and pre-bending techniques

The blues can be expressed in many different ways, and banjo players can take advantage of other bending techniques to find new things to say on their instruments. *Bend-and-release* and *pre-bending* chokes are two other common ways to bend and stretch your strings (and your loved ones) into a variety of blue moods.

Playing bend-and-release chokes

With the bend-and-release choke, you'll play the choke as you did in the previous section, but this time *don't* release the fretting pressure. You'll now hear the pitch go up and then come back down to its original starting point as you bend and return the string to its original position. Be careful not to let up the fretting pressure at any time with a bend-and-release choke.

Tab 6-22 (Audio Track 35) will take you up and bring you down again with this choke.

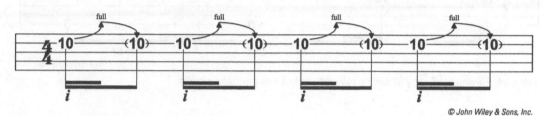

© John Wiley & Sons, Inc.

Tab 6-22: Playing bend-and-release chokes.

Playing pre-bend chokes

When you stretch the string before striking it and then return it back down to its normal pitch after playing it, you're picking a *pre-bend choke.* Check out Tab 6-23 (Audio Track 35) to see how this technique appears in written form. The arrow clues you to bend the note upward before playing it with a picking-hand finger.

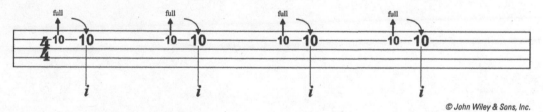

© John Wiley & Sons, Inc.

Tab 6-23: Playing pre-bend chokes.

Mixing chokes and pre-bend chokes with the Foggy Mountain roll

To conclude your string-bending experiments, try mixing chokes with pre-bend chokes, integrating these fretting-hand techniques into the Foggy Mountain roll. Expect a fiery musical combustion to occur very soon!

Tab 6-24 (Audio Track 35) shows you how Earl played it in 1949! In this measure, you choke the second string twice, starting from the tenth-fret position. After playing the second choke, continue to bend the second string until you strike it again. (This effect is indicated in the tab with the 12th fret, second string in parentheses in this example.) Don't forget to check out Video Clip 11 for a review of all the bending exercises and phrases covered in this section.

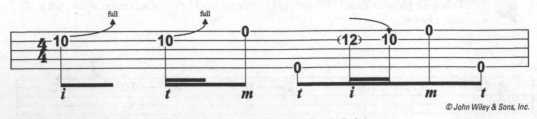

Tab 6-24: Playing the Foggy Mountain roll with chokes and pre-bend chokes.

Chapter 7

Getting Bona Fide: Playing Licks and Classic Tunes

In This Chapter

▶ Exploring licks and songs that combine roll patterns and fretting-hand techniques

▶ Using essential licks to enhance your solos

▶ Performing ten classic banjo jam-session standards

▶ Access the audio tracks and video clips at www.dummies.com/go/bluegrassbanjo

"*L*et's pick!"

This is the universal clarion call you'll hear when someone wants you to break out your banjo to play in a bluegrass jam session. You've been working toward this moment ever since the thought crossed your mind that you could someday, somehow be a bluegrass banjo player. Now the time has come: You're about to experience the joy of playing music with other musicians. There's no turning back now, but no worries! With the help of the licks and songs in this chapter, you'll play with confidence, sound great, and be invited back when these folks get together again.

This chapter is designed to help make your transition to playing music with others a smooth one by offering up an essential collection of classic roll-based (Scruggs-style) bluegrass banjo licks, along with ten solidly authentic but very playable arrangements of tunes that you're likely to hear at just about any jam session. You'll work through these licks and tunes much more quickly if you have a thorough understanding of the picking-hand roll patterns presented in Chapter 5 and the fretting-hand techniques covered in Chapter 6. Head back to those chapters if you need a refresher. I'll be here patiently waiting for you — I've got some practicing to do, too.

And if you're ready, well then, get that banjo out of its case and let's pick!

Playing and Using Licks

A *lick* is a short, standard musical phrase that can be used interchangeably in a variety of songs. Licks are the building blocks of bluegrass banjo playing. They enable you to easily assemble solos using tried-and-true musical formulas. There are licks that begin a song (called *kick-offs*), licks that you can use when there's a pause in the musical action (called *fill-in licks*), and *tag* and *ending licks* that you can use at the end of your solo or when it's time to finish a song entirely. You can play licks that match just about any chord you can fret either up or down the neck of your banjo and, best of all, you even can create licks of your own.

There's a lot to love about licks! You can use licks to create a solo on the fly to a song you've never heard before, or you create variations on a tune you're already playing with a few well-placed, tasty licks that add variety to your solo.

The anatomy of a lick

You want to get to know licks — as many of them as possible! This chapter gets you started with more than 40 absolutely essential roll-based bluegrass banjo licks played down the neck. Before you jump in, check out this complete guide to understanding what licks are all about and some tips on how they're used:

- ✔ **Licks are associated with chords.** Licks usually work best when used with one particular chord, and banjo players tend to think about licks in this way. G licks are used for those moments in a song where the chord progression is a G chord, C licks for a C chord, and so on.

- ✔ **Licks are often interchangeable.** If a C lick works well in one song, it will most likely work well in another song when the C chord is being played. This is what makes licks so useful in bluegrass banjo: When you get comfortable using a lick that goes with one particular chord, you can use it whenever that chord comes up again in any other song.

- ✔ **Licks have different lengths.** Some licks are just one measure long; others stretch out the banjo excitement to four or more measures. Be aware of these differences in length as you swap out licks from one song to another.

- ✔ **Licks can be joined together to form longer mega-licks.** One of the most exciting moments in bluegrass banjo is when you hear several well-known licks played one after another in new combinations at the end of a solo. Keep this formula in mind as you create your own outstanding licks.

✔ **Licks are used in lead and backup playing.** Certain licks sound best when accompanying others; other licks sound great when playing a solo. It's all part of the bluegrass banjo tradition. Active listening to your favorite artists and to recordings of classic bluegrass is the best way internalize how to use banjo licks.

✔ **Licks sound best when used sparingly.** Licks are real attention-getters. Although it's important to use licks in the right places, be careful not to overshadow a singer or another instrumentalist with licks that are too frantic or played too loudly.

REMEMBER

Licks can stand alone or they can be such an integral part of a song that they become identified with that tune. Licks can also be associated with particular roll patterns or fretting-hand techniques. All these characteristics can help you to keep straight which lick works best for a particular situation.

Most of the songs that banjo players love to play are in the key of G, and the chords most associated with this key are the G, C, and D chords. You'll need licks for all three of these chords. In the following sections, you try out ten licks for each chord along with classic fill-in licks you can use to end your solos.

Ten essential G licks

Banjo players live in the world of G! The open strings of your banjo are tuned to a G chord, most of the songs you play will be in the key of G, and you'll encounter the G chord most frequently in chord progressions. For all these reasons, you simply can't have enough G licks. The phrases you'll encounter in this section lay the foundation for great bluegrass banjo playing. I bet you'll even recognize many of these phrases from hearing them in your favorite songs. Now it's time to play them yourself!

Check out these ten classic G licks to start your lick collection (see Tab 7-1):

✔ **G lick 1:** Great licks combine different fretting-hand techniques in small musical spaces. This lick joins an alternating thumb roll pattern to slides, pull-offs, and hammer-ons to create a phrase that's often used in the second half of "Cripple Creek."

✔ **G lick 2:** By slightly altering a roll pattern or by using a different fretting-hand technique, you can dramatically alter the sound of a lick. Lick 2 adds a third-string pull-off to the mix to create a phrase that's used in "Shucking the Corn" and "Doing My Time."

✔ **G lick 3:** Lick 3 is two separate licks combined. The forward-reverse lick in the first measure is used in a long list of songs, from "Flint Hill Special" to "Long Journey Home." When combined with the forward roll-based lick in the second measure, you're playing a phrase that captures the first part of the melody of "Your Love Is Like a Flower."

✔ **G lick 4:** This lick is used frequently in "Roll in My Sweet Baby's Arms" and is a combination of three separate licks. If you have any trouble playing through the tricky second measure, isolate the picking-hand pattern without fretting to play the roll pattern with a steady rhythm. Then move on to add the fretting-hand pull-off and slide.

✔ **G lick 5:** When you need to emphasize an important melody note, be sure to include it in the roll pattern you're choosing for the lick. Lick 5 comes in handy for songs like "Will the Circle Be Unbroken" and "Fireball Mail" when you're directing attention to the third-string G note. Note how the forward roll extends beyond the first measure to create a driving sound. This phrase is also used in down-the-neck backup (see Chapter 9).

✔ **G lick 6:** Here's an interesting variation of lick 5 where you delay the fourth-string slide for a few notes to add a bit of rhythmic interest and even more drive to the lick.

✔ **G lick 7:** Lick 7 puts the focus on the first-string D note, again calling upon a forward roll that extends into a second measure. This phrase is a familiar one from the classic instrumental "Earl's Breakdown."

✔ **G lick 8:** A variation of lick 7 that adds a first string, second fret to the mix, this lick can be played at the beginning of "Sitting on Top of the World."

✔ **G lick 9:** Here are the first three measures to one of the all-time classic bluegrass banjo instrumentals, "Foggy Mountain Breakdown." Note that in measure three, you'll be using the same order of picking fingers as in measures one and two, but moving over to the third string to play a 3–2 pull-off.

✔ **G lick 10:** This four-measure lick fills up all sorts of vast G spaces. Be careful with the picking-hand fingering of the Foggy Mountain roll in measure two. You'll want to begin the roll with the picking-hand index finger but then follow it with the thumb picking the second string.

Listening and watching is crucial so don't forget to check out Audio Track 36 and Video Clip 12.

Tab 7-1: Ten classic G licks.

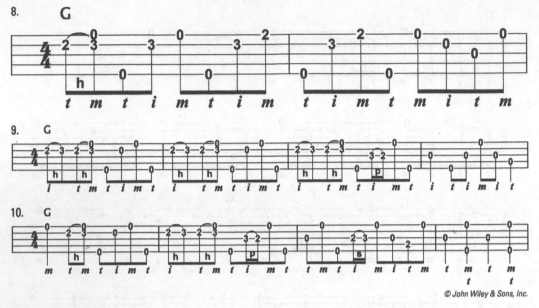

Tab 7-1: Continued.

Ten essential C licks

Banjo players can't live by G alone, no matter how much they may wish this were true! It's now time to look at ten great-sounding licks based around the C chord, which is the chord you'll often encounter just after you play a G lick in a song (and sometimes — as in the songs "This Land Is Your Land" and "John Hardy" — the C chord is the first chord you'll play). As you try each of the following C licks, fret the full chord first before you play the lick.

Check out the following ten C licks (see Tab 7-2):

- ✔ **C lick 1:** This one-measure lick is used in "Cabin in Caroline," among many other songs. It works perfectly for a melody that moves down to the open fourth-string D note that begins the measure two G chord lick.

- ✔ **C lick 2:** Lick 2 is a memorable phrase first heard in Earl Scruggs's "Flint Hill Special." Note that it combines two four-note phrases in measure one, which are then reversed in order in measure two. Your fretting-hand middle finger has a lot of work to do as it moves back and forth between the third and fourth strings. Keep your index and ring fingers fretting the rest of the C chord on the second and first strings, and you'll have this lick sounding great in no time!

✔ **C lick 3:** Lick 3 uses an alternating thumb followed by a forward roll, with the fretting-hand middle finger moving from the third to the fourth strings. You'll hear this lick in "Blue Ridge Cabin Home," among other tunes.

✔ **C lick 4:** Here's a great lick that works for down-the-neck backup, as well as in solos. Note that you'll lift off the C chord with the fretting hand for the last four notes of measure one, but then immediately fret the C chord again at the beginning of measure two.

✔ **C lick 5:** The forward-reverse roll is a great pattern to use when you need to play melody notes that move between the third and fourth strings, as is the case with this C lick. You'll use licks like this for the C chord in songs like "Long Journey Home" and "Worried Man Blues."

✔ **C lick 6:** This forward-roll-based pattern is used in "John Hardy," which you play later in this chapter. In measure two, fret the third fret, first string with your pinky finger while also continuing to fret the rest of the C chord. All you then have to do to complete the lick is lift up the pinky at the end of the second measure to play the last first string at the second fret.

✔ **C lick 7:** Forward-roll-based licks add drive to both your solo and backup playing. Here's a great C lick that works well as an all-purpose C chord down-the-neck roll pattern backup lick. When you need to fill two measures of C space, call up lick 7!

✔ **C lick 8:** A variation on lick 7, lick 8 is designed to lead you nicely back to a G chord as you shift to a D7 fretted position briefly in the last four notes of the lick's second measure.

✔ **C lick 9:** It's time to use the Foggy Mountain roll with a C lick that uses two different C-chord positions. As you shift to the C chord at the fifth fret at measure two, take note of the fingering indications above the tab staff for smooth sailing between these chords.

✔ **C lick 10:** You're going to love this lick! It's a classic C7 phrase that Earl Scruggs played in "Bugle Call Rag," among other tunes. You're mixing backward and forward roll segments to create some incredible excitement with lick 10. You have my permission to play this as much as you like until you're banished to the garage to practice.

Although the tab is a valuable resource, spend as much time as you can with Audio Track 37 and Video Clip 13 to get the sound of each lick in your head.

Tab 7-2: Ten essential C licks.

Tab 7-2: Continued.

© John Wiley & Sons, Inc.

Ten essential D licks

D licks can be real banjo attention getters. This is probably because bluegrass banjo players have come up with a lot of creative things to play when this chord inevitably pops up in a song. As in the previous sections, most of these licks are based around different roll patterns. If you grasp the picking-hand moves first, you can then more easily add fretting-hand techniques to play each phrase smoothly.

Check out the following ten D licks (see Tab 7-3):

✔ **D lick 1:** Lick 1 uses a forward-reverse roll and two different D positions to play a phrase that you can use in the banjo favorite "John Hardy." You'll want to shift from the first D-chord position on the second and third strings to the next position that you fret on the third and fourth strings just as you approach measure two.

✔ **D lick 2:** This is another forward-reverse roll lick, but this time there's activity on the first string as you use your ring and pinky fingers to climb from the second to the fourth fret. A standard G lick follows the D phrase in this and many examples in this section, in order to get your flow going as you move from one chord to the next in a real song.

✔ **D lick 3:** You only need to fret the third and fourth strings to play this forward-roll-based lick. This all-purpose and absolutely essential D phrase is used in many songs, such as "Your Love Is Like a Flower," in both lead and backup scenarios.

✔ **D lick 4:** Old-school masters J. D. Crowe, Sonny Osborne, and Earl Scruggs specialize in ingenious variations on standard licks. Lick 4 is a finger-busting variation on lick 3, where you shift quickly from a forward to a backward roll. J. D. Crowe uses this phrase in his classic "Old Home Place" solo.

✔ **D lick 5:** Get ready to use your picking-hand middle finger on the second string with this ingenious lick that has you playing forward rolls on the inside strings of your instrument. There's a quarter note midway through measure two, so don't forget to give this note the breathing room it needs to allow you to complete the lick in good rhythm.

✔ **D lick 6:** Lick 6 is one of those rare licks that works well for both D and G chords. Here, the open fourth string indicates that it's a D lick. The chord progression that's shown in this lick (one measure to G moving to one measure of D that then moves to two measures of G) is one you'll encounter frequently in songs like "Little Maggie" and "Nine-Pound Hammer." This phrase can be used either for a solo or as backup when encountering this chord progression in any song.

✔ **D lick 7:** Exercise care with the picking-hand rhythm on this lick from Earl Scruggs's classic "Ground Speed," as the mix of quarter and eighth notes is tricky for just about everyone who tries it. You'll want to get the sound of the lick in your head first with this lick, so feel free to dive into the audio track and video clip for this section first before consulting the tab to reinforce the details.

✔ **D lick 8:** Everybody needs a two-measure D lick to use at the end of a solo, and this one's just the ticket! Use your thumb to pick the second-string hammer-on note in measure one to give this lick the drive and power that it needs to put this over the top.

✔ **D lick 9:** Lick 9 provides another great two-measure D alternative, this time featuring third-string hammer-ons. You may not recognize the roll pattern used in measure two: It's a Foggy Mountain roll using a third-string variation.

✔ **D lick 10:** J. D. Crowe has created a number of memorable D licks that reflect his interest in rock and blues guitar techniques. This lick from the song "You Don't Know My Mind" reflects those influences. Check out the picking-hand indications below the staff to try out J. D.'s own preferences for this lick.

Tab 7-3: Ten essential D licks.

Tab 7-3: Continued.

Start your D-lick adventures by checking out Video Clip 14, where you can see and hear me demonstrate the fretting and picking details of every lick. Audio Track 38 allows you to take the sound of each lick with you wherever you may roam.

Ten (plus two) essential fill-in licks

Fill-in licks comprise a special category of phrases that are treated by banjo players with special reverence. You call upon a fill-in lick when there's a break in the musical activity of some kind, as when a singer takes a breath between the lines of a song lyric. You can also use one or more fill-in licks to raise the musical temperature for the final measures of your next banjo solo.

Fill-in licks put the focus on you and your banjo, and they're an important part of your identity as a bluegrass banjo player. Each of the ten licks (plus two bonus licks) in this section is worthy of your attention — you'll want to play them all well. We owe a huge debt of eternal banjo gratitude to Earl Scruggs for coming up with almost all the ideas used in these licks.

Check out the following fill-in licks (see Tab 7-4):

- **Fill-in lick 1:** This is absolutely, positively the most important lick in all of bluegrass banjo. You can use it for the final G chord for just about any song you play, and you'll convince everyone that you have true bluegrass street cred (well, at least for a moment!). If you're a newbie, take care to play every note of the roll correctly. This is a bit tricky as the roll changes direction halfway through the measure, first going forward and then backward. This lick is so crucial that the roll pattern that goes along with it is called the "lick" roll, by the way.

- **Fill-in lick 2:** Banjo players live and breathe by the slight variations that separate one version of a lick from another. Although no one else may care, we do! Lick 2 is a *lot* like lick 1 with the addition of a fourth-string pull-off that makes it sound totally different — okay, not totally. The second measure offers up a nifty forward-roll phrase that presents a different way to exit the lick than the pinch pattern in lick 1.

- **Fill-in lick 3:** If lick 1 is number one on the all-time great fill-in lick popularity chart, this lick holds down the number-two spot. As you gain experience with more and more licks, you'll experiment with breaking down the parts of licks to combine them in unique ways to create new sounds. The last four notes of measure one are the last four notes of a forward-reverse roll. This phrase segment appears in many different contexts in all kinds of licks.

- **Fill-in lick 4:** You may have guessed this one was coming! As early as the late 1940s, Earl Scruggs started combining licks, and it's time for you to do the same. Lick 4 combines licks 1 and 3 to create a frequently used sequence that's ideally suited for the end of any solo.

- **Fill-in lick 5:** This lick has the same effect as licks 1 and 2 but uses a different roll pattern. This one is good to use when the song is at a rocking, medium tempo.

- **Fill-in lick 6:** A great fill-in lick can make you jump out of your seat when you hear it for the first time, and that's exactly what happened to me when I heard Earl Scruggs play this phrase in his classic instrumental "Earl's Breakdown." You'll follow the first third-string hammer-on with a new maneuver: a hammer-on followed by a pull-off. There are also quite a few consecutive index fingers you'll pick in this lick as well. Take it slow and check out the audio and video examples to get every detail correct.

- **Fill-in lick 7:** A growling variation on lick 3 that adds a first-string third-to second-fret pull-off to the mix. If you move downward with the fretting fingers for your pull-off, you'll really be able to snap that first string all the way to Nashville. Earl Scruggs and J. D. Crowe employ this lick in "Down the Road."

✔ **Fill-in lick 8:** Things really start to happen when you combine shorter licks into longer phrases to extend the length of the end of your solo. Here are three separate licks that work well when combined into one mega-lick.

✔ **Fill-in lick 9:** Lick 9 pulls in elements of lick 6, but take note of the unique timing and fingering. This is the kind of lick that J. D. Crowe often plays to end a hot solo on a medium-tempo song.

✔ **Fill-in lick 10:** Speaking of J. D. Crowe, here's a frequent way that he ends solos on such favorites as "Blue Ridge Cabin Home" and "Your Love Is Like a Flower." You can use this longer lick just about anytime you're ending a banjo solo in the key of G but you want to keep your momentum going for another couple of measures. Keep your rolls driving as you add the fretting-hand techniques, and you'll soon sound just as good as J. D.!

✔ **Fill-in lick 11:** Lick 11 combines lick 1 with a lick commonly used in "Roll in My Sweet Baby's Arms." Earl Scruggs played this kind of fill-in lick early in his career on songs such as "Little Girl in Tennessee."

✔ **Fill-in lick 12:** This is probably the most complicated fill-in lick you can play down the neck! You can hear Earl Scruggs play this lick in "I'll Stay Around." It combines elements of licks 6 and 7. Don't try to tackle a lick like this just from examining the tab. It's absolutely essential to listen and watch to get the sound of this lick just right.

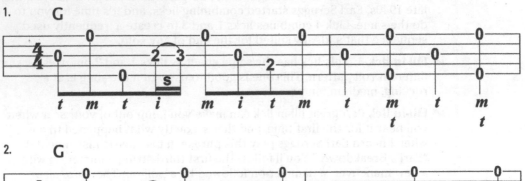

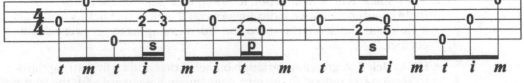

Tab 7-4: Essential fill-in licks.

Tab 7-4: Continued.

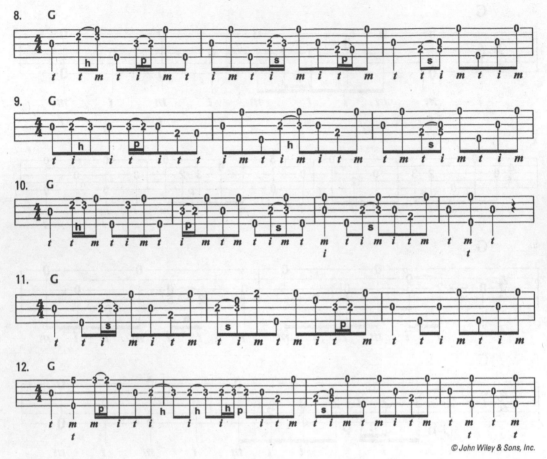

Tab 7-4: Continued.

Be sure to access Audio Track 39 and Video Clip 15. You'll want to hear and see the licks in this section. Although the tab shows you the mechanics of the licks, the audio and video examples convey the sound and feeling. You need all these things to play well, but especially the sound and feeling, so don't forget to access these online resources as you add these fill-in licks to your banjo toolbox.

Playing Classic Songs

Playing bluegrass banjo connects you with a worldwide community of musicians who love bluegrass music just as much as you do. When musicians get together at festivals or jam sessions to make music, they can often immediately start playing songs together, even if they're just meeting each other for the first time. This amazing phenomenon is able to take place because bluegrass musicians all over the world perform a shared repertoire.

It's time for you to get in on the action! When it's your turn to suggest a tune in a jam session, choose any one of the banjo-friendly standards in this section and play it at whatever speed works best for you. (For more information on the skills and techniques you use when playing with others, check out Chapters 9 and 10.)

If you can figure out which roll patterns are being used as you work through any song, you'll internalize the music in larger segments as you identify the patterns you already know. You'll be able to play songs more smoothly from the very beginning using this analytical approach (and defy all those who say that banjo players don't use their brains very much).

"Banjo in the Hollow": A great first song!

If this is the very first bluegrass banjo song you've ever tried to play, you've landed in exactly the right place with just the right song. "Banjo in the Hollow" is easy to play, sounds great, and won't cause your loved ones to head out of the house to catch a movie while you're practicing it. There are no slides, hammer-ons, pull-offs, or chokes to worry about, and you can even use the same fretting fingers for the three different positions used in this song.

For "Banjo in the Hollow," a forward-reverse roll is used for most of the song, with a half-measure of an alternating thumb roll making a special guest appearance at the last measures of lines one and three, as you can see in Tab 7-5 (Audio Track 40, Video Clip 16).

"Cripple Creek" (in four versions!)

One of the wonderful things about bluegrass banjo music that's a bit mystifying to newcomers is that there never is one definitive version of any song. That's certainly the story with the banjo favorite "Cripple Creek." There are probably as many versions of this song as there are banjo players who play it, and because this is the one song that just about every banjo player plays, that's a *lot* of versions!

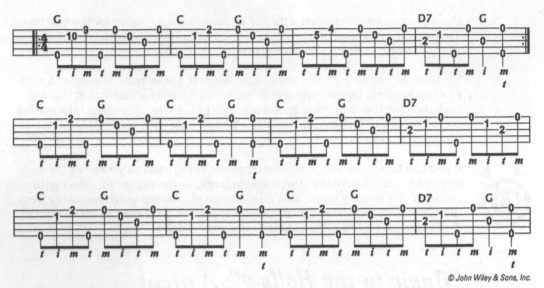

© John Wiley & Sons, Inc.

Tab 7-5: "Banjo in the Hollow."

"Cripple Creek" provides a great opportunity to get insight into the many different ways that the same tune can be played. Musicians will play simple or more difficult versions of pieces based on their experience level, what they're comfortable playing, and what they're wanting to express musically at that moment. There's always something new that you can bring to any song, even "Cripple Creek." This is what makes playing bluegrass banjo such a lifelong and rewarding creative process — you're never finished!

Check out Audio Track 41 and Video Clip 17 to experience each "Cripple Creek" variation. Then check out Tabs 7-6 through 7-9 to catch what's different. (Here's a hint in this regard: You can make any version more complex by adding more fretting-hand techniques and by adding different roll patterns.) After you're comfortable playing a couple of these versions, you've got the green light to come up with a new version using your own unique combination of licks and phrases.

"John Henry"

It just makes sense that a classic American folk song about man versus machine would be converted in a full-tilt banjo breakdown. This straightforward basic version (Tab 7-10; Audio Track 42) is ideal for beginning players.

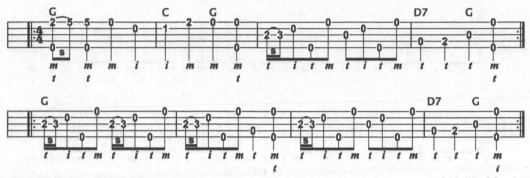

© John Wiley & Sons, Inc.

Tab 7-6: "Cripple Creek," version 1.

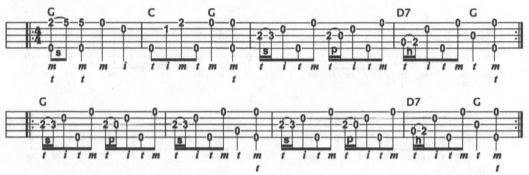

© John Wiley & Sons, Inc.

Tab 7-7: "Cripple Creek," version 2.

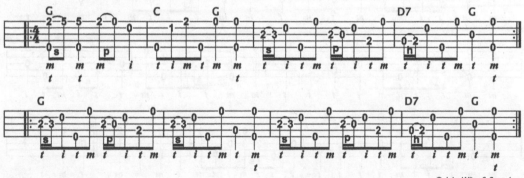

© John Wiley & Sons, Inc.

Tab 7-8: "Cripple Creek," version 3.

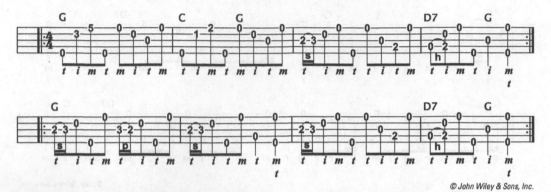

Tab 7-9: "Cripple Creek," version 4.

Tab 7-10: "John Henry."

"John Hardy"

Historians don't agree on whether John Henry really did exist, but there's no question that there was indeed a late 19th-century murderous West Virginia villain named John Hardy. This banjo version (Tab 7-11; Audio Track 43) moves up a notch in difficulty, adding more fretting-hand techniques along with a few of the G licks you encounter earlier in this chapter.

"Boil the Cabbage Down"

File this song under the group of all-important culinary bluegrass banjo songs that includes "Feast Here Tonight" (in which a rabbit is the main course) and

© John Wiley & Sons, Inc.

Tab 7-11: "John Hardy."

"Ground Hog." Now, that's good eatin'! To make this tune really cook, you'll pull in a few more licks from earlier in this chapter and use a greater variety of roll patterns (Tab 7-12; Audio Track 44).

© John Wiley & Sons, Inc.

Tab 7-12: "Boil the Cabbage Down."

"Buffalo Gals"

When you figure out a banjo version of a melody you're already familiar with, you're also discovering more about the inner workings of bluegrass banjo style. This version of "Buffalo Gals" (Tab 7-13; Audio Track 45) introduces you to the index leading and middle leading rolls. (Check out Chapter 5 for a complete inventory of essential picking patterns.)

Tab 7-13: "Buffalo Gals."

"Train 45"

Banjo players often play this hard-driving classic associated with J. D. Crowe in the key of B with their capos at the fourth fret. You'll work through the standard way of playing "Train 45" in lines one and two before trying out a well-known variation in lines three and four (Tab 7-14; Audio Track 46). Many of the techniques used in this song are also used in Earl Scruggs's "Foggy Mountain Breakdown."

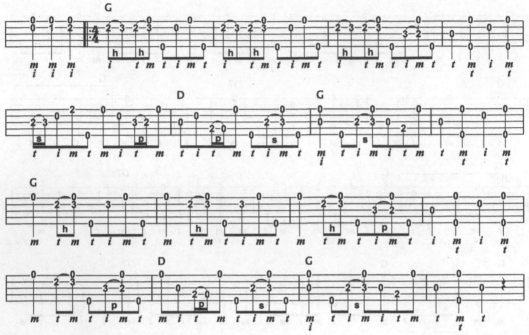

© John Wiley & Sons, Inc.

Tab 7-14: "Train 45."

"Old Joe Clark"

This song is usually played in the key of A, with the capo at the second fret. "Old Joe Clark" uses a form that's standard with many fiddle tunes, with a first and second part that are both repeated (this is sometimes called an *AABB form*). In the B part of "Old Joe Clark," you'll need an F chord. Check the tab to see how this chord is fretted on your banjo, or turn to Appendix A to find a chord diagram for this new chord (Tab 7-15; Audio Track 47, Video Clip 18).

"Cumberland Gap"

"Cumberland Gap" is a *barn burner* (a song that's played really fast). However, you can get a lot of enjoyment out of playing this classic at whatever speed works best for you. After the basic statement of this very short melody, you'll try two variations (Tab 7-16; Audio Track 48). Line two shows

© John Wiley & Sons, Inc.

Tab 7-15: "Old Joe Clark."

you an up-the-neck version that uses a fretted position you'll call upon frequently in other songs. The next variation is mine — I like it and I hope you do, too!

"Lonesome Road Blues"

It's time to try a version of a song that's entirely up the neck (Tab 7-17; Audio Track 49, Video Clip 19). Check out the fingering suggestions above the staff, and take note that in many cases you only need to fret the first and second strings to get the shapes you need. Don't forget to really bend those second-string, tenth-fret chokes!

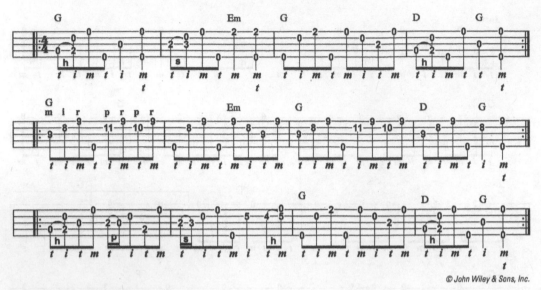

Tab 7-16: "Cumberland Gap."

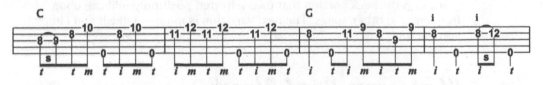

Tab 7-17: "Lonesome Road Blues."

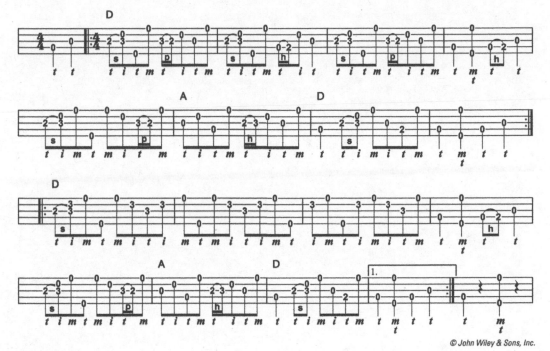

Tab 7-18: "Reuben."

"Reuben"

As a young boy, Earl Scruggs worked out his three-finger picking technique while playing this song. "Reuben" (Tab 7-18; Audio Track 50) is played in D tuning. To get into this tuning, just lower your third and fifth strings one fret to an F♯ and also lower your second-string two frets to an A; then touch up your first and fourth strings to make sure that they're both tuned to D notes. Now you're ready to go! The basic melody is presented in lines one and two and is almost always played using mostly alternating thumb rolls, just as Earl did when he was about ten years old!

Chapter 8

Working Up Your Own Scruggs-Style Solos

In This Chapter

▶ Finding simple melodies on your banjo

▶ Choosing the best roll patterns to create solos

▶ Using licks to enhance your solo

▶ Playing up-the-neck solos and modal tunes

▶ Access the audio tracks and video clips at www.dummies.com/go/bluegrassbanjo

I t's a great feeling to be able to move beyond memorized songs to make your own music on the five-string banjo. With just a little experience, you can begin to create your own arrangements in bluegrass style, combining what you know in unique ways to create your own sound.

It can be a challenge to play songs in your own way that still sound like real bluegrass banjo music. In this chapter, you discover how to do this by matching roll patterns and fretting-hand techniques to song melodies to create great-sounding bluegrass banjo arrangements. You build solos by finding the basic melody before moving on to choose the best roll patterns and licks to capture those melodies in bluegrass banjo style.

You find tips for creating solos in the upper regions of your banjo fretboard, see how to use licks to enhance your arrangements, and even check out a few classic solos for inspiration. This is the chapter where you step out on your own, calling upon your heart and soul — as well as your fingers — to find your own musical voice on the five-string banjo.

Finding the Melodies

"What's the difference between one bluegrass banjo song and another?"

"The titles."

If it takes a few moments to understand the punch line to this old banjo joke, don't worry. This means you're beginning to think like a bluegrass banjo player, for better or worse! To those unfamiliar with the sound of the banjo (and this often includes our families and friends), what you play may sound alike from one song to the next. However, if you base solos on the melody of the songs and you understand how to capture melodies in bluegrass banjo style, every song you play should sound different and be unique. You owe it to those you love (and who have to live with you as a banjo player) to bring as much melody as you can to everything you play.

You'll rely on your ear to develop many of the skills that are covered in this chapter. The fastest way to master ear-training skills is to adopt an attitude of musical fearlessness and try what comes to mind, even if at times you're only making your best guesses. Mistakes aren't really mistakes if you realize what you can do differently the next time around. The only mistake you can make is if you stop trying! Keep your ears engaged as you try different solutions to musical problems and go with what sounds right to you.

Finding the G scale

Melodies are based around scales and built around chord progressions. You'll encounter the G-major scale in a couple of places in this book for good reason: It's the basic set of notes that are put together to form many of the melodies you play as a bluegrass banjo player, whether you're using roll-based techniques or melodic and single-string styles (which you can try out in Chapters 11 and 12).

Tab 8-1 (Audio Track 51) names and locates the notes of the G-major scale on the lower frets of your banjo. Remember that because the fourth and first strings are both tuned to a D note in G tuning, any notes you play on the first string you can also play on the fourth string.

When using roll-based techniques, banjo players usually don't think about moving up and down the G-major scale as they do when playing melodic and single-string banjo. If you're playing a three-chord song in the key of G, you

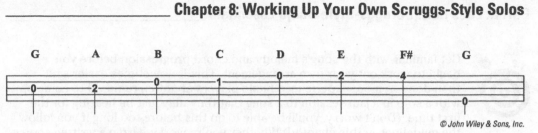

© John Wiley & Sons, Inc.

Tab 8-1: Finding the notes of the G-major scale on your banjo.

follow the chord progression of the song and begin to create a solo by finding the melody notes that are found in the chords, whether it's the open G chord or the fretted chords.

The G and C chords, along with two versions of the D chord, together contain all the notes that are in the G-major scale. Compare the chord diagrams in Figure 8-1 with the scale in Tab 8-1 to see this relationship (I've included two ways of playing the D chords because you'll use both positions often when playing solos).

Figure 8-1:
Chord dia-
grams for
(a) G, (b) C,
and (c, d) D
chords.

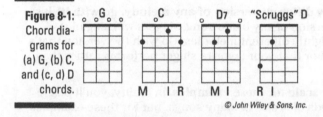

© John Wiley & Sons, Inc.

Mapping out melodies

It's a great ear-training exercise to find simple melodies on your banjo (without roll patterns) to everything from "Happy Birthday" to "Dueling Banjos" (paddle faster, I hear banjos!). In this section, you locate the unembellished melody to three bluegrass jam favorites — "I'll Fly Away," "Long Journey Home" (sometimes known as "Two Dollar Bill"), and "You Are My Sunshine" — on your banjo fingerboard in preparation for working up solos to each tune using bluegrass roll patterns and licks.

Get familiar with the song's melody and chord progression before you begin to work out your own arrangement. This is sometimes easier said than done — more experienced banjo players are often required to come up with a solo in a jam session to a song that they may just be hearing for the first time. (Don't worry, you'll be able to do this before too long if you follow the guidelines in this chapter!) Whether you're working from a written source or watching the guitar player's fretting hand, discover and get comfortable with the chord progression and be able to sing the song (silently to yourself if you must, but out loud is better) *before* attempting to find the melody on your banjo.

Here are few more tips to making finding melodies easier:

- **Fret full chords as you work through a song.** As the song moves to a C chord, for instance, fret all three notes of that chord. It's likely that your first melody note will be part of that fretted chord.

- **Use your ear before consulting the tab.** These are ear-training exercises, not a vision test! You'll learn from your mistakes, so don't be afraid to make them.

- **If you hear a slightly different version of any melody, go with it!** Just as there is no one version of any banjo song, singers will sing blue-grass songs using slightly different melodies. Go with the version that's already in your head or that your favorite singer performs rather than what's in any book.

- **Keep to the G-major scale for these examples.** In reality, you'll pull in notes from other kinds of scales in many songs. but for these examples, make it easy on yourself and just stick to the notes of the G-major scale.

- **Be patient!** You'll be surprised at how the most familiar melodies can be downright tricky to locate on your banjo fingerboard. Don't forget that every time you've successfully worked out one phrase, you've stored just a bit more information in the melody-finding part of your brain that you'll call upon again as you work on another song or lick.

"I'll Fly Away"

One of the most popular of all bluegrass jam-session tunes, your first adventure in melody hunting will be to work out the verse to this song (the chorus has the same chord progression but a different melody). Take note of how many of the melody notes in "I'll Fly Away" are made up of open strings for the G-chord phrases with just a few fretted notes at measures 3 and 11. Melody notes that are also part of the chord being played at that moment are called *chord tones,* while the scale notes that connect one chord tone to another are called *passing tones.* For the G chord, the passing tones are the fretted notes.

As you're figuring out a melody for the first time, look for patterns of repetition as you move from one line to the next. In the case of "I'll Fly Away" (Tab 8-2; Audio Track 52), line three (measures 9 to 12) is an exact repetition of the melody and chord progression of line one (measures 1 to 4).

© John Wiley & Sons, Inc.

Tab 8-2: "I'll Fly Away" basic melody.

"Long Journey Home"

Southwest Virginia's Stanley Brothers (Ralph and Carter) may have been the first artists to record a bluegrass version of this song. I'm old enough to remember when the $2 bill came back into circulation, but you may never have seen one of these before.

As with "I'll Fly Away," you'll play lots of open strings for the melody of "Long Journey Home" (Tab 8-3; Audio Track 53). The chord progression is characterized by relatively brief one-measure C and D7 chords with a whole lot of G measures in between. There are really only three separate lines of music to learn in this song, because line three is a repetition of line one.

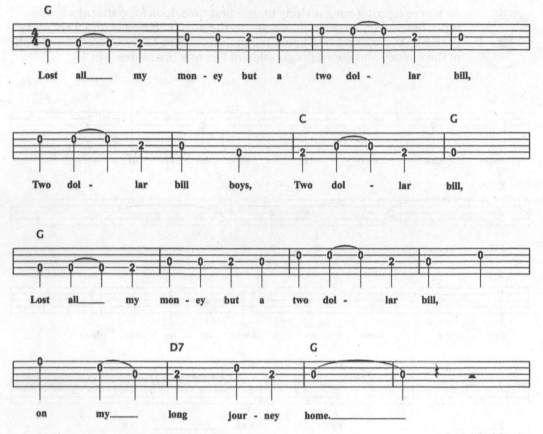

Tab 8-3: "Long Journey Home" basic melody.

"You Are My Sunshine"

It's great to finesse your ear-training abilities with songs you've heard before or already know well. In the key of G, the melody to "You Are My Sunshine" (Tab 8-4; Audio Track 54) is found on the first, second, and third strings of your instrument. On the two occasions where you'll fret a C chord, lift up just the first-string fretting finger to play the open first-string passing note heard in the second measure of each of the two C phrases.

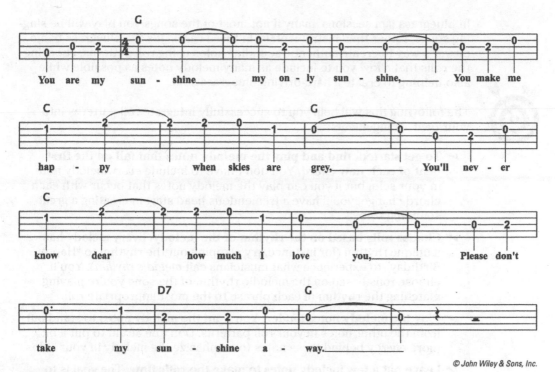

You are my sun - shine_____ my on - ly sun - shine,_____ You make me

hap - py_____ when skies are grey,_____ You'll nev - er

know dear_____ how much I love you,_____ Please don't

take my sun - shine a - way._____

© John Wiley & Sons, Inc.

Tab 8-4: "You Are My Sunshine" basic melody.

Matching Rolls to Melodies

When roll patterns are added to melodies, you bring both the bluegrass and the banjo elements to the music you're creating. It's the crucial step that turns your banjo playing into great-sounding bluegrass music. The following section explores the ways that banjo players use roll patterns to create bluegrass banjo solos based around the melody. You discover how the notes and rhythm of the melody help determine your choice of rolls and how you can vary rolls to include as many melody notes as possible in your arrangements.

Bluegrass banjo players play a *lot* of notes when taking a solo, but not all these notes are melody notes. Guitar and mandolin players and fiddlers play songs primarily by using scales, but bluegrass banjo players build solos from the roll patterns themselves. When banjo players create solos in this way, they surround the melody with these notes, playing eight roll notes for every one to four melody notes (if you need to get in touch with those all-important roll patterns, check out Chapter 5). The roll-pattern notes that are not melody notes are almost always notes that are part of the chord being played at that moment in the song.

In bluegrass jam sessions, many if not most of the songs you play will be singing songs, rather than instrumentals. In these cases, it's the bluegrass banjo player's way to create authentic-sounding solos using roll patterns, choosing the rolls that allow you to include as many melody notes as possible while also helping to create a hard-driving bluegrass solo.

The following tips will help you to successfully integrate roll patterns into your own arrangements:

- **To get started, find and play the melody notes that fall on the first beat of each new chord.** You don't have to include *every* melody note in your solo, but if you can play the melody notes that occur with each chord change, you'll have a tremendous head start in creating a great-sounding solo.

- **Choose rolls based on the rhythm of the melody.** Every melody has a unique rhythm (for instance, try clapping out the rhythm to "Happy Birthday" to experience what musicians call *melodic rhythm*). You'll choose rolls based on the melodic rhythm of the song you're playing, matching the rhythm of each phrase to the most appropriate roll.

- **Play the melody notes louder.** You want the melody notes to stand out from the other notes in your roll patterns. Don't be afraid to put a bit more energy behind these notes to emphasize the melody in your solos.

- **Leave out a few melody notes to make the rolls flow.** The goal is to include enough melody notes so that your listeners will recognize what you're playing, but it's also important to keep the rolls flowing. If you miss melody notes, or if a melody note falls in an unexpected place in the roll, no worries — simply keep rolling!

- **Use roll variations to grab melody notes.** Think of the roll patterns as a basic framework that you can alter to get the notes you need.

- **Break up rolls with quarter notes and pinch patterns to create phrases.** Just as a singer has to take a breath, there are times when you want to stop the flow of roll notes to emphasize the end of one line and the beginning of the next (these lines are called *phrases*). Using pinch patterns to finish phrases is a good way to break up the flow of rolls to mark off the phrases of the song you're playing.

Chapter 5 presents a complete overview of the many roll patterns commonly used in bluegrass banjo playing. The next few sections of this chapter show how the most important of these patterns can be used in solos to capture melodies.

A roll-pattern review

It's time to take a look at how roll patterns are commonly used to capture melody notes in bluegrass banjo playing. Don't forget that you can create variations on each of these patterns by striking different strings using the same picking-hand sequence, a topic that's covered in full in Chapter 5.

In the following examples, *MN* doesn't stand for the great state of Minnesota — it stands for "melody note."

Forward-reverse roll

The forward-reverse roll is used to play melody notes that are found on your banjo's fourth and third strings, which are the first and seventh notes of this roll (see Tab 8-5). You'll use this roll to play "Long Journey Home." It also works well for songs like "She'll Be Coming 'Round the Mountain."

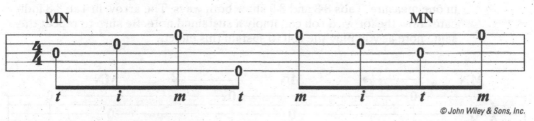

© John Wiley & Sons, Inc.

Tab 8-5: Forward-reverse roll melody notes.

Alternating thumb roll

The alternating thumb roll is typically used when two to four melody notes on the third and fourth strings are needed in a single measure. Tabs 8-6 and 8-7 show two different ways that alternating thumb rolls capture melody notes. You'll use this roll to play "I'll Fly Away." It also works well on such classics as "Grandfather's Clock." "Cripple Creek," a banjo favorite presented in Chapter 7, also uses this roll extensively.

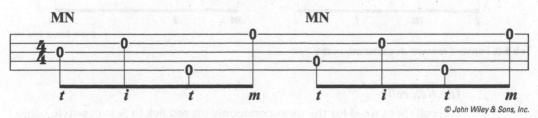

© John Wiley & Sons, Inc.

Tab 8-6: Alternating thumb roll with two melody notes.

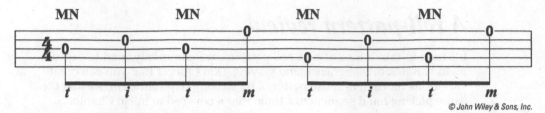

© John Wiley & Sons, Inc.

Tab 8-7: Alternating thumb roll with four melody notes.

Forward roll

Forward rolls add drive and power to bluegrass banjo playing. Forward rolls are often used in solos to represent a melody note that is of long rhythmic duration (just as when a singer sings one note and holds it for a few beats) on the second, third, and fourth strings.

Forward rolls can also be used when two or three melody notes are needed in one measure. Tabs 8-8 and 8-9 show both ways. The arrow in Tab 8-8 indicates how the forward roll can imply a sustained note. Be sure to repeat this same note as you play the roll to sustain this effect.

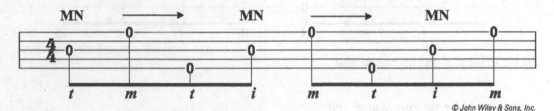

© John Wiley & Sons, Inc.

Tab 8-8: Forward roll with sustained melody note.

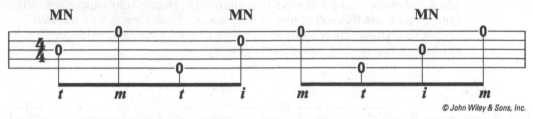

© John Wiley & Sons, Inc.

Tab 8-9: Forward roll with three melody notes.

The lick roll

The roll that's used for the most commonly played lick in Scruggs-style banjo can also be used for melodies in solos. Note that the first five notes of this roll are the same as the forward roll. The lick roll is frequently used when a melody note is needed on the third or fourth string at the fourth beat of the measure, as shown in Tab 8-10.

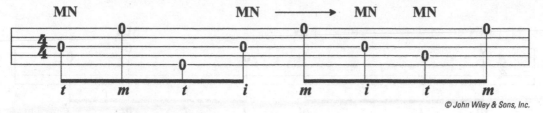

© John Wiley & Sons, Inc.

Tab 8-10: The lick roll with four melody notes.

The Foggy Mountain roll

If you need two melody notes one right after the other at the beginning of a measure on the second or third strings, the Foggy Mountain roll is just the thing you need. Tabs 8-11 and 8-12 show the second- and third-string variations.

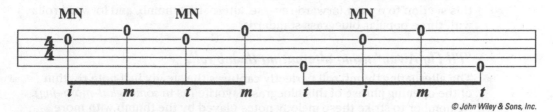

© John Wiley & Sons, Inc.

Tab 8-11: Foggy Mountain roll with second-string melody notes.

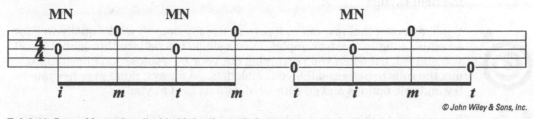

© John Wiley & Sons, Inc.

Tab 8-12: Foggy Mountain roll with third-string melody notes.

Backward roll

The backward roll is ideal for those melody notes that are found on the banjo's first string. As in the case with the forward roll, the backward roll can play either three separate first-string melody notes or convey the feeling of a sustained pitch on this string. Take a look at Tab 8-13 to see how this works, and give a listen to Earl Scruggs's "Home Sweet Home" and "Ground Speed" for some classic recorded examples.

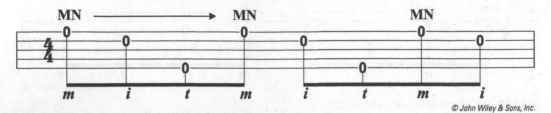

Tab 8-13: The backward roll with first-string melody notes.

Using rolls in banjo solos

There's no substitute for trying rolls with a few different songs to get a clearer understanding on how bluegrass banjo players match roll patterns to melodies to create bluegrass banjo solos. Check out the three examples in this section to try out forward-reverse, alternating thumb, and forward rolls with three popular bluegrass standards.

"I'll Fly Away" using alternating thumb rolls

The alternating thumb roll perfectly captures the steady half-note rhythm of the opening phrase of this bluegrass favorite (as in *some–glad–morn–ing*). Remember to strike these melody notes played by the thumb with more volume than the other notes in this roll. At measures 6 and 14, the alternating thumb roll also allows you to play the melody notes for "fly away" in exactly the right rhythm.

You'll discover that just one roll pattern usually doesn't work equally well for an entire song. In these examples, I use a single roll pattern throughout to get you started, but when you're working out your own solos, don't hesitate to mix the rolls to better match your melodies. As always, don't ever hesitate to try multiple options and go with what sounds best to you!

I've included a third-string slide in several places in this arrangement of "I'll Fly Away" (Tab 8-14; Audio Track 55). In the next section, you'll add additional fretting techniques as a final step to finesse each of these solos.

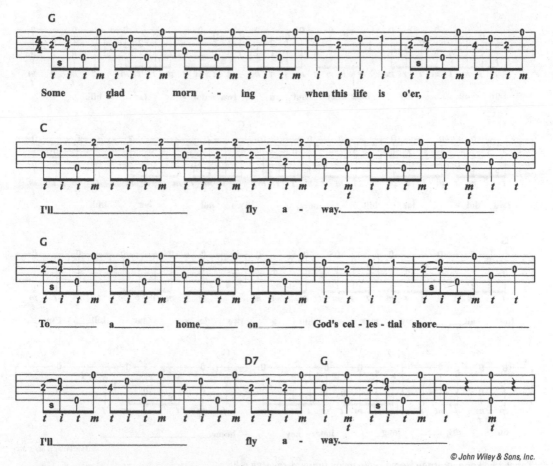

Some glad morn - ing when this life is o'er,

I'll_____ fly a - way._____

To_____ a_____ home_____ on_____ God's cel - les - tial shore_____

I'll_____ fly a - way._____

© John Wiley & Sons, Inc.

Tab 8-14: "I'll Fly Away" solo using alternating thumb rolls.

"Long Journey Home" using forward-reverse rolls

Banjo players use the forward-reverse roll in all kinds of situations to capture melodies in solos. It's easy to play, and it always sounds great! In the case of "Long Journey Home" (Tab 8-15; Audio Track 56), the forward-reverse roll grabs two of the three melody notes needed in each measure. Note how the use of quarter notes and pinch patterns at the end of each line helps to define the four phrases of this melody.

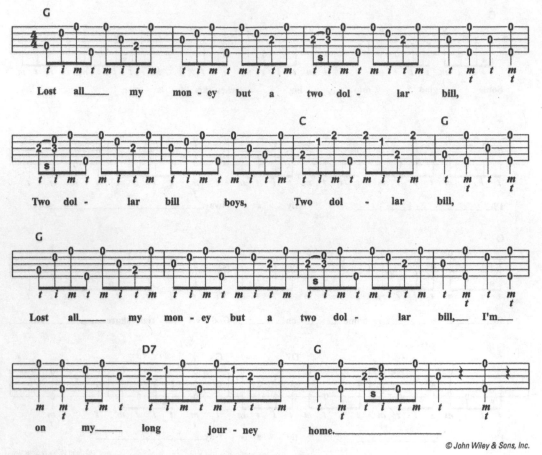

© John Wiley & Sons, Inc.

Tab 8-15: "Long Journey Home" solo using forward-reverse rolls.

"You Are My Sunshine" using forward rolls

In this arrangement of "You Are My Sunshine" (Tab 8-16; Audio Track 57) forward rolls create the sense of a single sustained note (as in measure 7 at *gray* and measure 13 at *take*) and are also used to play multiple melody notes in a single measure (as in measure 14 with *sun–shine–a–way*). Forward rolls can lend considerable bluegrass cred to your solos, so try to use them whenever possible!

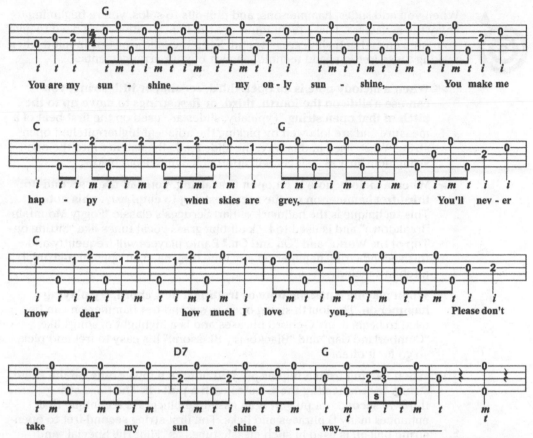

© *John Wiley & Sons, Inc.*

Tab 8-16: "You Are My Sunshine" solo using forward rolls.

Adding Fretting Techniques to Solos

When asked about his approach to creating solos, Earl Scruggs would often reply that he made an attempt with every solo he created to "play the syllables" on his banjo that the vocalist sings. Singers seldom hit notes straight on as if playing a melody on a piano. They move up and down into notes with slides and embellish phrases with passing notes, which connect the main melody notes.

When you add slides, hammer-ons, and pull-offs to solos, you're beginning to "play the syllables." These techniques are the final additions you need to give your solo an authentic bluegrass sound. Keep the following tips in mind when making these fretting-hand techniques part of your arrangements:

- **When a melody note is an open third, second, or fifth string, you can use a slide on the fourth, third, or first strings to move up to the pitch of that open string.** Typically, slides are used on the first beat of a measure and are followed by picking the adjacent higher-pitched open string. When used in this way, the slide leads the listener into the open-string note, just as a singer will approach a note from below.

- **When a melody note is an open first string, you can use a second- to third-fret hammer-on on the second string to emphasize this note.** This technique is the hallmark of Earl Scruggs's classic "Foggy Mountain Breakdown" and is used to kick off bluegrass vocal tunes like "Sitting on Top of the World" and "On and On." Banjo players will frequently add this second-string hammer-on any time they need an open first-string D pitch in a melody.

- **When playing a passing note or fretting a new chord, try playing a hammer-on.** The fourth-string open to second-fret hammer-on can be used to begin many C-chord phrases and is a highlight of songs like "Cumberland Gap" and "Blackberry Blossom." It's easy to fret and pick, so go for it often!

- **When moving from a higher-pitched note to a lower note on the same string, try connecting these notes with a pull-off.** The third-string third- to second-fret pull-off is an essential bluegrass technique that enhances many G phrases and licks. The first-string second-fret to open-string pull-off is used in such classic tunes as "Flint Hill Special" and "Shortening Bread."

It's important to not lose track of the roll patterns you're playing when adding fretting techniques to solos. Keep the rolls flowing smoothly, adding slides, hammer-ons, and pull-offs without interrupting the steady rhythm of your rolls. This will help lend your playing the driving rhythm that all bluegrass banjo players strive to achieve.

Putting it all together

You're taking a huge step forward in your understanding of the inner workings of bluegrass banjo style, as well as taking a big leap forward in your playing ability as you get comfortable playing through these songs once again, but this time with the addition of fretting-hand techniques.

As you work through each of these songs, compare these versions with the previous two versions that presented the basic melody alone and then the basic melody with roll patterns. Keep track of the roll patterns that are used in the following arrangements and match the song lyrics to the tab above to find the melody notes.

"I'll Fly Away" using fretting techniques

The alternating thumb roll remains the picking-hand foundation of this arrangement of "I'll Fly Away" (Tab 8-17; Audio Track 58; Video Clip 20) based on the playing of banjo great Sonny Osborne (of the Osborne Brothers and "Rocky Top" fame). Note how the slides, hammer-ons, and pull-offs connect one melody note to the next, just as a great singer would do, to create a flowing arrangement.

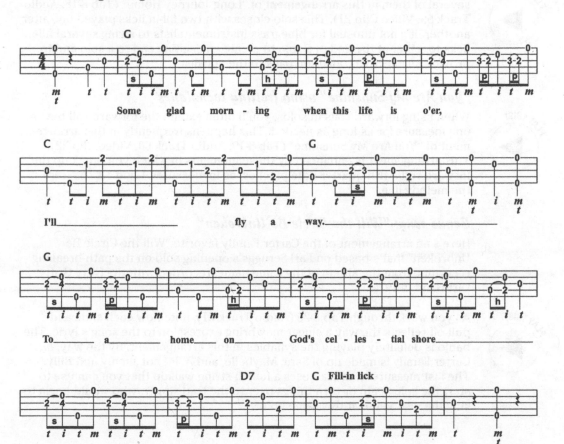

© John Wiley & Sons, Inc.

Tab 8-17: "I'll Fly Away" solo using fretting techniques.

A great way to end your solo is to play a fill-in lick at the final G chord (visit Chapter 7 for a handful of great fill-in licks). You'll play the classic, all-purpose version of this lick at the close of this arrangement of "I'll Fly Away." You'll play this lick more than any other single phrase in all your bluegrass banjo playing! It even uses its own roll pattern, called the "lick roll," of all things. It's a tricky pattern, requiring a 180-degree shift in picking-hand direction halfway through the measure as the hand shifts from a forward to a backward flow of notes. Practice this roll at first without the left hand to make the picking-hand moves second nature before adding the fretting techniques to complete this essential lick.

"Long Journey Home" using fretting techniques

If you've reviewed all the great licks presented in Chapter 7, you'll recognize several of them in this arrangement of "Long Journey Home" (Tab 8-18; Audio Track 59, Video Clip 21). This solo closes with two fill-in licks played one after another. It's not unusual for bluegrass instrumentalists to string several fill-in licks together at the end of a solo to create an exciting end to a solo and to provide an effective transition back to the vocalist.

"You Are My Sunshine" using fretting techniques

When using forward rolls in solos, you'll often extend the forward roll beyond one measure for as long as needed. This happens frequently in this arrangement of "You Are My Sunshine" (Tab 8-19; Audio Track 60, Video Clip 22). This arrangement is enhanced by those moments in which you break up the forward rolls with quarter-note pinches, as in measures 1 and 13, to stress the melody line.

Bonus song: "Will the Circle Be Unbroken"

Here's an arrangement of the Carter Family favorite "Will the Circle Be Unbroken" that's based on Earl Scruggs's opening solo on the path-breaking recording from the album of the same name, recorded with the Nitty Gritty Dirt Band in 1972.

As you work through Tab 8-20 (Audio Track 61), note how each slide and pull-off reflects the way a singer may bring expression to the song's lyric. The banjo is definitely playing the syllables in this arrangement. By the way, *this* Carter Family is made up of Sara, Maybelle, and A. P., not Jimmy and Billy. The last measure in the tab uses a fourth-string walkup that you can use to start the solo again or turn things over to the lead singer, who would begin to sing the next verse at this same point.

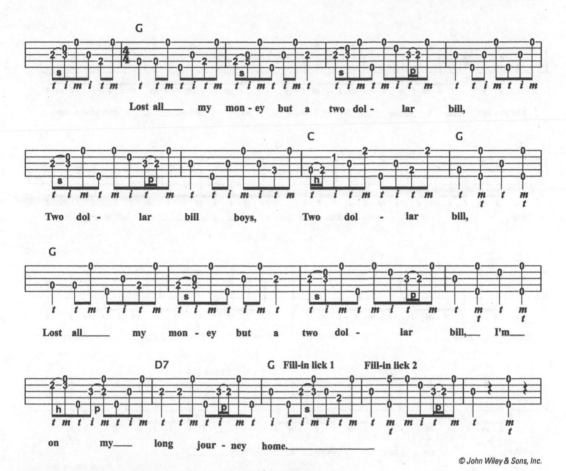

Tab 8-18: "Long Journey Home" solo using fretting techniques.

Working out modal solos

The melodies of bluegrass songs and instrumentals aren't just assembled from the notes of the major scale. There's a category of song that banjo players just love to play that they describe as "lonesome." It uses the kind of scale that's just perfect for murder ballads or songs that frequently use the word *sorrow*.

Although I've never heard any banjo player use this term, the kind of scale that is used for songs like "Clinch Mountain Backstep" and "Wild Bill Jones"

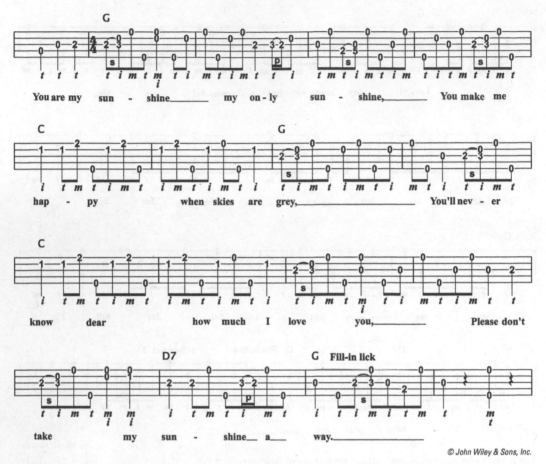

Tab 8-19: "You Are My Sunshine" solo using fretting techniques.

is called a *pentatonic minor* scale. *Pentatonic* refers to a five-note scale, while a *minor scale* is created by lowering the third and seventh notes of a major scale by one fret each.

Tab 8-21 (Audio Track 62) shows the notes of a G pentatonic minor scale, including the two notes you can play using this mode on fourth string.

"Man of Constant Sorrow" basic melody

Of all the songs that use this most lonesome of scales, "Man of Constant Sorrow" is perhaps the best known. Although it dates from the early 20th

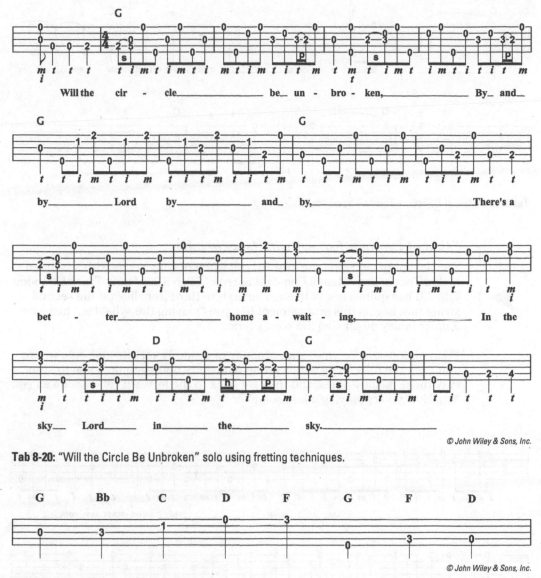

© John Wiley & Sons, Inc.

Tab 8-20: "Will the Circle Be Unbroken" solo using fretting techniques.

© John Wiley & Sons, Inc.

Tab 8-21: The G pentatonic minor scale.

century, its timeless quality comes from the pentatonic minor scale that comprises the song's melody.

As you play through Tab 8-22 (Audio Track 63), check out my fingering suggestions above the tab staff.

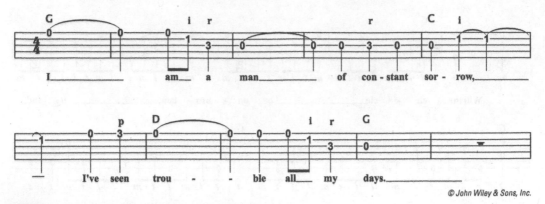

Tab 8-22: "Man of Constant Sorrow" basic melody.

"Man of Constant Sorrow" with forward rolls

You'll want to call upon the forward roll when playing songs with sustained melody notes and "Man of Constant Sorrow" (Tab 8-23; Audio Track 63, Video Clip 23) has quite a few of these. The first- to third-fret slide on the second string that begins this arrangement has you "playing the syllables," just as Ralph Stanley might sing the song's lyric.

"Man of Constant Sorrow" is an example of a simple yet effective solo where you keep the rolls going until a group of melody notes requires you to stop. Play those melody notes, and then get back to the forward roll as soon as you can. Now you're playing it lonesome!

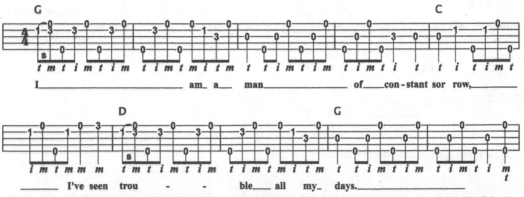

Tab 8-23: "Man of Constant Sorrow" solo using forward rolls.

Playing a modal instrumental classic: "Cluck Old Hen"

To conclude this section on playing melody-based solos, here's "Cluck Old Hen," a tune commonly heard at both bluegrass and old-time jam sessions (Tab 8-24; Audio Track 64). This particular arrangement is a step up in difficulty in comparison to the other songs presented in this chapter. You'll use many of the same fretting positions here as you did in "Old Joe Clark," which you can find in Chapter 7.

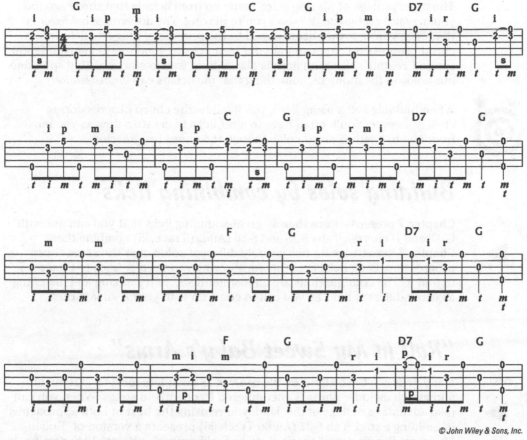

© John Wiley & Sons, Inc.

Tab 8-24: Playing it lonesome with "Cluck Old Hen."

Assembling Solos from Licks

In addition to creating solos based on the melody, you can improvise solos using licks that match the chord progression of the song you're playing. This is a great strategy to follow if you're hearing a tune for the first time in a jam session or if you want to play something different when you have the opportunity to play a second solo.

The disadvantage of playing solos made up from licks is that those around you may not recognize the song you're playing. The advantage however is that once you've grown accustomed to the process of plugging licks into a chord progression, you can put your best licks to good use in many different songs. Creating solos with licks is also a great way to start creating spontaneous solos in the moment, something that musicians call *improvisation*.

When building solos using licks, you'll follow the chord progression as closely as ever. You'll often have to alter licks to create a flow as you move from one to another as you play though the chord progression.

Building solos by combining licks

Chapter 7 presents more than 40 great-sounding licks that you can use with G, C, and D chords. Tabs 8-25 and 8-26 (Audio Track 65) combine these Chapter 7 licks to create two entirely different solos over the same chord progression. Each lick is numbered, allowing you to refer back to Chapter 7 to find it. The combinations are almost limitless, so try mixing and matching as many different licks as you can to come up with your own favorites.

"Roll in My Sweet Baby's Arms"

Many licks can both stand by themselves as complete musical statements and match melodic phrases encountered frequently in songs. When you can take advantage of licks of this kind, you're using the best of both approaches in building a solo. Tab 8-27 (Audio Track 66) presents a version of "Roll in My Sweet Baby's Arms" that's close to Earl Scruggs's original 1949 version. In this example, the solo is filled with licks that you'll hear in other songs, but these licks also match the melody well.

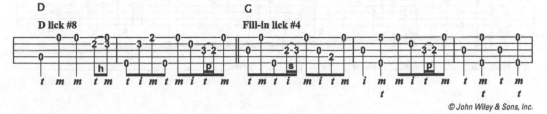

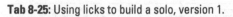

© John Wiley & Sons, Inc.

Tab 8-25: Using licks to build a solo, version 1.

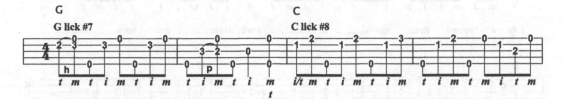

© John Wiley & Sons, Inc.

Tab 8-26: Using licks to build a solo, version 2.

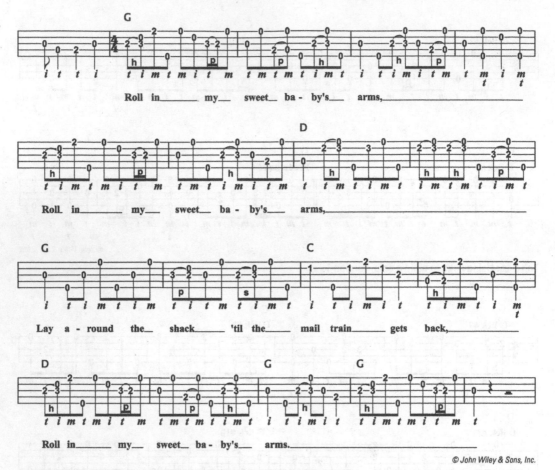

Tab 8-27: "Roll in My Sweet Baby's Arms," building a solo using licks.

Heading Up the Neck to Play Solos

Some of the most exciting moments in bluegrass banjo playing happen when you play solos up the neck. In this section, you gain experience with essential up-the-neck licks and chord positions that you can use in just about all your upper-range musical explorations.

Although banjo players are concerned with matching roll patterns and licks to melodies for down-the-neck solos, interchangeable licks are much more frequently employed when playing solos up the neck. The licks in the following section are designed for G, C, and D chords, but you can transpose these licks to other places on your banjo fingerboard to use for other chords that you'll encounter.

Basic up-the-neck G-lick position

One the biggest initial challenges for new players is getting used to an up-the-neck G position that is used in backup and is also an integral part of tunes like "Cumberland Gap" and "Sally Goodin'." Check out Figure 8-2 for the chord shape for this position.

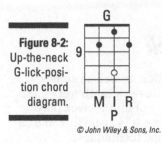

Figure 8-2:
Up-the-neck
G-lick-position chord
diagram.

© John Wiley & Sons, Inc.

The basic position requires you to use your middle, index, and ring fingers on the eighth and ninth frets, which is easy enough. However, the tough part in playing the licks associated with this position is touching down with the pinky finger on the 11th fret while holding down the other three fretting fingers, as shown in Figure 8-3.

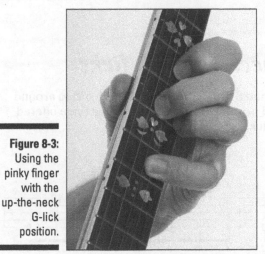

Figure 8-3:
Using the pinky finger with the up-the-neck G-lick position.

Photograph by Anne Hamersky

Try a second-string variation of the lick roll to play this up-the-neck G fill-in lick, as shown in Tab 8-28 (Audio Track 67).

© John Wiley & Sons, Inc.

Tab 8-28: Up-the-neck G fill-in lick.

The Foggy Mountain bend lick

Another essential G lick that generates a lot of attention as well as smiles from other musicians and listeners is the iconic up-the-neck tenth-fret, second-string choke lick that's heard in a wide variety of up-the-neck playing. You encounter this lick back in Chapter 6, but here it is again in Tab 8-29 (Audio Track 67), with pre-bend and choke-and-release techniques.

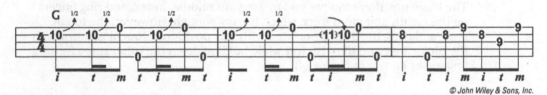

© John Wiley & Sons, Inc.

Tab 8-29: Up-the-neck G lick using bends.

Essential up-the-neck C and D licks

These licks, shown in Tabs 8-30 and 8-31 (Audio Track 67) are based around the same F-shape movable chord position. Note the nice blues tinge offered in the second measure of the D lick.

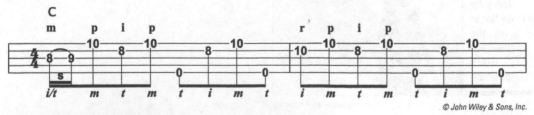

© John Wiley & Sons, Inc.

Tab 8-30: Up-the-neck C lick.

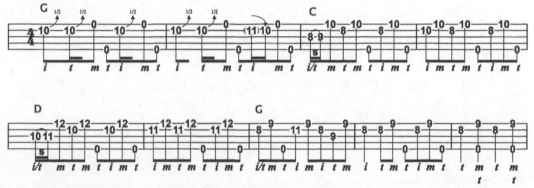

Tab 8-31: Up-the-neck D lick.

Putting the licks together

If you put these licks together (Tab 8-32; Audio Track 68, Video Clip 24), you'll hear an effective up-the-neck solo that contains elements of "Foggy Mountain Breakdown," "Lonesome Road Blues," and other up-the-neck bluegrass banjo classics. Enjoy!

Tab 8-32: Creating an up-the-neck solo from G, C, and D licks.

Part III
Playing in the Band: Backup Essentials

Photograph by Anne Hamersky

Get a jam survival checklist in an article at www.dummies.com/extras/
bluegrassbanjo.

In this part . . .

✔ Understand the role of the banjo in group playing.

✔ Discover accompaniment techniques to make other bluegrass musicians sound their best.

✔ Develop your backup abilities using roll patterns in one- and two-measure combinations to create great-sounding down-the-neck bluegrass banjo backup.

✔ Explore movable chord positions in different keys and use these positions to accompany songs using vamping techniques.

✔ Discover up-the-neck picking patterns and classic licks to give your accompaniment a professional bluegrass sound.

Chapter 9

Getting Started: Playing Down-the-Neck Backup

....

In This Chapter

▶ Playing basic roll patterns to accompany others

▶ Using the forward roll to create driving bluegrass backup

▶ Utilizing target tones to make your playing flow

▶ Accompanying fiddle tunes in the keys of G and D

▶ Access the audio tracks and video clips at www.dummies.com/go/bluegrassbanjo

....

*B*luegrass banjo playing isn't just all about playing blazingly fast and virtuosic solos that amaze (and maybe amuse) your loved ones, who sometimes get to hear you play when you forget to shut the basement door. Bluegrass banjo playing is also designed for making music with others, whether it's in an honest-to-goodness bluegrass band or in your friendly neighborhood folk-gospel-whatever jam session.

When banjo players accompany other musicians, it's called playing *backup*. Getting comfortable with backup techniques is an essential part of becoming a good player. You'll be a bluegrass banjo convert for life after you've experienced how much fun it is to play music with others, and the really exciting news is that you only need to master a few basic backup skills to get started.

In this chapter, you get familiar with the fine art of playing roll-based down-the-neck backup with a special emphasis on how to use forward rolls to capture the drive and power that's characteristic of the best ensemble playing. You'll understand much better what's expected of the banjo in a group context, and you'll even begin to unlock the secrets of knowing what to play when hearing new songs for the first time in a jam session.

Before you jump in, you should know your roll patterns. Check out Chapter 5 to review these essential building blocks of bluegrass picking techniques. Then you'll be more than ready to emerge from that basement and become a great, aboveground bluegrass band player.

Using Basic Roll Patterns in Backup

If you listen carefully to any great bluegrass band, you'll hear that each instrument has a unique job to do. Whether you're playing just a few notes (like the bass player) or a *lot* of notes (like, well, the banjo player!), it's everyone's responsibility to contribute to the precise rhythm of the total band.

It's true that banjo players *do* get to play more notes than any other bluegrass musician, but this is a big responsibility! When you play smoothly and in good rhythm, you're laying down a groove that locks in with the patterns that other musicians play to create the irresistible drive that defines great bluegrass music.

The banjo accomplishes this primarily through playing roll patterns, using these picking techniques for both featured solos and backup playing. *Down-the-neck backup* refers to playing picking patterns while fretting chords in the first position on the lower frets of your banjo (close to where the tuners are). You'll sound great using the basic chords you already know for all the examples in this chapter.

Before you can mix and match roll patterns with other backup techniques, you'll need to get comfortable using the basic roll patterns as your primary backup. In the following sections, you find your picking groove using alternating thumb, forward-reverse, and forward rolls to accompany three bluegrass classics. Your job is to play these rolls smoothly and in good rhythm, not stopping as you move from one chord to the next.

Using alternating thumb rolls

The alternating thumb roll is a great way to get started with using roll patterns to play banjo backup. Tab 9-1 (Audio Track 69) shows you how to use this roll as accompaniment to the Kentucky coal-mining classic "Nine Pound Hammer."

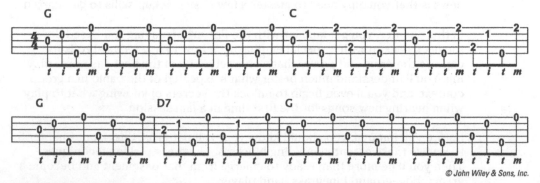

© John Wiley & Sons, Inc.

Tab 9-1: Using alternating thumb rolls to play backup to "Nine Pound Hammer."

Using forward-reverse rolls

The forward-reverse roll is another way to effectively accompany others using down-the-neck backup techniques. Try this roll as an accompaniment to the Carter Family favorite "Will the Circle Be Unbroken" (Tab 9-2; Audio Track 70).

TIP

Although it's natural to check out the tabs for all these examples, try not to stare at the written music as you play. If you're already comfortable playing the roll patterns you need, it's better to just play along with the audio track without looking at the tab. If you listen for the chord changes as you play through the tune, you'll be using the same skills that you'll need in real jam sessions.

Using forward rolls

Forward rolls put the drive and power into down-the-neck roll-based backup playing, and these are the primary rolls that professional players use for this type of accompaniment. Because of the nature of the forward roll — which by definition contains some combination of notes played by the picking-hand thumb, index finger, and middle finger in succession — it can be a challenge to fit the forward roll into one-measure patterns.

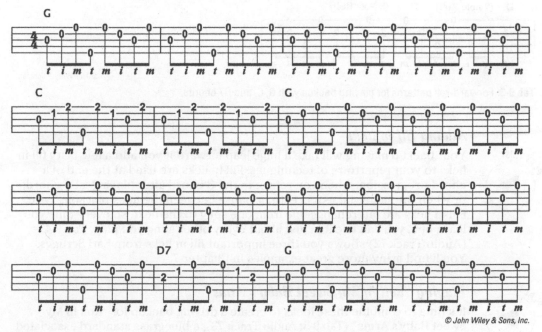

© John Wiley & Sons, Inc.

Tab 9-2: Using forward-reverse rolls to accompany "Will the Circle Be Unbroken."

Choosing forward rolls

Check out Tab 9-3 (Audio Track 71), which lays out some great choices for these patterns. You can play a seven-note roll, where the first note is a quarter note that takes up the rhythmic space of two roll notes, or you can pick the conventional eight-note roll. If you're just getting used to playing forward rolls, try the seven-note patterns first as written out for the G, C, and D7 chords, and then shift over to the eight-note patterns when you're ready.

When deciding which roll to play for backup, it's a great idea to choose a roll variation that includes the strings that you're fretting for the C and D7 chords. As you play through the examples in Tab 9-3, note that although the order of picking-hand fingers remains the same, you'll strike different strings for each chord. Playing the second string for the C chord reinforces to the listeners that this is the chord you want them to hear. For the D7 example, you play the third and fourth strings to create the same effect.

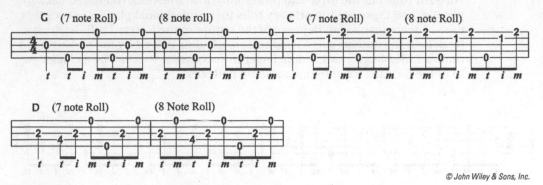

© John Wiley & Sons, Inc.

Tab 9-3: Forward-roll patterns for playing backup with G, C, and D7 chords.

Adding fill-in licks

Your backup playing will take a huge leap forward if you add a few tasty fill-in licks to your repertoire of techniques. Fill-in licks are used at the end of a chord progression, when you return to the G chord after playing a D7 chord, or when the singer takes a breath or pause between the lines of a song lyric. Fill-in licks are interchangeable from one song to the next, so every time you learn one, you can use it in just about every other song you play. Tab 9-4 (Audio Track 72) shows you three important fill-in licks from Earl Scruggs. You'll find many more great examples in Chapter 7.

Playing "Roll in My Sweet Baby's Arms"

It's time to combine these ideas to create a driving backup for "Roll in My Sweet Baby's Arms" (Tab 9-5; Audio Track 73), a bluegrass standard associated with Flatt & Scruggs. Take care to adjust the roll patterns to highlight the fretted strings for each chord, and don't forget to add those fill-in licks whenever you get the chance.

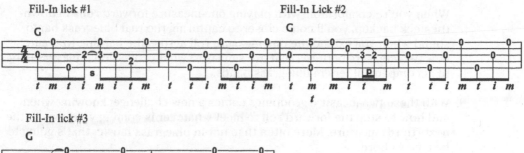

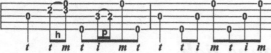

© John Wiley & Sons, Inc.

Tab 9-4: Three essential Scruggs-style fill-in licks.

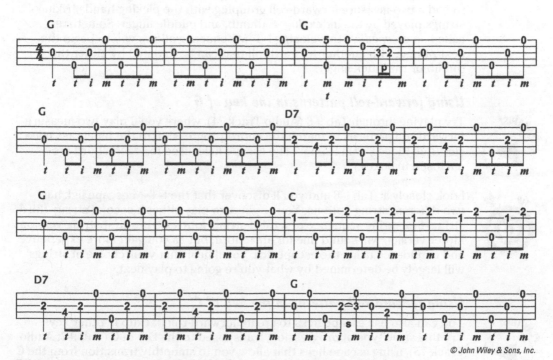

© John Wiley & Sons, Inc.

Tab 9-5: Forward-roll backup for "Roll in My Sweet Baby's Arms" using fill-in licks.

Using Two-Measure Forward Rolls in Backup

When you're comfortable with playing one-measure forward rolls in down-the-neck backup, you'll come closer to capturing the real bluegrass banjo sound when you extend the one-measure roll across the bar line to create new two-measure patterns that are similar to what professional players play to accompany others in bluegrass bands.

With these two-measure groupings comes a new challenge: knowing when and how to stop the forward roll to meet whatever is coming your way in the next (third) measure. More often than not in bluegrass music, that's going to be a new chord.

Capturing the escape lick

The formula that skilled players use to organize these longer patterns is to end a two-measure forward-roll grouping with the picking-hand striking strings played by the index finger, thumb, and middle finger. Sometimes called an *escape lick,* this closing I–T–M sequence allows you to begin the next phrase with another forward roll that can be initiated by either the thumb or the index finger.

Using forward-roll patterns in the key of G

Try playing through Tab 9-6 (Audio Track 74), where you'll play two-measure forward-roll patterns to match the chord progression to the bluegrass classic "Blue Ridge Cabin Home." The escape licks used for each chord are enclosed in boxes.

Look closely at Tab 9-6 and you'll discover that the I–T–M escape lick has two different string options: You're going to play either a second-string–third-string–first-string sequence or a third-string–fourth-string–first-string version. Either version will sound fine for any chord, but as you gain more experience and confidence using the escape lick, you'll hear that your choice of strings will largely be determined by what you're going to play next.

Using forward-roll patterns in the key of C

You can also use escape licks to create forward-roll backup in other keys. Try this same type of progression, transposed to the key of C (Tab 9-7; Audio Track 75), using escape licks that allow you to smoothly transition from the C to the F and G chords.

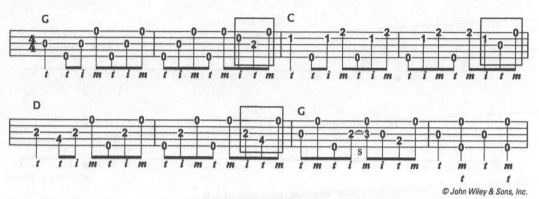

© John Wiley & Sons, Inc.

Tab 9-6: Two-measure forward-roll backup for "Blue Ridge Cabin Home" progression.

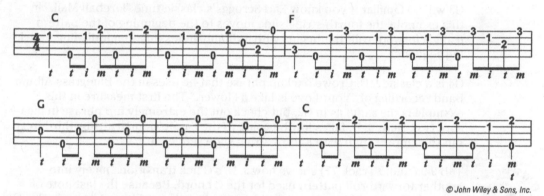

© John Wiley & Sons, Inc.

Tab 9-7: Two-measure forward-roll backup in the key of C.

Adding slides to forward-roll patterns

Now it's time to make your forward-roll accompaniment sound even better by adding slides to several different G forward-roll phrases. Tab 9-8 (Audio Track 76) introduces you to four different backup licks that you can insert into any song that has a two-measure G-chord sequence (and that includes a *lot* of songs!). Note that each of these examples concludes with an escape lick that leads into the next phrase or chord.

G1 is built on the same roll pattern used in Tab 9-6 with the addition of a fourth-string slide at beat two. Note how adding this slide immediately makes this phrase sound infinitely cooler! G2 builds upon G1 by adding an additional roll note just after beat one to create an unending flow of roll notes through the two measures.

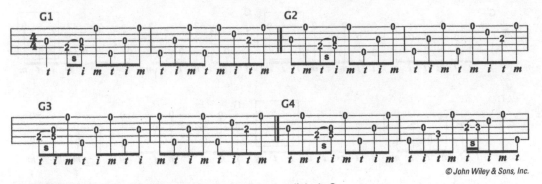

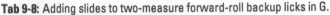

Tab 9-8: Adding slides to two-measure forward-roll backup licks in G.

G3 will be familiar if you know Earl Scruggs's classic tune "Fireball Mail." In this example, the fourth-string slide moves to the beginning of the pattern, using a forward roll that begins with a thumb–index-finger–middle-finger picking sequence.

G4 is a classic J. D. Crowe backup phrase that he uses in the Bluegrass Album Band recording of "Your Love Is Like a Flower." The first measure in this example is the same as in G2, but check out the extremely hip phrase in measure two. Here, J. D. fakes low by going to the F note (fourth string, third fret) but then moves high with a third-string slide sequence.

Tab 9-9 (Audio Track 77) shows how J. D.'s G lick transitions nicely into another forward-roll pattern used for the C chord. Because the last note of the G phrase is a fifth-string picked by your thumb, you'll need to begin this C phrase with an index finger instead of the usual thumb.

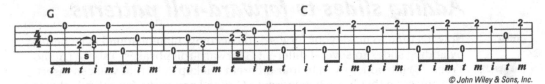

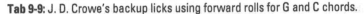

Tab 9-9: J. D. Crowe's backup licks using forward rolls for G and C chords.

Perfecting your backup with target tones

One of the last steps in getting a professional sound to your down-the-neck backup playing is to give some thought as to how you can use escape licks to transition smoothly from one chord to the next in a chord progression.

A helpful concept in this regard is to use *target tones* to chart a course through a chord progression.

A *target tone* is the note you're choosing to play on the first beat of a chord change as you move through the chord progression of a song. Although choosing the target tone is important, even more crucial is the creation of a forward-roll sequence that convincingly leads into the target tone of the new chord.

You can think of a target tone as your destination, but as in much of life itself (not to mention bluegrass banjo playing), it's the journey to that destination that provides the challenge and the thrill.

When playing a bluegrass song, the target tone will be one of the notes in the new chord you're about to play. It's that simple! If you can locate your target tone on the second, third, or fourth string, it's possible to pick that note with the right-hand thumb to launch into another two-measure forward-roll pattern that you can play over the new chord.

A target tone can be fretted or unfretted, but it makes sense to choose a target tone in the new chord that isn't shared by the chord you're moving from. For instance, both the G and C chords share the third-string open G note. For this reason, choosing that string as a target tone for the C chord usually won't be as strong a choice as either the fourth string or the second string, which are both fretted for the C chord. Your choice of target tone will often determine which strings make the most sense to play for the escape roll that leads into that target tone.

Mixing Backup Techniques

Great players mix and match techniques when they play down-the-neck backup. The two-measure forward-roll sequences discussed in this chapter can be the foundation of your backup strategy, but you should also feel free to insert licks that you've picked up along the way to add even more energy to your backup playing. To conclude this section on forward-roll backup techniques, take a look at two more examples that combine the techniques presented in the last few sections while adding a few more new ideas along the way.

Tab 9-10 (Audio Track 78, Video Clip 25) works with the chord progression for "Blue Ridge Cabin Home," while Tab 9-11 (Audio Track 79) matches the chord progression of another Flatt & Scruggs favorite, "Your Love Is Like a Flower." Each is a no-holds-barred example of what a banjo master like Sonny Osborne or Earl Scruggs would play down the neck when backing up a singer in a bluegrass band.

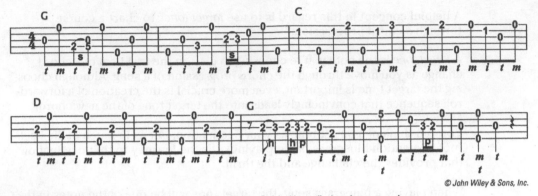

© John Wiley & Sons, Inc.

Tab 9-10: Mixing backup techniques for "Blue Ridge Cabin Home" chord progression.

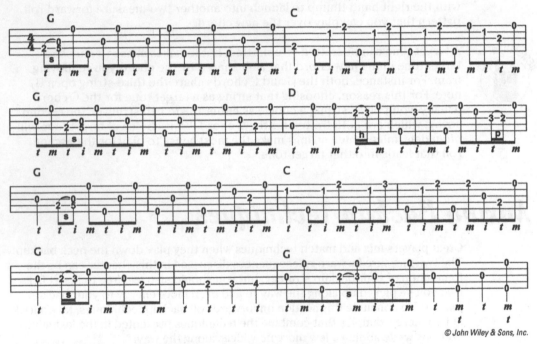

© John Wiley & Sons, Inc.

Tab 9-11: Mixing backup techniques for "Your Love Is Like a Flower" chord progression.

Playing Fiddle-Tune Backup

Some of the most satisfying music that you can make on the banjo is when you back up a fiddle. As part of every Flatt & Scruggs live show, fiddle and banjo aficionados would anxiously wait for that moment in the concert when the Foggy Mountain Boys would leave the stage, allowing Earl and his fiddler to play one or two of the old fiddle tunes just by themselves. Earl Scruggs perfected the banjo's role in the fiddle and banjo duet through his work in the 1950s and 1960s with the fiddlers who played in his band: Benny Martin, Jim Shumate, Paul Warren, and Chubby Wise.

When you play with a fiddler, you're sustaining one of the oldest and most important traditions in American folk music. You want to make sure that your banjo playing is holding up its end of the deal! Great fiddle-tune backup calls upon the banjo to not only play the forward roll patterns you encounter in the previous sections of this chapter, but also utilize a variety of other techniques to create an active and rhythmic counterpoint to the fiddler's melody.

In this section, you discover backup techniques that you can use to accompany the fiddle in the keys of G and D. You also get acquainted with two of the best-known fiddle classics in bluegrass music, "Sally Goodin'" and "Whiskey Before Breakfast."

Playing fiddle-tune backup in G

"Sally Goodin'," "Katy Hill," "Leather Britches," and "Grey Eagle" are just a few of the fiddle tunes that can be accompanied on the banjo using similar backup roll-pattern techniques. All these tunes share a similar chord progression that's very easy to remember: three measures of G, followed by a half-measure of D, then back again to a half-measure of G. (Truth be told, if fiddlers decide to play "Sally Goodin'" in the key of A, you can still use all the same G licks and techniques presented in this section by placing your capo at the second fret to play in the key of A.)

Following Earl's lead, banjo players have adopted a consistent set of backup techniques to accompany these kinds of fiddle tunes. For the four-measure chord progression that these tunes all share, try playing a two-measure forward-roll G pattern, followed by a one-measure G lick and then concluding with another one-measure lick that moves from the D chord back home to the G.

Check out Tab 9-12 (Audio Track 80) for phrases and licks that you can use to accompany a fiddler through four repetitions of "Sally Goodin'."

Playing fiddle-tune backup in D

Fiddlers love to play in the key of D, and because banjo players just love to play with fiddlers, we've developed some great-sounding techniques to keep up in this key.

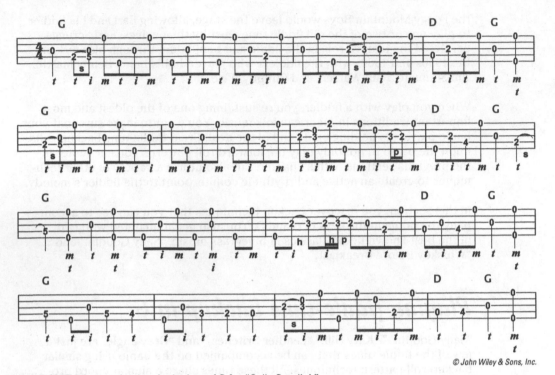

© John Wiley & Sons, Inc.

Tab 9-12: Fiddle-tune backup in the key of G for "Sally Goodin'."

Much of what you can play to accompany fiddle tunes in the key of D you can borrow from the techniques you're already familiar with from playing tunes in the key of G. For instance, two-measure forward-roll backup patterns will also sound great in the key of D, but you'll need to shift strings a bit to emphasize the fretted notes of the D-major chord.

In addition, many D fiddle tunes have fast-moving chord progressions where chords change every measure and sometimes even every *half*-measure. Never fear! You'll find that the forward-reverse roll is designed just for these situations. It's time to seize the day in the key of D by trying out some accompaniment techniques for another fiddle-tune favorite, "Whiskey Before Breakfast."

Besides having a fantastic song title, "Whiskey Before Breakfast" is also one of the most frequently played jam-session instrumentals. Although "Whiskey" seems to be relatively easy to play on the fiddle, mandolin, and guitar, it's one of those tunes that strikes fear into even experienced banjo players.

Maybe it's the wide-ranging, challenging melody line (which is hard to remember and even harder to play!), or it could be the fast-moving chord progression, or maybe it's just playing in the key of D that makes some of us want to crawl back into our banjo caves and just stick to playing

"Cripple Creek" and "Foggy Mountain Breakdown." Whatever your excuse, it's time to shed your inhibitions and experience a bit of attitude adjustment in the key of D by trying out this backup to "Whiskey Before Breakfast." I promise that you'll be a forever-changed banjo player!

You'll want to raise your fifth string to A to play in the key of D without a capo for this version of "Whiskey Before Breakfast" (Tab 9-13; Audio Track 81). Use forward-roll backup when a chord lasts for more than one measure, but don't be afraid to shift into using forward-reverse rolls for the many times in this tune where the chords change every measure or every half-measure. You'll have a blast playing the last line of the song, where you'll move from the 12th fret all the way down to the first position, using forward-reverse rolls to negotiate one of the fastest-moving chord progressions in bluegrass music. Enjoy!

In a jam session, it's not essential that you take a solo on every song — *especially* on fiddle tunes. What's more important in this situation is being able to quickly pick up chord progressions by watching the other musicians (particularly the guitar player) and asking questions when you get stuck. When you've learned the chords, you'll want to try working up a good-sounding and comfortable-to-play roll-pattern backup. After you've mastered the backup, you can worry about creating a solo.

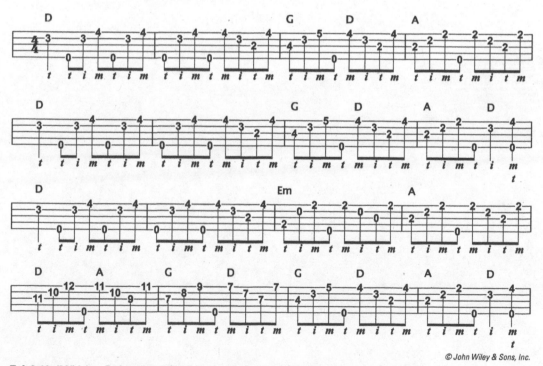

© *John Wiley & Sons, Inc.*

Tab 9-13: "Whiskey Before Breakfast" backup in the key of D, fifth string tuned to A.

Chapter 10

Taking It Higher: Playing Up-the-Neck Backup

In This Chapter

▶ Locating up-the-neck chords

▶ Accompanying others with vamping

▶ Trying out up the neck-picking patterns and classic licks

▶ Playing backup for slower songs

▶ Access the audio tracks and video clips at www.dummies.com/go/bluegrassbanjo

*B*anjo players often claim that playing in a support role to other musicians is more fun — and more challenging — than being the featured soloist. When you hear a bluegrass band that's really cooking, the banjo player will use a variety of standard accompanying techniques that define the sound of the banjo in a bluegrass band context and make everyone else sound great. These techniques are collectively called *backup*. Some of the most exciting and attention-getting of these moments occur when you venture to the upper reaches of your fingerboard to play up-the-neck backup patterns and licks.

If you're playing in a four- or five-piece bluegrass band, you'll spend a lot of your time supporting other musicians. In Chapter 9, you can get acquainted with basic accompaniment techniques using roll patterns and fretting down-the-neck chords (called *down-the-neck backup*). In this chapter, you vastly expand the repertoire of what you can play with up-the-neck ideas and techniques that you can use in almost all the songs you'll encounter at your next jam session.

First, you find the up-the-neck chords needed to play in a variety of keys and use these chords to get started with up-the-neck backup by playing vamping techniques. Then you move on to wrap your fingers around some of the greatest up-the-neck backup patterns and licks in bluegrass banjo history as played by Earl Scruggs, J. D. Crowe, and Sonny Osborne.

If you've been wondering how to play some of the mind-blowing phrases and licks you've heard on your favorite bluegrass recordings, this chapter shows you how. Roll up your sleeves and get ready to move your playing to the next level by heading up the neck.

Mapping Out Up-the-Neck Chords

Whether you're picking lead or playing backup, the first step to playing up the neck with confidence is to get comfortable fretting the chords you need anywhere on your banjo fingerboard. In this section, I show you the six movable chord positions you use to play major and minor chords. I also unlock the secrets of how to move these positions up and down the neck to play chord progressions and songs in different keys.

Fretting movable major chords

A *movable* chord position is a chord shape that can be shifted up and down the neck to play chords at different frets on the banjo fingerboard. The great thing about movable positions is that you can fret a *lot* of chords using the same shape. The challenge is that you need to fret four strings — the fourth, third, second, and first strings — to create a chord that can be moved around the fingerboard in this way.

The three shapes used to fret movable major chords are commonly called the F, D, and barre shapes (see Figure 10-1). When fretting the F shape at the third fret (with your ring finger fretting the fourth string at this fret), you're playing a first-position F chord. When you fret D shape at the fourth fret (with your ring finger fretting the fourth string at this fret), you're sounding a first-position D chord. The open strings of your banjo form a G chord. The barre shape transfers this open chord up the neck and is relatively easy to fret: Just place your index finger across the fourth through the first strings to create chords using this shape. When you use a barre shape at the second fret, you're playing an A chord.

Figure 10-1: Fretting the (a) F, (b) D, and (c) barre shapes for major chords.

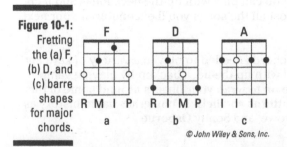

© John Wiley & Sons, Inc.

You create new chords by moving these three shapes up and down the fingerboard, being careful to keep the relative positions of each fretting finger the same for each shape. The letter name given to each chord is determined by which shape you're using and where you're fretting the chord.

For the F shape, the letter name of the chord is determined by the name of fourth- and first-string notes you're fretting (these are the same note, one octave apart). For the D-shape chord, the letter name of the chord is determined by the note you're fretting on the second string and with the barre shape, the chord's letter name is determined by the note you're fretting on the third string. These strings are indicated for each movable position in Figure 10-1.

Appendix A provides the note names for each string from the open position to the 12th fret and can be used as a guide for naming your movable position chords. You'll also become familiar with many of the chords you need as you proceed through the techniques and licks presented in this chapter.

Fretting movable minor chords

Although you won't encounter minor chords nearly as often as major chords in bluegrass music, you'll use minor chords in everything from "Rocky Top" to "Foggy Mountain Breakdown." Some bluegrass songs, like "Little Sadie," "Wayfaring Stranger," and "Jerusalem Ridge," are in a minor key, and their chord progressions are made up mostly of minor chords.

As with movable major chords, there are three movable minor chord shapes. Figure 10-2 shows you these positions for the F minor, D minor, and A minor chords. You can move each shape up the neck to find all the other minor chords.

Figure 10-2: Fretting the (a) F-minor, (b) D-minor, and (c) A-minor movable chord shapes.

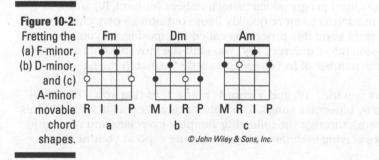

© John Wiley & Sons, Inc.

The letter name for each minor chord is determined in the same way as for the corresponding major-chord shapes: the fourth- and first-string notes you fret name the F-minor-shape chord, the second-string note names the D-minor-shape chord and the third-string note for the A-minor-shape chord. Check out Appendix A for a guide to the note names on each string.

The most efficient way to master these movable positions is to get comfortable with these shapes one at a time, as you encounter them in new songs. The following sections point you in the right direction as you use the F-major and D-major chord shapes with vamping patterns.

Understanding I–IV–V progressions

Great bluegrass banjo players seem to move effortlessly from one chord shape to another, using the entire length of the fingerboard to fret the chords they need. How do they accomplish this seemingly impossible feat? The chord progression of the song provides the road map that banjo players follow to determine what to play, and the movable positions are the destination points along the way. Understanding how chords and movable positions relate to one another in chord progressions will unlock the mysteries of playing up the neck on your banjo.

Many bluegrass songs use only three chords. If you're playing in the key of G (using a G-major scale), these chords are G, C, and D or D7. Chord progressions can also be described using numbers that represent the chords built from the notes of the scale of the key of the song. In the key of G, the G chord (the I chord) is built on the first note of the G-major scale, the C chord (the IV chord) is the chord that's built on the fourth note of the G-major scale and the D or D7 chord (the V chord) is built on the fifth note of this scale.

Bluegrass singers choose a key that best matches their singing range, so it's important to get comfortable over time playing in a variety of keys on your banjo. Describing chord progressions using numbers (either I, IV, and V or 1, 4, and 5) allows musicians to more quickly figure out how to play chord progressions in different keys; this process is called *transposing*. As you transpose a chord progression into a different key, you shift the movable chords up or down the neck the number of frets needed in order to match the new key.

Table 10-1 shows you the I, IV, and V chords in the keys that you'll most frequently use to play bluegrass songs. This reference will come in handy in this chapter as you work through the following vamping exercises and when you need to negotiate playing in different keys using the capo at your next jam session.

Table 10-1	Naming the I–IV–V Chords in the Most Frequently Used Bluegrass Keys		
Key	I	IV	V
G	G	C	D
A	A	D	E
B♭	B♭	E♭	F
B	B	E	F♯
C	C	F	G
D	D	G	A
E	E	A	B
F	F	B♭	C

Using Vamping in Up-the-Neck Backup

Whether you're backing up a mandolin solo, making room for another banjo player in your jam session, or just generally trying not to attract a lot of attention for a verse or two in the course of a song, there are times when it's best to support other musicians with something that's less hectic than roll patterns. Vamping techniques perfectly fill the bill for these situations.

Vamping is a percussive backup technique using movable chord positions that propels the rhythm of the whole band. Vamping is just the thing for when you're still figuring out the chord progression to a new song or when the tempo of a song is too fast for you to keep up by playing rolls. It's also the quickest way to get comfortable using up-the-neck movable chords.

Now's the time to discover the uncharted regions of your banjo fretboard with techniques you'll use every time you play with others. Find those finger-picks and get ready to vamp!

Getting both hands into vamping

Although the picking-hand moves are relatively straightforward in vamping, there's quite a bit of fancy fingerboard work involving movable chords and muting techniques that will keep your fretting hand more than busy with this new playing technique.

Picking the basic vamping pattern

Play the fourth string with your thumb, followed by a pinch on the third, second, and first strings played with the thumb, index finger, and middle finger, striking the strings at the same time. Then repeat! Believe it or not, that's all there is to it for the picking hand.

TIP

When vamping, you'll want to position your picking hand away from the bridge, striking the strings over the banjo head close to the neck in order to pull a mellower tone from your banjo (see Figure 10-3).

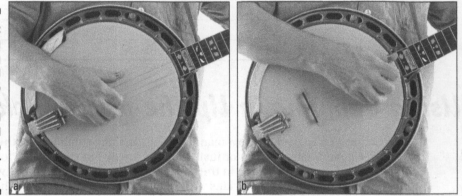

Figure 10-3:
Positioning the picking hand (a) close to the bridge for lead playing and (b) close to the neck for vamping.

Photographs by Anne Hamersky

Fretting and muting with vamping patterns

Vamping patterns are used almost exclusively with movable chords and are characterized by fretting-hand muting techniques that give a percussive, snare drum–like sound to this technique. These muting techniques are the same as what mandolin players play when they provide backup to the banjo in a bluegrass band. (Mandolin players, being the individualists that they are, call this *chopping*.)

REMEMBER

Getting the desired muting effect in vamping is a bit like patting your head and rubbing your stomach at the same time — there's a bit of coordination required between the picking and fretting hands to get the sound you want. Just after playing the pinch, lift your fretting fingers off the strings just enough to mute the sound of the chord. Keep your fingers in contact with the strings, because they'll be needed to press down and fret the same movable chord position once again to play the fourth string, which is always fully sounded when vamping.

As you move from one chord to another along the fingerboard, keep those fretting fingers in touch with the strings and in position for the chord you're about to fret. You'll then be able to more quickly fret the new movable chord when you've arrived at the appropriate fret.

Some players like to let the notes of the chord ring for just a moment before muting with the fretting hand; other banjo players time this effect to occur just as they play the third-second-first-string pinch pattern, giving an even more percussive sound to vamping.

Playing the basic vamping pattern with G, C, and D chords

It's time to try a basic vamping exercise with movable F-shape major-chord positions for the G, C, and D chords. You use the same movable shape for all three chords, moving the position up the neck from the G chord to fret the C and D chords. Your fretting-hand middle and pinky fingers will fret the fourth and first strings at the 5th fret for the G chord, the 10th fret for the C chord, and the 12th fret for the D chord.

Take a look at Video Clip 26, where I demonstrate how to coordinate both hands to get the percussive effects you'll want when vamping. Then check out Tab 10-1 to get the hang of the basic vamping technique, and give a listen Audio Track 82 to hear how you want your vamping to sound.

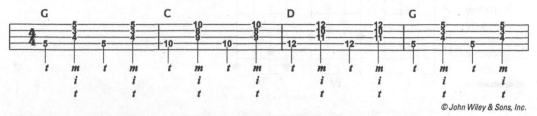

© John Wiley & Sons, Inc.

Tab 10-1: Basic vamping pattern using F-shape movable position for G, C, and D chords.

Playing F-shape chords a in different keys

Bluegrass banjo players spend most of their practice time at home playing in the key of G. However, the moment you venture out to play with others in jam sessions, you'll need to get comfortable playing along to songs in other keys. When this happens, you'll be glad you spent some time finding the movable chords you'll need to play in these new keys.

The chord progressions for many bluegrass songs consist of chords built upon the first, fourth, and fifth notes of the major scale of the key of the song (called the I, IV, and V chords when using the number system that's explained earlier in this chapter). When you transpose a song from the key of G into a new key, the relationship of the chords remains the same. The location of the movable chords on the fingerboard will shift, depending upon the new key. However, the distance along the fingerboard from one chord to another remains consistent for all keys.

Calculating distances between chords in the key of G

You remember that the I, IV, and V chords in the key of G are G, C, and D, right? Take a look at Figure 10-4, which shows the relative position of these chords using the F movable shape.

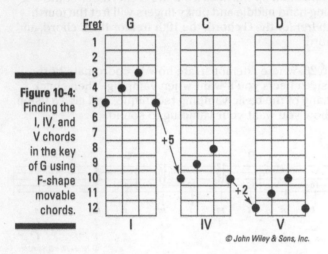

Figure 10-4:
Finding the I, IV, and V chords in the key of G using F-shape movable chords.

© John Wiley & Sons, Inc.

Keeping track of the distances between chords is the secret for more easily negotiating vamping in different keys. Whether you're fretting the F, D, or barre shapes in vamping, the distance from the I chord to the IV chord will always be five frets up, and the distance from the IV chord to the V chord will be two frets up, *when using the same movable chord shape* for both chords.

Calculating distances between chords in the keys of C and D

Consulting the chart presented earlier in this chapter, you'll discover that the I, IV, and V chords in the key of C are C, F, and G and in the key of D are D, G, and A. Take a look at Figures 10-5 and 10-6, which map out the position of the I, IV, and V chords in these keys along the first 12 frets of your banjo fingerboard, using movable F shapes.

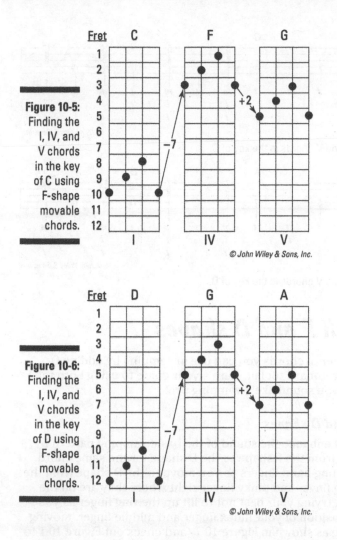

Figure 10-5:
Finding the
I, IV, and
V chords
in the key
of C using
F-shape
movable
chords.

© John Wiley & Sons, Inc.

Figure 10-6:
Finding the
I, IV, and
V chords
in the key
of D using
F-shape
movable
chords.

© John Wiley & Sons, Inc.

TIP

Note that for the keys of C and D, you have the choice of moving down seven frets or up five frets to play the IV chord. When moving down, you're fretting the IV chord one octave (or 12 frets) below your higher option. Many players choose this lower position in these keys for a richer sound when vamping. Try both ways, and go with what's easiest and sounds best to you.

PLAY THIS!

Now try playing the basic vamping pattern in the keys of C and D using F-shape movable chords. Tables 10-2 and 10-3 and Audio Track 83 show you how it's done.

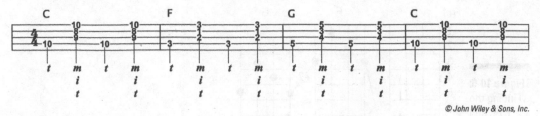

© John Wiley & Sons, Inc.

Tab 10-2: Basic vamping pattern for I, IV, and V chords in the key of C.

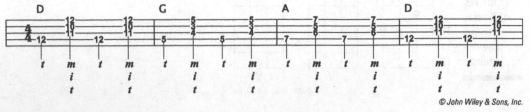

© John Wiley & Sons, Inc.

Tab 10-3: Basic vamping pattern for I, IV, and V chords in the key of D.

Vamping with F and D shapes

You'll double the number of chords you can use in vamping by adding D-shape chords to your fretboard toolkit. Here's your guide to using both the F and D shapes to make you sound like a vamping pro!

Moving between F and D shapes

Most banjo players will enhance the sound of the basic vamping pattern by moving back and forth from the F shape to the D shape for the same chord. To reposition your fretting-hand fingers as you move to the D shape from the F shape, keep your ring finger and pinky finger right where they are on the fourth and first strings, trying your best not to lift up the ring finger as you shift. Next, trade the position of your index finger and middle finger, moving each to the other string as shown in Figure 10-7 (and check out Figure 10-1 to take a look at the chord diagrams for these two shapes).

The location of the D-shape chord is always four frets higher than the F-shape chord *for the same letter name chord.* When you become accustomed to shifting positions in this way, you'll want to frequently use both shapes for all kinds of chords in vamping. Figure 10-8 shows the relationship between these two positions on your banjo fingerboard.

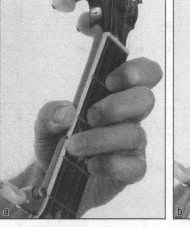

Figure 10-7: Moving from the F-shape to the D-shape movable positions.

Photographs by Anne Hamersky

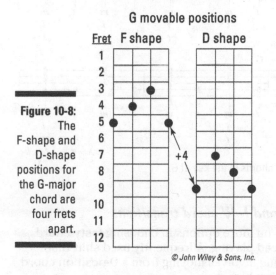

Figure 10-8: The F-shape and D-shape positions for the G-major chord are four frets apart.

© John Wiley & Sons, Inc.

Now try playing the exercise in Tab 10-4 (Audio Track 84), where you practice alternating F and D shapes first in one measure and then in half-measure groupings for the I, IV, and V chords in the key of G. When you can shift confidently between these shapes for different major chords, you're using the techniques that the best banjo players typically employ for vamping.

© John Wiley & Sons, Inc.

Tab 10-4: Vamping using F and D shapes for I, IV, and V chords in the key of G.

Using D and F shapes for V–I and I–IV chord transitions

Using both D and F shapes gives you more options in choosing tasty chord transitions for both backup and lead playing. A frequently used shift that comes in handy for almost any song involves moving from a D-position chord to an F-position chord that's one fret higher.

In the key of G, this position shift can be used in two different ways:

- ✔ When moving from a D chord to a G chord at the fourth and fifth frets
- ✔ When moving from a G chord to a C chord at the ninth and tenth frets

The economy of motion that results from moving up only one fret from one chord to another makes vamping easier. It also sounds great to lead from one chord into another in this way.

PLAY THIS!

Figure 10-9 shows where these shifts occur on the banjo fingerboard. Try putting these transitions to use in Tab 10-5 (Audio Track 85) playing the chord progression to the bluegrass standard "Nine Pound Hammer."

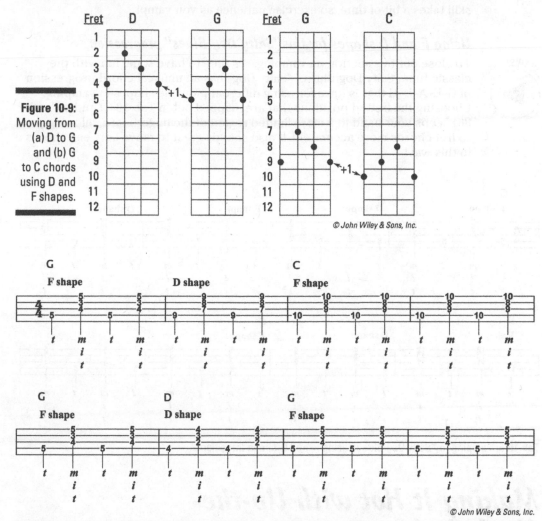

Figure 10-9: Moving from (a) D to G and (b) G to C chords using D and F shapes.

© John Wiley & Sons, Inc.

Tab 10-5: Vamping to "Nine Pound Hammer" using D- to F-shape transitions.

© John Wiley & Sons, Inc.

TIP

Keeping the fretting-hand fingers in position as you shift between the F- and D-shape positions is tricky. The ring finger is the usual culprit because it often wants to lift off of the fourth string entirely and follow the middle finger when it moves from the third to the second string when changing chord shapes. Practice moving back and forth between the two positions, being careful to train the ring finger to stay in contact with the fourth string as you move your index finger and middle finger to fret the next position. Next, try keeping both the ring finger and pinky finger lightly touching the fourth and first strings as you move up and down the neck to fret different chords. This skill takes a bit of time, so exercise patience as you vamp!

Using F and D shapes for the "Salty Dog Blues" progression

To close out this section on vamping, it's time to have some fun with the classic tune "Salty Dog Blues." "Salty Dog" has an unusual chord progression of G–E–A–D–G that is ideal for using different movable shapes in vamping. Choosing the fretted positions that are mapped out in Tab 10-6 (Audio Track 86) keeps your hand in a more limited region of the fingerboard, allowing you to fret chords more accurately. It also sounds great to move between chords in this way!

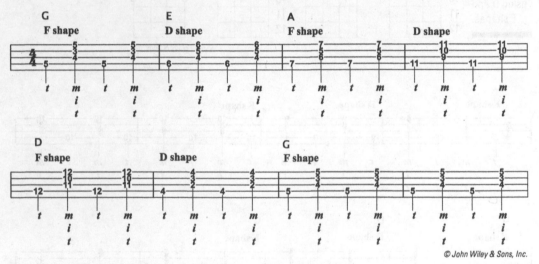

© John Wiley & Sons, Inc.

Tab 10-6: Vamping to "Salty Dog Blues" using F- and D-shape transitions.

Making It Hot with Up-the-Neck Picking

A great bluegrass band performance is dynamic, with the role of each instrument changing from verse to verse in a song. When vamping or playing down-the-neck roll-pattern backup (see Chapter 9), you're creating a space for other musicians to play their unique backup patterns and licks in support of a singer or another instrumentalist. However, at some point in every song, it will be your turn to be the featured support player, and that's a great time to play up-the-neck backup using picking patterns and licks.

Some of the most exciting moments in bluegrass banjo playing happen when you play the techniques and licks presented in this section. These are the classic patterns used by bluegrass banjo greats such as J. D. Crowe, Sonny Osborne, and Earl Scruggs.

Up-the-neck picking patterns and licks are based around the movable chord positions presented in the first half of this chapter. You'll want to be familiar with these positions before tackling the picking techniques covered in the following sections. Because up-the-neck backup is made up of patterns and licks that you can use in a variety of songs and in different keys, when you get comfortable with these patterns, you can use them in all kinds of songs. You can get a lot of musical mileage out of playing just a few of these techniques well while understanding how to use them for different chords and keys.

Getting "In the Mood" patterns

If you're under the age of 60, you may not know the big-band favorite "In the Mood," but there's no question that Earl Scruggs heard this song a lot as a budding young professional musician in the early 1940s. One of the most useful of the up-the-neck backup picking patterns, the "In the Mood" lick is Earl's restatement on the banjo of the short main theme of this song.

Playing the basic "In the Mood" pattern

Most banjo players use "In the Mood" patterns with F-shape movable chords. In Chapter 9, I introduce you to playing forward rolls in down-the-neck backup. The forward roll is the picking pattern you'll also use for the "In the Mood" lick.

Tab 10-7 presents "In the Mood" patterns in one- and two-measure versions for a C chord fretted at the tenth fret using the F shape. Check out the picking-hand rhythm in the second measure of the two-measure version of this lick. The tie indicates that the note played in the middle of this measure is given the rhythmic space of a quarter note. Check out Audio Track 87 to experience the sound of this lick.

If you're comfortable playing both the one- and two-measure versions of the "In the Mood" pattern, you can then mix and match them to work with all kinds of different chord progressions.

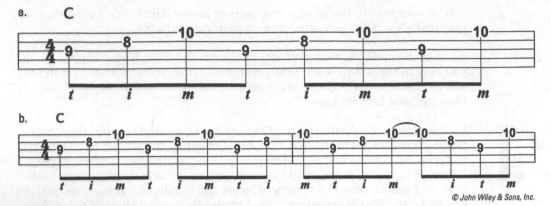

Tab 10-7: (a) One-measure and (b) two-measure "In The Mood" patterns.

 Tab 10-8 (Audio Track 88) shows how this can work using the chord progression to "Nine Pound Hammer" as an example.

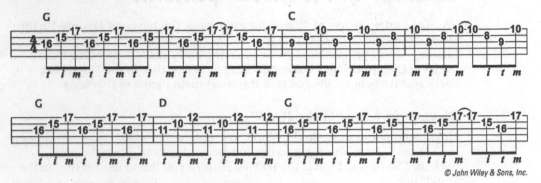

Tab 10-8: Playing "In the Mood" patterns for "Nine Pound Hammer."

Adding slides to "In the Mood" patterns

When playing through Tab 10-7, you may have experienced some difficulty moving quickly enough from one chord to the next to get a clean sound out of all the fretted notes, especially the first and last notes of each pattern.

Banjo players have solved this problem by playing slides to move more easily from one chord to the next. You can also lift off your fretting hand for the very last note of each pattern, giving the hand a head start as it heads for its next fretted destination.

 Tab 10-9 (Audio Track 89) presents "Nine Pound Hammer" once again, this time including slides at each new chord.

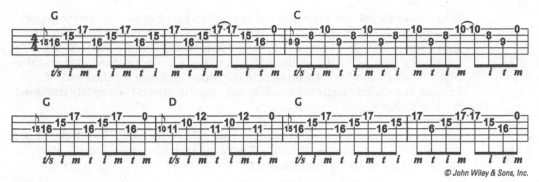

© John Wiley & Sons, Inc.

Tab 10-9: Playing "In the Mood" patterns with slides for "Nine Pound Hammer."

Earl Scruggs often started "In the Mood" patterns with a booming fourth-string slide up to the desired chord position. Tab 10-10 (Audio Track 90) shows this variation.

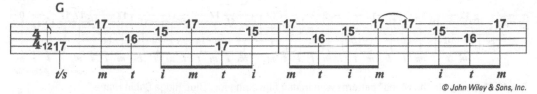

© John Wiley & Sons, Inc.

Tab 10-10: The "In the Mood" pattern with a fourth-string slide.

Adding the fifth string to "In the Mood" patterns

You can increase the cool factor considerably with "In the Mood" patterns by fretting the fifth string to add color to the basic major chord. Because all four of your fretting-hand fingers will be busy fretting the movable chord, you'll have to use your thumb to fret the fifth string, as you can see in Figure 10-10.

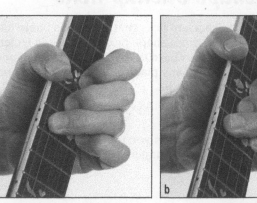

Figure 10-10: Fretting (a) seventh and (b) sixth chords with a fretted fifth string.

Photograph by Anne Hamersky

When your thumb frets the fifth string on the same fret as your index finger is using on the second string, you're forming a seventh chord. You can also move the thumb down one fret to create something called a sixth chord, which is a major chord with the addition of the sixth note of the major scale. Sixth chords sound great with the "In the Mood" pattern for the I and IV chords in a chord progression, while the seventh chord is perfectly designed for the V chord.

Here's an up-the-neck backup example using these techniques with the chord progression that matches the Flatt & Scruggs standard "Blue Ridge Cabin Home" (see Tab 10-11; Audio Track 91).

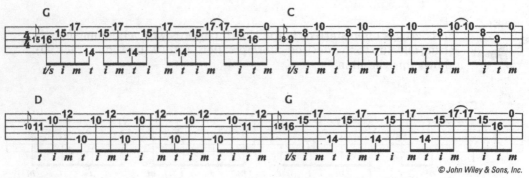

© John Wiley & Sons, Inc.

Tab 10-11: Using "In the Mood" patterns with fretted fifth string for "Blue Ridge Cabin Home."

There's no question that it's quite a fretting-hand stretch to successfully reach both the fifth string *and* the movable chord for these "In the Mood" patterns. Try working out these licks up the neck first, where the distances between the frets aren't as great, before venturing down the neck to try these patterns.

Digging D-shape backup licks

Another set of up-the-neck backup licks that bluegrass banjo players love to play are those based around the D-shape movable chords (refer to Figure 10-1 for a chord diagram of this chord). As with the "In the Mood" patterns, these D-shape licks can be used any place along the neck where you find yourself fretting one of these chords.

Playing the basic D-shape lick

Many of the up-the-neck backup licks you play are based around chord positions where you move one or more fingers to get the notes you need, while keeping the chord fretted with your other fingers. With this basic D-shape backup lick, you'll want to keep your index finger, middle finger, and pinky finger fretting the third, second, and first strings while moving the ring finger from the fourth to the third string and back again.

Tab 10-12 (Audio Track 92) introduces you to this lick by first getting you accustomed to moving the fretting-hand ring finger in measure one. Measure two presents the basic lick, which is a favorite of the great bluegrass banjo player and singer Ralph Stanley. The fretting-hand fingering is indicated above the tab staff.

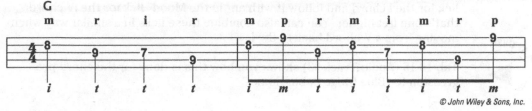

© John Wiley & Sons, Inc.

Tab 10-12: The basic D-shape lick.

Playing D-shape licks just like J. D. and Earl

After getting acquainted with the basic D-shape lick, you can move on to some of the classic phrases played by J. D. Crowe and Earl Scruggs. Both of these licks involve some unusual picking-hand moves, so take a look at the tab carefully before diving in. If you use the suggested finger choices, you'll get closer to the sound you're looking for with these licks.

Tables 10-13 and 10-14 (Audio Track 92) are based on licks played often by Earl Scruggs and J. D. Crowe. In the key of G, these backup phrases work equally well for both the G and D chords.

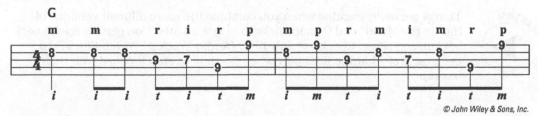

© John Wiley & Sons, Inc.

Tab 10-13: Earl Scruggs's D-shape lick.

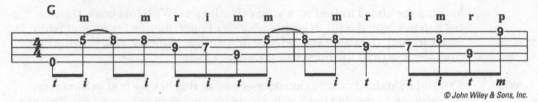

Tab 10-14: J. D. Crowe's D-shape lick.

Combining D-shape and "In the Mood" licks

A great way to start an up-the-neck backup sequence is to use a D-shaped lick for the I chord and follow it with an "In the Mood" lick for the IV chord that's one fret higher. You can also combine these licks in a similar way when moving from a V chord back to the I.

Tab 10-15 (Audio Track 93) shows you how this is done for the chord progression to "Blue Ridge Cabin Home."

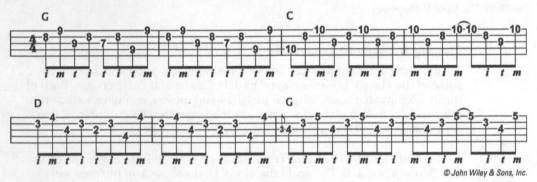

Tab 10-15: Using basic D-shape and "In the Mood" licks together.

Things get *really* exciting when you combine the more difficult versions of the "In the Mood" and D-shape licks to create an attention-getting up-the-neck backup sequence. Check out Tab 10-16 (Audio Track 94, Video Clip 27) to get a taste of what the pros play when it's time to step forward with their backup.

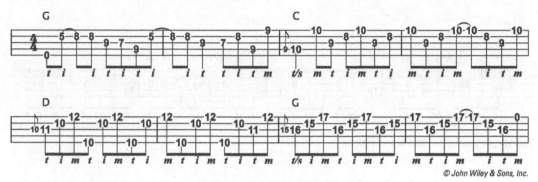

Tab 10-16: Combining more advanced D-shape and "In the Mood" licks.

Trying out classic backup licks

There are a handful of classic licks that banjo players will use to make their up-the-neck backup even more interesting. The best of these tried-and-true licks are found right here in this section! Pay close attention to both the picking- and fretting-hand fingerings indicated in the tablature examples, and be sure to spend time with the audio tracks to get the sound of each lick in your head *before* you try to play it.

The "Six White Horses" lick

This lick is ideal for medium-tempo pieces where you need to add a bluesy (or as Earl Scruggs would say, "boo-gee woo-gee") element to your backup playing. The "Six White Horses" lick (from the song of the same name) is designed to be played with F-shape movable chords anywhere you find them along the banjo fingerboard. It can be used either sparingly as a fill-in lick at the ends of phrases or as a lick you can insert at the beginning of each new chord.

TIP

The "one-finger-per-fret" rule applies to the fretting-hand fingering for this lick. From the F-shape position, move fingers across strings (rather than up or down frets) to find the notes you need.

PLAY THIS!

Take a look at Tab 10-17 (Audio Track 95, Video Clip 28) to try out two variations of this lick for yourself. The fretting-hand fingering is indicated above the tab staff. You'll also discover some repetition of picking-hand fingers in the right hand. This is how J. D. and Earl pick this lick, but many others use an alternation of their thumb and index finger. I've indicated both choices in the tab. As you've heard me say before, try it both ways and go with what works for you!

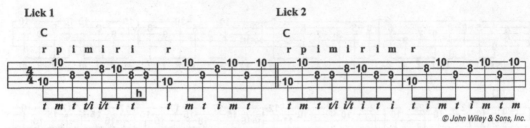

Tab 10-17: The "Six White Horses" licks.

The "Salty Dog Blues" lick

It was December 8, 1962, when Earl Scruggs, Lester Flatt, and their band, The Foggy Mountain Boys, stepped onto the stage of Carnegie Hall for the first time. Earl kicked off the bluegrass standard "Salty Dog Blues" to thunderous applause. As Lester Flatt finished singing the second verse, Earl played a thunderous lick that has been indelibly associated with this tune ever since.

Back in the day, you had to slow down the LP to figure out how Earl played such great stuff, but now you've got Tab 10-18 (Audio Track 96, Video Clip 28) to show you how it's done.

Tab 10-18: The "Salty Dog Blues" lick.

The "Blue Ridge Cabin Home" and "Your Love Is Like a Flower" licks

You know you're becoming addicted to bluegrass banjo when you're listening to a classic performance and just waiting on the edge of your seat for that really hot backup lick to emerge from out of nowhere at the end of a verse or between the lines of a chorus. That's just how I experienced the following two licks, which are hallmarks of the two Flatt & Scruggs performances of these songs.

There are a number of ways to fret these licks. Just make sure that whatever way works out for you, you're not using the same finger to fret the notes along the first string. Try my suggestions, indicated above the staff for Tables 10-19 and 10-20 (Audio Track 96, Video Clip 28).

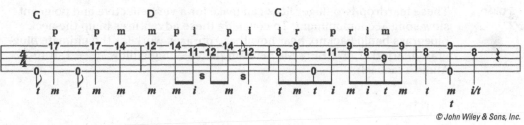

Tab 10-19: The "Blue Ridge Cabin Home" up-the-neck fill-in lick.

Tab 10-20: The "Your Love Is Like a Flower" up-the-neck fill-in lick.

Two-finger "teardrop" slow-song backup

Bluegrass music has lots of sad songs. When played at slow tempos, slow *and* sad songs can be almost pitiful. In order to not get too choked up by the singer's lyrics, banjo players have developed their own set of backup licks and phrases for slow songs that are often called *teardrop licks.*

These licks are also known as *two-finger licks* because they're usually played with just two of the three picking-hand fingers. Earl, Sonny, and J. D. play these licks with their index and middle fingers, but you can use the thumb in place of the index finger.

Tab 10-21 (Audio Track 97) offers up one- and two-measure examples of teardrop licks. If you fret the second string with your index finger and the first string with your middle finger for these phrases, that will give you enough reach to use the pinky finger to climb up on the first string in these licks.

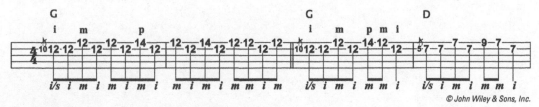

Tab 10-21: Playing one- and two-measure teardrop licks.

These teardrop/two-finger licks can make for a very effective and poignant slow-song accompaniment. To conclude these adventures in up-the-neck bluegrass banjo backup, hear how these phrases work for the ultimate bluegrass tearjerker, "Go Bury Me Beneath the Weeping Willow" (see Tab 10-22; Audio Track 98).

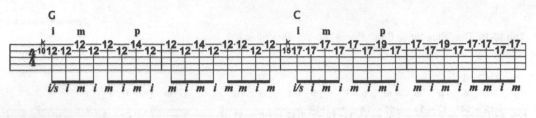

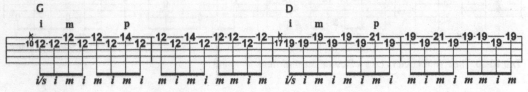

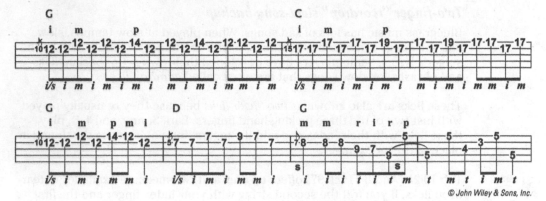

© John Wiley & Sons, Inc.

Tab 10-22: Using teardrop backup for "Go Bury Me Beneath the Weeping Willow."

Part IV

Progressive Banjo: Melodic and Single-String Styles

Photograph by Anne Hamersky

Part IV

Progressive Banjo: Melodic
and Single-String Styles

In this part . . .

- ✔ Explore the world of progressive banjo playing by trying out melodic and single-string banjo techniques.

- ✔ Work out scales in basic and up-the-neck positions and play classic instrumentals in melodic banjo style in the keys of G, C, D, and A major.

- ✔ Get comfortable with single-string picking techniques using both two and three picking fingers.

- ✔ Explore the banjo fingerboard with playing scales using open- and closed-position single-string fretting techniques.

- ✔ Play six great-sounding bluegrass, Irish, and blues-tinged single-string arrangements.

Chapter 11

Melodic-Style Banjo

In This Chapter

▶ Understanding how scales and melodies are played in melodic style

▶ Exploring melodic banjo technique in first position and up the neck

▶ Playing bluegrass favorites in the keys of G, C, D, and A

▶ Access the audio tracks and video clips at www.dummies.com/go/bluegrassbanjo

Banjo players today can play just about any kind of music using a variety of three-finger picking techniques. While hard-driving, roll-based bluegrass is what most people expect to hear from our instruments, musicians have developed other ways of playing that have launched the banjo into classical, jazz, rock, and other outlying musical realms. There's no question that these days it's not just your grandpa's music that you can play on the banjo.

Melodic style is the most widely used of these modern techniques. This approach enables you to play scales and note-for-note melodies while still taking advantage of the power and speed that roll-patterns provide (hence the name *melodic*). Melodic licks and techniques add an exciting new dimension to your playing that will considerably raise your bluegrass banjo game.

In this chapter, you tackle four scales and apply these new skills to dive into a great collection of instrumental bluegrass classics. The tabs provide complete fingering instructions, and the online audio and video examples are patiently waiting to provide 24/7 emergency support. So, what are you waiting for? It's time to get melodic!

Understanding Melodic Technique

Bluegrass banjo players have difficulty playing the fast-moving, demanding melodies of fiddle tunes using only the tried-and-true roll patterns associated with Scruggs style (see Chapter 5). If fiddlers, mandolin players, and guitarists are able to play *every* single melody note to such favorites as "Sailor's

Hornpipe" and "Turkey in the Straw," how can banjo players do this, too? Melodic technique solves this musical/technical banjo problem.

Melodic banjo allows you to play scales and melodies using picking techniques that are familiar from your roll-based Scruggs-style explorations. It was developed by Bill Keith and Bobby Thompson in the early 1960s and immediately captured the imagination of bluegrass players everywhere. Melodic style is great for everything from fast bluegrass instrumentals to arrangements of J. S. Bach pieces and everything in between.

Here are some things to keep in mind as you explore this way of playing:

✔ **Even if you're an experienced player, take a look at my fingering suggestions.** It's important to make good choices from the very beginning so that when it comes time to play melodic-style tunes, your fingers will automatically go to the right strings and frets.

✔ **The fretted positions you use are dependent upon the key of the song.** In this chapter, you explore melodic style in the keys of G, C, D, and A. Each key has a slightly different set of fretting-hand fingerings because each scale is made up of different notes. (But don't stress about this — the tab, and accompanying audio and video will help you every step of the way!)

✔ **You can use melodic licks in all kinds of songs.** Melodic-style banjo doesn't need to be limited to just certain kinds of songs. You can work up short musical phrases, called *licks,* in melodic style to add some spice to just about any banjo situation (and visit Chapter 7 for essential Scruggs-style roll-based licks).

✔ **Memorizing melodic-style songs is challenging.** Because every note you pick in melodic style is usually a melody note, melodic-style tunes can be more of a challenge to memorize and to play fast. If it takes a lot more time for you to comfortably play a melodic-style tune, especially at first, this isn't because you should've taken up the tuba — it's because remembering tunes in this style is just more difficult. I've been playing for more than 40 years now, and it still can take a few months for me to successfully play up to speed a new tune that I've worked out in this style.

Figuring out scales in first position

Whatever kind of music you're playing, melodies are made up of individual notes. If you line up all the individual melody notes used in a song in order from low to high, these notes form a *scale.* There are all kinds of scales available to musicians; in bluegrass banjo playing, we mostly use the *major scale.* Even if you've never played a lick on any instrument in your life, you're still familiar with the sound of the major scale because most of the songs you've heard all your life are assembled from major-scale notes.

Playing the G-major scale in melodic style

Tab 11-1 lays out the notes of the G-major scale on your banjo fretboard, with the letters above the staff indicating the notes in this scale. Take a moment to find these notes on your banjo and listen to the bright, happy sound of the major scale. (I told you that you'd recognize it!)

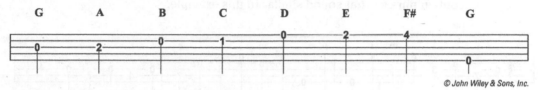

© John Wiley & Sons, Inc.

Tab 11-1: Finding the notes of the G-major scale on your banjo.

When you play the G-major scale in this way, you're picking several consecutive notes on the same string. This is difficult to do when using a different picking finger for each successive note. However, if you relocate most of the fretted notes of this scale (the A, C, E, and G notes) to a lower string, each successive note can now be played on a different string, making it much easier to use roll-pattern picking techniques to play the scale.

When you make music in this way, you're playing melodic-style banjo! When you work out melodic scales on the lower frets, that's working out of the *first position.* Check out Tab 11-2 (Audio Track 99) to try this out. Also, take a moment to watch Video Clip 29 to see me play these G-major scales.

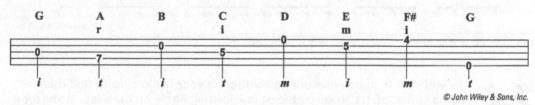

© John Wiley & Sons, Inc.

Tab 11-2: Playing the G-major scale in first position using melodic techniques.

Banjo tablature can convey a lot of information if you know what to look for! In Tab 11-2, the letters above the staff indicate which fretting-hand fingers to use, while the letters below the staff suggest which picking-hand fingers work best. The most challenging aspect of melodic banjo is picking a *higher-*sounding note on a *lower* string. When you get used to this idea, you'll be off and picking!

Playing extended G-major scales

Melodies seldom are confined to just one octave of the major scale. You'll almost always need to grab notes above and below to get what you need to play songs.

Tab 11-3 (Audio Track 100; Video Clip 29) shows you how to play an extended G-major scale that adds one note below and another above the basic eight notes. In this case, your fretting hand doesn't have to move out of position to grab these extra notes as you move across the strings. Many fiddle tunes contain phrases that sound similar to this example.

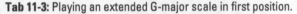

© John Wiley & Sons, Inc.

Tab 11-3: Playing an extended G-major scale in first position.

Sooner or later, you'll have to move out of the first position to grab higher and lower notes as needed. Tab 11-4 (Audio Track 100; Video Clip 29) shows how this is done, using an up-the-neck position (second string, tenth fret and first string, ninth fret) that's played in the instrumental classic "Blackberry Blossom," among many other tunes.

© John Wiley & Sons, Inc.

Tab 11-4: Playing an extended G-major scale that shifts position.

As you shift from one position to another on your banjo neck to find the notes you need, try to keep at least one fretting finger on the same string for both fretted positions if you can. If you keep that finger lightly touching the string as you move, you'll stay connected to your instrument, enabling you to reach new positions much more quickly.

In Tab 11-4, you're using your middle and index fingers to fret the second string, fifth fret and first string, fourth fret (these are the E and F♯ notes of the G-major scale). You'll want to keep those two fingers in position on the same strings as you shift to the second string, tenth fret and first string, ninth fret (these are the A and B notes of a higher-octave G-major scale).

Playing melodic style up the neck

Playing up-the-neck scales over more than one octave in melodic style can require some fretting prestidigitation. You'll use all four fretting fingers and even your thumb to perform some amazing sleight of hand in the upper reaches of your banjo neck as you work through this section. All the hard work you're about to do will pay off as you open up vast new fretboard regions for future high-flying melodic explorations.

When you're comfortable with the exercise in Tab 11-4, try extending the G-major scale to include a few more upper-scale notes, following the fingering indications in Tab 11-5 (Audio Track 101; Video Clip 30). You'll use your fretting-hand thumb to play the fifth string, tenth fret with this G-major scale.

© John Wiley & Sons, Inc.

Tab 11-5: Playing an extended G scale using the thumb to fret the fifth string.

Not so easy, right? Remember that melodic banjo technique requires you to use a different picking finger to play a different string with each successive note. At some point, you simply have to fret the fifth string to grab a note you need in these upper fretting regions. The good news is that you don't *have* to use the thumb to do this. As an alternative, you can use one of your four fingers, but this requires you to alter other fretting fingers.

Try wrapping your fingers around Tab 11-6 (Audio Track 101), which presents the exact same scale but with different fretting-hand fingering. Here you'll use the middle finger to fret the fifth string and your ring finger to fret the second string. Video Clip 30 shows both ways of fretting these up-the-neck scales.

© John Wiley & Sons, Inc.

Tab 11-6: Playing an extended G scale using the middle finger to fret the fifth string.

Players just naturally get accustomed to one way or the other of fretting these positions, depending upon what they're more easily able to reach and which position feels the most natural. If you have larger hands, you may prefer fretting the fifth string with your thumb. If you have smaller hands, you'll likely want to use your middle finger.

Figure 11-1 shows how your fretting hand will look using either the thumb or the middle finger to fret the fifth string in Tabs 11-5 and 11-6.

Figure 11-1:
Fretting
upper
melodic-
style
positions
with (a) the
thumb
and (b) the
middle
finger.

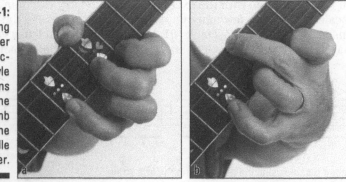

Photographs by Anne Hamersky

There are many possible fretting pathways you can create to play the notes of the G-major scale all up and down your banjo neck. As you move into these up-the-neck regions, you'll often have to perform sudden fretting-hand shifts as well as fret the fifth string to reach the consecutive notes of a scale.

Check out Tab 11-7 (Audio Track 102), which covers two entire octaves of the G-major scale to see how this works.

© John Wiley & Sons, Inc.

Tab 11-7: Playing a two-octave G-major scale in melodic style.

Figure 11-2 shows the suggested fingering for the highest reaches of the two-octave G-major scale, which you'll need at the end of the second measure in Tab 11-7.

Figure 11-2:
Up-the-neck
G-major
fretting-
hand
position.

Photograph by Anne Hamersky

Exercises like these are useful for discovering fingering positions, but the real fun comes with playing tunes and licks in melodic style. Banjo players use the knowledge gained from working through scale exercises to create their own great-sounding phrases that are often easier to play than the scales themselves.

Check out this cool melodic lick in Tab 11-8 (Audio Track 103) that uses many of the up-the-neck positions introduced via the scale exercises in this section.

© John Wiley & Sons, Inc.

Tab 11-8: Melodic lick using up-the-neck positions.

Melodic style also allows you to play long extended passages of cascading notes that can be assembled into great-sounding licks. The six-measure G lick in Tab 11-9 (Audio Track 103) starts high up on your banjo neck with a fret-ted position where you'll need to call on your pinky and ring fingers to fret the first and second strings at the 12th fret and your thumb to fret the fifth string at the 10th fret. Fortunately, it's all musically downhill from there.

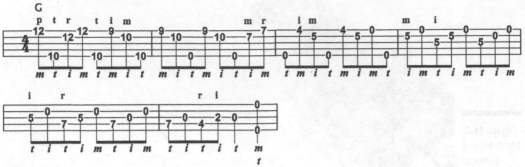

Tab 11-9: A cascading melodic lick in G.

 If you're familiar with the fretted positions for the G-major scales presented earlier in this chapter, conquering challenging licks like this will be a breeze. As your piano teacher told you many years ago, practice those scales, kid!

Playing Melodic Tunes in G

You've got the picking-hand moves down, and you're solid with your fretting positions up and down the banjo fingerboard for the G-major scale. You've done your homework, and you're champing at the bit to finally play some tunes. Let's do this! In this section, you wrap your ears and fingers around four popular bluegrass instrumentals that will familiarize you with some of the most important aspects of playing in melodic style.

 Be patient with your progress when working out melodic tunes for the first time. Even for experienced players, melodic-style songs are more difficult to memorize and to play up to speed. Break down each tune into sections, getting familiar with just one or two measures at a time, playing each phrase smoothly before moving on to the next. Most of these melodies have repeated phrases, so when you've mastered the first section of a new song, you've likely figured out at least half of the second section as well!

"The Girl I Left Behind Me"

Many instrumental bluegrass favorites have their origins in the music of the British Isles, and that's the case with this Irish song, which dates back to the late 1700s. Also an American Civil War favorite, "The Girl I Left Behind Me" is mostly performed these days as an instrumental, but you'll occasionally hear it sung with either Irish or English lyrics, depending upon which continent you find yourself on.

"The Girl I Left Behind Me" is a great melodic banjo starter piece. The entire song is played in first position and there's lots of space in this arrangement for your fingers to get used to moving up and down the G-major scale to locate the melody notes. If you've never tried melodic style before, Tab 11-10 (Audio Track 104) is the tune to get you started.

© John Wiley & Sons, Inc.

Tab 11-10: "The Girl I Left Behind Me," an Irish melody from the late 1700s.

Spend some time with the audio tracks to internalize the melody first before you begin to play. When you can't get the melody out of your head, you can start to play the tune, using the tab as a reference to check on all the individual picking- and fretting-hand moves you'll be making. Try this the next time you tackle a brand-new piece, and see how much more quickly you'll be able to grasp a new song.

"Devil's Dream"

"Devil's Dream" was one of the first tunes that melodic innovator Bill Keith performed with bluegrass great Bill Monroe in 1963, so it was perhaps inevitable that this tune would become an essential melodic banjo classic. Although Bill Keith played the tune *fast,* luckily, this melody also sounds great played more slowly.

Dating back to the early 19th century, "Devil's Dream" (Tab 11-11; Audio Track 105) has a unique chord progression that moves from the G-major to A-minor chords. The notes in the A-minor chord — A, C, and E — are the second, fourth, and sixth notes in the G-major scale. You'll continue to use the fingerings you've already worked out for the basic G-major scale over both chords in this song.

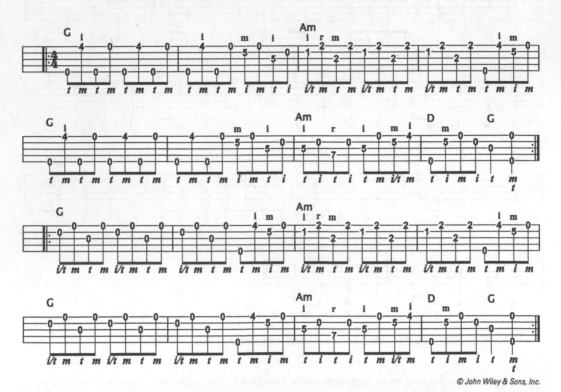

© John Wiley & Sons, Inc.

Tab 11-11: "Devil's Dream," a melodic banjo classic first played bluegrass style by Bill Keith.

"Devil's Dream" has two distinct sections, each of which is played twice. This form, sometimes labeled AABB, is so common to fiddle tunes that musicians call it *fiddle-tune form*. You'll encounter it in every other tune in this chapter! Grasping the form of a new piece as you first hear it opens the door to quicker mastery and is a skill that will develop naturally as you listen to recordings and to other musicians.

When playing melodic-style banjo, you sometimes have more than one choice as to which strings you can use to fret different melody notes. In Tab 11-11, I suggest playing the A-minor chord down the neck (see measures three and four). Bill Keith chooses to play the three notes of the A-minor chord on lower strings, which lay out perfectly using the standard fingering for the G-major melodic scale. Check out Tab 11-12 for this variation, which you can then use for measures 3 and 4 and 11 and 12 in Tab 11-11.

© John Wiley & Sons, Inc.

Tab 11-12: A minor variation for "Devil's Dream."

"Katy Hill"

"Katy Hill" requires you to shift out of first position in your fretting hand to move up the neck to capture all the notes that fiddlers play on this well-known breakdown piece. You should be more than ready for this challenge if you've spent time with the up-the-neck melodic exercises presented earlier in this chapter. (In case you're wondering what a breakdown is, it's a tune that's played *really* fast!)

In the second half of "Katy Hill," you'll also encounter some new picking-finger moves. In measures 9, 11, and 13, you'll use your middle finger to pick the second string. But no worries, it's just in a day's work for any melodic-style banjo picker!

Check out Audio Track 106 to hear the tune and Video Clip 31 to watch me play it. Then take a look at Tab 11-13 for all the up-the-neck melodic fingering details.

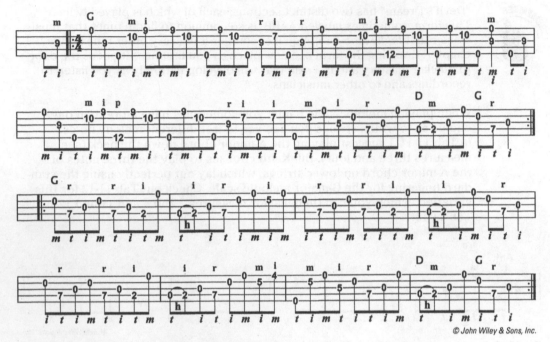

© John Wiley & Sons, Inc.

Tab 11-13: "Katy Hill," using up-the-neck melodic fingering techniques.

"Cherokee Shuffle"

A jam-session favorite, "Cherokee Shuffle" (Tab 11-14; Audio Track 107) combines a unique chord progression with a fast-moving and memorable melody. You'll stick mostly to first-position fingerings in this version and there's even a bit of roll-based Scruggs licks included to add some contrast in the tune's second half (and yes, you're allowed to mix Scruggs and melodic techniques at any time in the same tune!).

If you're like me, the first thing you might do to check out a new tune is to find it on YouTube and listen to a few versions as played by the most famous musicians that turn up in your search. You'll experience an amazing number of variations with a tune like "Cherokee Shuffle." Keep in mind that there is never just one way to play any tune; musicians will frequently use the form and chord progression of a fiddle tune to create jazzlike improvisations. Playing all the classic pieces in this chapter can be a lifelong process. Great musicians continually evolve their own ways of playing a song as they bring in new licks and techniques that reflect their musical knowledge and experiences. You can do this, too, by getting started today! Don't ever hold back from working up your own version of any song.

© *John Wiley & Sons, Inc.*

Tab 11-14: "Cherokee Shuffle" played using melodic banjo techniques.

Playing Melodic Tunes in C, D, and A

Melodic banjo technique is right at home in the key of G, but it can be used effectively in other keys as well. Fiddle tunes are often associated with particular keys, and it's both challenging and fun to try to play tunes in the same keys that fiddlers and mandolin players typically use.

In the following sections, you try out scales and introduce yourself to more classic fiddle tunes in the keys of C, D, and A. In all these examples, you find that just one or two fretting adjustments is all you need to navigate these exciting new musical pathways.

Playing in the key of C

The C-major scale shares the same collection of notes as the G scale with the exception of just one note. In a C scale, you play an F note instead of the F♯ note that's found in the G scale. Tab 11-15 (Audio Track 108) shows you one way to play a C-major scale in melodic style. The F note is found on the third fret of the first string in this example.

© John Wiley & Sons, Inc.

Tab 11-15: The C-major scale in melodic style.

"Soldier's Joy"

"Soldier's Joy" (Tab 11-16; Audio Track 109), another tune of British Isles origin, is very likely the most popular fiddle tune of all time. Fiddlers play this tune in the key of D, but it makes for a great melodic banjo workout in the key of C. To play this arrangement with other musicians, you'll need to put your capo on the second fret and raise the pitch of your fifth string two frets to A.

"Billy in the Lowground"

"Billy in the Lowground" (Tab 11-17; Audio Track 110) is associated with Texas fiddling traditions, which are characterized by elaborate melodies that blend folk and jazz sounds. "Billy" is, indeed, a sophisticated tune that will require you to use some up-the-neck fretted positions to play in melodic style. This is a more challenging arrangement — the key to success is to work through each measure slowly, using the fretting-hand indications that are above the tab staff.

Tab 11-16: "Soldier's Joy" in melodic banjo style in the key of C.

Playing in the key of D

Bluegrass banjo players have come up with several different ways to make great music in the key of D (check out Chapter 7 to discover the open-D tuning used for Earl Scruggs's classic tune "Reuben," for instance). If you're in a jam session and someone calls out a tune to play in this key, the quickest way to get your banjo ready is to raise your fifth string the equivalent of two frets in pitch, from a G to an A note. Your fifth string is tuned to one of the three notes found in the D-major chord (the D-major chord is made from the D, F♯, and A notes) and can now be unapologetically picked at all times in this key.

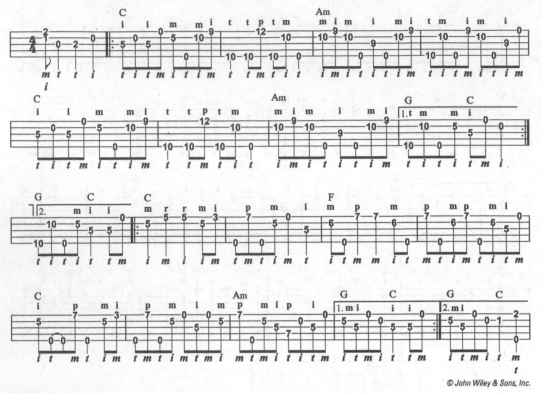

Tab 11-17: "Billy in the Lowground," using up-the-neck melodic techniques in the key of C.

In this section, you encounter new fingering positions in the key of D that you can use to play two more classic tunes, "Angeline the Baker" and "St. Anne's Reel." Because the G note isn't available on the open string in this tuning, you'll need to find that note on the first string at the fifth fret.

The D-major scale shares the same collection of notes as the G scale with the exception of just one note. In a D scale, you'll play a $C\#$ note instead of the C note that's part of the G scale. Tab 11-18 (Audio Track 111) introduces you to a D scale that covers two octaves. You'll find $C\#$ notes on the third string at the 6th fret and on the first and fifth strings at the 11th fret.

Tab 11-18: The D-major scale in melodic style, two octaves.

"Angeline the Baker"

This melodic arrangement of "Angeline the Baker" (Tab 11-19; Audio Track 112) will get you accustomed to the new fretting positions that you have to use when the fifth string is tuned to A. Although "Angeline" is played with the familiar AABB fiddle-tune form, musicians are equally divided as to which section is supposed to be played first.

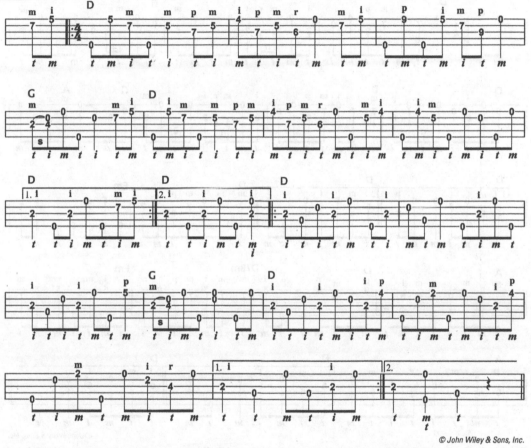

© John Wiley & Sons, Inc.

Tab 11-19: "Angeline the Baker" in melodic banjo style in the key of D, fifth string tuned to A.

"St. Anne's Reel"

When you play tunes in melodic style that are in the same key, you'll use many of the same fretted positions from one tune to the other. That's the case here with "St. Anne's Reel" (Tab 11-20; Audio Track 113), which adds a few more fretted notes to the positions you've already worked out for "Angeline the Baker."

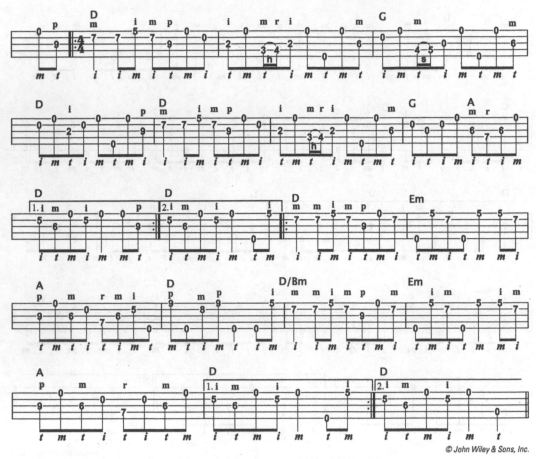

© John Wiley & Sons, Inc.

Tab 11-20: "St. Anne's Reel" in melodic banjo style in the key of D, fifth string tuned to A.

In "St. Anne's Reel," you'll need to fret a wildly stretched-out position that's common to this key and tuning. You can do this! Check out measure one, where you'll fret the first string at the fifth fret with your index finger, the second string at the seventh fret with your middle finger, and the third string at the ninth fret with your pinky finger. You'll use this position throughout the tune, so it's important to get used to this as soon as you can. The good news is that you don't have to fret all three notes at once — you can put down a fretting finger just before you need it.

Playing in the key of A

Melodic style works well when the scales you're playing include as many of the open strings of your banjo as possible. A few popular tunes, such as "Old Joe Clark" in Chapter 7 of this book and "Red-Haired Boy" in *Banjo For Dummies,* are normally played in the key of A but with a seventh note that is one fret lower than in a regular major scale.

Musicians who like to show off will call a major scale with a lowered seventh note a *Mixolydian scale.* However, I've never heard this phrase used by any self-respecting banjo player. Although we may not know exactly what to call it, we love the bluesy sounds and tunes that come out of our banjos when we play songs that are made up of the notes used in this scale.

Check out Tab 11-21 (Audio Track 114) to explore the finger positions used for this A scale.

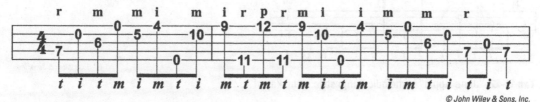

© John Wiley & Sons, Inc.

Tab 11-21: A Mixolydian scale in melodic style.

To close this exploration of melodic-style banjo, check out "June Apple," played in the key of A without a capo (Tab 11-22; Audio Track 115).

© John Wiley & Sons, Inc.

Tab 11-22: "June Apple" in melodic banjo style in the key of A.

Chapter 12

Single-String Banjo

In This Chapter

▶ Discovering picking patterns in single-string style

▶ Finding open- and closed-position scales up and down the neck

▶ Playing great tunes in single-string style

▶ Access the audio tracks and video clips at www.dummies.com/go/bluegrassbanjo

The most exciting breakthrough in bluegrass banjo technique over the last several decades has come with single-string banjo. Single-string banjo is the playing technique that enables you to shred like the heaviest heavy-metal guitarist, wail like the hippest jazz saxophone player, or hold your own with an Irish fiddler at your next ceili. When used in combination with roll-based and melodic styles, single-string playing will also considerably expand your bluegrass banjo horizons.

Contrary to its name, you actually pick more than one string when using this playing technique! Single-string banjo enables you to play scales and scale-based melodies using fretting-hand techniques similar to those that guitar and mandolin players commonly use. Unlike roll-based and melodic styles, with single-string banjo you play the same string for two or three notes con-secutively before moving up or down to another string. To accomplish this feat, you'll call upon techniques where the picking-hand fingers imitate the motion of a guitarist's or mandolin player's flatpick.

If you're dazzled by the single-string exploits of such banjo virtuosos as Béla Fleck and Noam Pikelny and you want to try out these techniques for your-self, this chapter is for you! From picking-hand exercises, you'll move on to scales up and down the banjo neck, as well as wrap your fingers around six great tunes in single-string style.

Single-string banjo is a great way to gain a more thorough understanding of your banjo fretboard, and that knowledge will come in handy with everything you play on the banjo. Read on to become a better player by single-stringing it!

Understanding Single-String Technique

Single-string playing utilizes techniques in the fretting and picking hands that are different from what you're used to with roll-based and melodic-style banjo. You'll even think about making music in a different way when using single-string techniques. Opening up new possibilities on the banjo is terrific — and this is just what single-string playing does!

Examples of single-string playing can be found in the classic banjo music of the early 20th century (check out my book *Banjo For Dummies* for an overview of this style). In bluegrass, banjo pioneers Eddie Adcock and Don Reno began incorporating single-string techniques into their playing in the 1950s. Beginning in the early 1980s, Béla Fleck expanded the range of what could be done with single-string techniques, influencing a new generation of younger players, like Ryan Cavanaugh and Noam Pikelny, to take up this approach.

Today, single string is an exciting stylistic option that provides another way for you to find the notes you need to make the music you want to play. Like melodic style, it's an important part of the musical vocabulary of the modern bluegrass banjo player.

As you work through the exercises and songs in this chapter, here are a few guidelines to make your single-string transition as smooth as possible:

✔ **Practice new techniques slowly, and be patient!** Single-string banjo isn't quite like learning a new instrument, but it's pretty close to it! Work for a smooth, even sound as you practice the exercises in this chapter. Don't worry about speed until the basic techniques start to become second nature to your fingers and brain.

✔ **Trust your own hands.** There are frequently several ways to play something using single-string techniques. As with guitar and mandolin playing, you can find the same notes on more than one string and in more than one place on the banjo fretboard in single-string style. You'll also have a choice as to which picking-hand fingers to use. Try not to get overwhelmed with these options! Work with the choices that I recommend, try something different if you like, and go with what feels the most natural to you.

✔ **Don't play single string when you're playing backup.** Single-string is great for lead playing, not so great for backup. Just as with melodic-style picking, single-string banjo is designed for when you need to be in the spotlight. When you're accompanying others in bands or in jams, you'll want to rely on the backup techniques in Chapters 9 and 10.

Exploring picking-hand techniques

The picking-hand fingers strike the same strings consecutively in single-string banjo, and this is one of the biggest challenges of mastering this playing technique. Most players use the thumb and index fingers to do this, much the same way as guitar and mandolin players use a flatpick in an up-and-down motion to get a similar result. More recently, banjo players have incorporated the middle finger, using parts of roll patterns to play single-string passages.

It's essential to get comfortable with the picking-hand moves as you embark upon your single-string explorations. Keep the following tips in mind as you tackle the following exercises:

- **Maintain the same basic picking-hand position that you use for roll-based playing.** Single-string style is usually used in conjunction with roll-based playing. In the course of a song, you'll need to shift back and forth between both ways of playing, so it makes sense to use the same picking-hand position for both styles. Turn to Chapter 4 for a complete guide to fitting fingerpicks and positioning the picking hand for optimal tone and volume.

- **Strike strings with equal volume with the thumb, index finger, and middle finger.** To get a flowing sound from your single-string picking hand, you'll want to strike the strings with equal volume with all fingers. This is trickier than it sounds because the thumb is accustomed to hitting the strings with more force. Practice single-string passages slowly at first to make sure you're pulling the same volume from each finger.

- **Play notes in an even rhythm.** Your single-string efforts will sound smoother if you let each eighth note equal every other note in rhythmic duration with no bounce or swing feel added to your playing. Even rhythm plus equal volume gives your single-string playing the poise and balance you'll need to execute long, complex lines with your fretting hand.

Basic single-string technique

The basic single-string picking-hand stroke sounds simple: Strike a string with your thumb, strike the same string with your index finger, and then repeat. That's it! However, things get a bit more complicated as you shift this picking sequence from one string to another.

Tabs 12-1 and 12-2 (Audio Track 116, Video Clip 32) will get you comfortable with shifting strings with the basic single-string sequence. Note that in Tab 12-2, you'll move more quickly between strings, much as you'll encounter when playing real tunes.

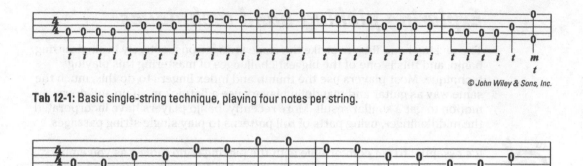

© John Wiley & Sons, Inc.

Tab 12-1: Basic single-string technique, playing four notes per string.

© John Wiley & Sons, Inc.

Tab 12-2: Basic single-string technique, playing two notes per string.

TIP

As you move from the fourth to the first strings and back again in these examples, try shifting your hand position ever so slightly as you move from string to string by pivoting on the ring and pinky fingers. The goal is to center the thumb and index finger over each string so that you can use the same precise movement and angle to strike each string (you don't want to have to reach farther with your thumb to play the first string than the fourth string, for instance). Don't be surprised if you hear a more balanced tone from your single-string efforts after you get used to striking the strings in this way.

Single-string crossovers

Your fingers have to go where the melodies take them, and there are times when you need to pick a lower string with your index finger just after your thumb has done its thing on a higher string. You'll frequently encounter single-string *crossovers,* but they don't necessarily come naturally to the picking hand. It makes sense to isolate this particular skill so that you're ready for it when you encounter it in songs.

PLAY THIS!

▶

Tabs 12-3, 12-4, and 12-5 (Audio Track 117, Video Clip 32) show you how it's done. Note that each successive exercise gets a bit more complex, but the picking hand maintains the steady alternation of thumb and index notes throughout, regardless of what string is being played. This is an important aspect of most of what you play in single-string style, so don't hesitate to "put the thumb to it," as Ralph Stanley likes to say.

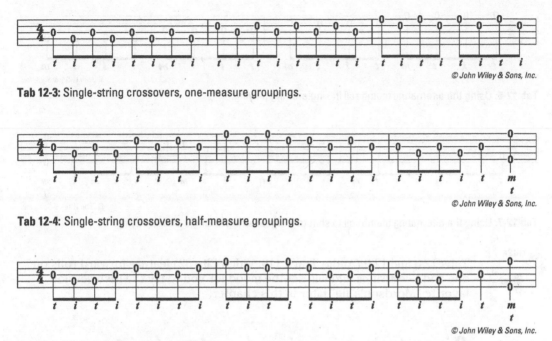

Tab 12-3: Single-string crossovers, one-measure groupings.

© John Wiley & Sons, Inc.

Tab 12-4: Single-string crossovers, half-measure groupings.

© John Wiley & Sons, Inc.

Tab 12-5: Mixing single-string crossovers.

© John Wiley & Sons, Inc.

Alternating thumb rolls in single-string style

When adding the middle finger to your picking-hand ingredients, you can cook up some spicy single-string phrases that take advantage of the roll patterns (see Chapter 5) that you already know. The alternating thumb roll, with its basic sequence of T–I–T–M, contains the essential ingredients of basic single-string technique, with the middle finger giving the index finger a momentary break in the action.

Tabs 12-6 and 12-7 (Audio Track 118, Video Clip 32) show you two ways that you can use the alternating thumb roll in single-string banjo. Note that in Tab 12-7, the middle finger is called into action when moving to a higher string. This is the way that most professional players use the middle finger in single-string technique.

Forward rolls in single-string style

Forward rolls are just the things to use in single-string style when you need six notes in a measure, as in an Irish jig. To play in 6/8 time, you count "ONE-two-three-FOUR-five-six" with a bit of an emphasis on the "one" and "four." This driving rhythm is a great match for a standard forward roll sequence of T–I–M.

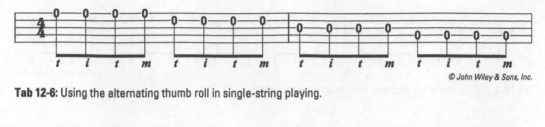

© John Wiley & Sons, Inc.

Tab 12-6: Using the alternating thumb roll in single-string playing.

© John Wiley & Sons, Inc.

Tab 12-7: Using the alternating thumb roll to shift to a higher string in single-string playing.

Tabs 12-8 and 12-9 (Audio Track 119, Video Clip 32) feature forward rolls on one and two strings and will set the mood for you to try the Irish session favorite "Morrison's Jig" later in this chapter.

Discovering fretting-hand techniques

The fretting hand has a lot of work to do in single-string banjo playing! Like melodic banjo (see Chapter 11), single-string style is based around assembling the notes of a scale into licks and melodies. However, with single-string playing, you often fret consecutive scale notes on the same string, something that's not usually done in melodic banjo playing.

© John Wiley & Sons, Inc.

Tab 12-8: Using the forward roll in 6/8 time in single-string banjo.

© John Wiley & Sons, Inc.

Tab 12-9: Using forward rolls to shift string in 6/8 time in single-string banjo.

Boxes and open and closed positions

Fretting in single-string banjo requires an alternative way of finding the notes you need and even a different way of conceptualizing the banjo fingerboard. In single-string style, players work out scale patterns up and down the neck of their banjos, using shifting positions that guitarists sometimes call *boxes*. A box is a three- to five-fret region where you find the fretted notes you need by moving horizontally across the fingerboard from one string to the next. Boxes are often but not always related to up-the-neck chord positions (see Chapter 10 for a cornucopia of up-the-neck chords).

Typically, you play two or three notes on an individual string before moving to another string, often staying within the same box to fret more notes. As you move the fretting hand up or down the banjo neck, you shift to a different box, or region, of your banjo fingerboard. Each box has a unique fingering based on where you are in the scale you're playing.

Banjo players play single-string phrases in *open position,* where you mix unfretted and fretted strings, usually in the lower five frets of the banjo, and in *closed position,* where every note of a phrase is played using fretted notes. Closed positions are typically used above the fifth fret and can be transposed to new keys by shifting any pattern up or down the fingerboard.

Finding a great fretting-hand position

Big stretches are sometimes required in single-string fretting, and many players will use a slightly different hand position than they use for roll-based and melodic playing. The larger the stretch, the more you may need to move your fretting-hand thumb to the middle of the back side of your banjo neck, providing your fingers with greater reach over the fingerboard (see Figure 12-1a).

You'll need for your fingers to be ready to spring into action at all times, so try to keep them as close to the strings as possible with fingertips aimed in the direction of the banjo fingerboard. You can even try stretching the fingers across the box position you're about to use, as shown in Figure 12-1b.

The key to becoming a great single-string player is to know your open- and closed-position scales, in as many areas of the fretboard as possible and in the keys you need, and be comfortable shifting your box positions up and down the fingerboard.

This sounds like an impossible challenge, doesn't it? Have no fear, intrepid single-string striver! This section unlocks the fretting mysteries of single-string style and puts you well on your way toward fingerboard mastery.

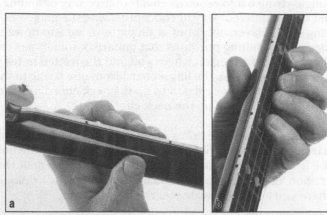

Figure 12-1:
(a) Placing the thumb on the back of the neck and (b) moving your fingers close to the strings for an optimal fretting-hand position for single-string stretches.

Photographs by Anne Hamersky

You'll need to *practice,* of course, but you'll know that you're investing your playing time well after spending time with the exercises and tunes presented in the rest of this chapter.

Working out open- and closed-position scales

It's time to put the fretting hand to work to make some music in single-string style. You'll understand a lot more clearly the differences between open- and closed-position fretting by working out both approaches for the G- and D-major scales, two of the most common keys you'll use for playing songs.

To get things started, play Tab 12-10 (Audio Track 120, Video Clip 33), which presents a G-major scale in open position, moving down through the fourth-string notes that are in this scale below the third-string open G.

© John Wiley & Sons, Inc.

Tab 12-10: Playing a G-major scale in open position.

PLAY THIS! ▶

PLAY THIS! ▶

REMEMBER

Now compare with Tab 12-11 (Audio Track 120, Video Clip 33), where you play the exact same note sequence, but this time using all fretted notes.

Before you catch your breath, try playing a D-major scale in open and closed positions in Tabs 12-12 and 12-13 (Audio Track 121, Video Clip 33).

Both open and closed positions are commonly used in all kinds of songs, but notice how the fingering in closed positions often follows a "one finger per fret" rule, where your closed-position box largely determines which fingers to use across the strings. It's not unusual to shift the index finger up a fret or two (as with Tab 12-11) as you move to a higher string, repositioning the closed-position box to extend the reach to higher frets along the second and first strings.

Different ways to play the same closed-position scale

In Tab 12-11, you fret the pinky finger on the fifth fret of the fourth string to play the G-major scale. This starting point defines the box you're using as

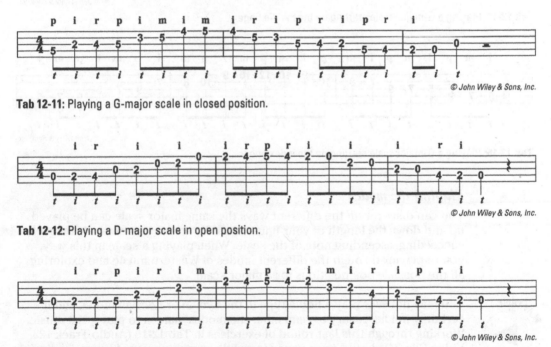

© John Wiley & Sons, Inc.

Tab 12-11: Playing a G-major scale in closed position.

© John Wiley & Sons, Inc.

Tab 12-12: Playing a D-major scale in open position.

© John Wiley & Sons, Inc.

Tab 12-13: .Playing a D-major scale in closed position.

extending from the second to the fifth fret of your banjo fingerboard and largely determines the other fingers you use to fret the rest of the scale. If you start this same G scale using a different finger, you play the same notes but use a different box, or fretted region. Each box extends the range of the scale in a different way.

Tabs 12-14 and 12-15 (Audio Track 122, Video Clip 33) show the fingerings for the G-major scale that result if you use the middle finger and then the index finger as your starting points. Note how different each way of playing this same scale feels under the hand and check out the range of notes that is possible with the different ways of fingering this scale.

© John Wiley & Sons, Inc.

Tab 12-14: Playing a G-major scale starting on the middle finger.

© John Wiley & Sons, Inc.

Tab 12-15: Playing a G-major scale starting on the index finger.

Playing the modes

You can discover *all* the different ways the same major scale can be played up and down the length of your fingerboard by starting a new scale on each succeeding, ascending note of the scale. When playing a scale in this way, you're playing through the different modes of Western music and exploring all the possible box positions for a major scale.

You may not ever play a fiddle tune in the Lydian or Locrian mode, and it's certainly not necessary to remember the modes' names to play great music. Working through this last round of exercises in Tab 12-16 (Audio Track 123, Video Clip 34) should open your ears while stretching your fingers, leading to new ideas and positions in the most friendly banjo key of G major.

© John Wiley & Sons, Inc.

Tab 12-16: Exploring the different ways to play a G-major scale using modes: (a) Dorian, starting on the second note of the G-major scale; (b) Phrygian, starting on the third note of the G-major scale; (c) Lydian, starting on the fourth note of the G-major scale; (d) Mixolydian, starting on the fifth note of the G-major scale; (e) Aeolian, starting on the sixth note of the G-major scale; and (f) Locrian, starting on the seventh note of the G-major scale.

Playing Single-String Tunes

This is no doubt the single-string moment you've been waiting for: It's time to (finally) play some tunes! You'll put everything you absorbed in the last section to good use with these six favorites. From open- and closed-position playing in the keys of G and D to an Irish sojourn, the hard work you've invested in getting comfortable with single-string picking-hand moves and fretting-hand positions is about to pay off as you work through these well-known instrumentals arranged in single-string style.

Don't forget to check out the audio tracks and video clips (when available) for each tune. If you've internalized the sound of each song and you follow my fingering choices, you'll have a lot more fun jumping the technical hurdles I've created for you with each arrangement. The techniques you use for all these tunes are the same as you use when creating your own arrangements of songs in any key, anywhere on your banjo fretboard.

"Sally Goodin'"

An American bluegrass fiddle favorite, this song provides a great way to get started playing full tunes in single-string style. You'll use open positions in the key of G to play the arrangement in Tab 12-17 (Audio Track 124).

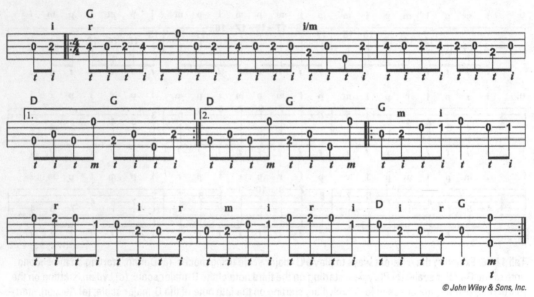

© John Wiley & Sons, Inc.

Tab 12-17: "Sally Goodin'," using open positions in the key of G.

"Whiskey Before Breakfast"

A tune of recent derivation, Tab 12-18 (Audio Track 125, Video Clip 35) is a jam favorite among mandolin and fiddle players. That fact alone makes this a good tune to learn! This arrangement uses a mix of open and closed positions in the key of D. Check out my fretting-hand fingering suggestions above the tab staff. You'll want to tune your fifth string up two frets to A in order to back up others when playing this tune in a jam session.

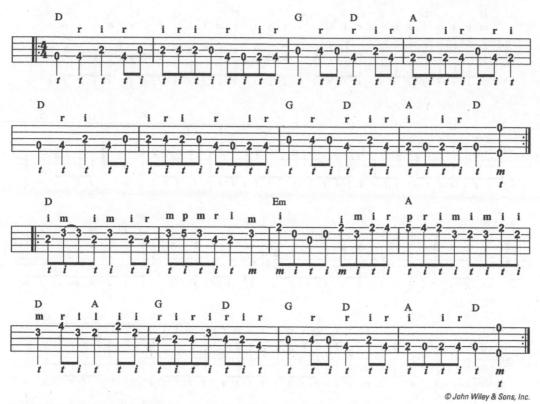

Tab 12-18: "Whiskey Before Breakfast," using open and closed positions in the key of D.

© John Wiley & Sons, Inc.

"Blackberry Blossom"

The tune in Tab 12-19 (Audio Track 126, Video Clip 36) is usually played in melodic style, but you can find the same notes using up-the-neck box positions. This arrangement represents a considerable step up in difficulty from the first two tunes, so work through this arrangement as slowly as you need to make it flow smoothly, following my fingering suggestions. Most of the first section of this song uses a box position based around the D-shaped movable G chord fretted by the ring and pinky fingers at the ninth fret.

"Lynchburg Blues"

I visited with bluegrass pioneer Don Reno at his home in the Lynchburg, Virginia, area in the early 1980s and was impressed by his generosity of spirit and his willingness to share everything he knew on the five-string banjo. I put together the tune in Tab 12-20 (Audio Track 127) in his memory, utilizing my versions of many of the closed-position licks he contributed to bluegrass banjo playing beginning in the 1950s.

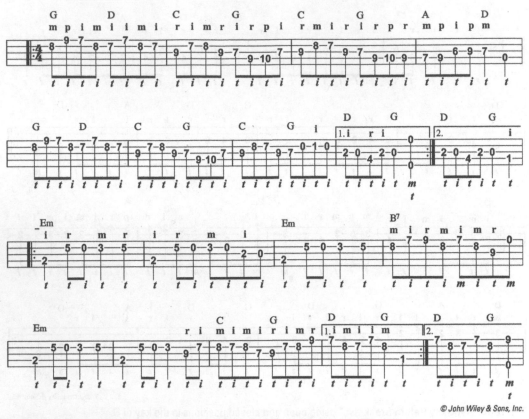

© John Wiley & Sons, Inc.

Tab 12-19: "Blackberry Blossom" using closed positions up the neck in the key of G.

There are a lot of fretting-hand position shifts in "Lynchburg Blues," which is how Don would've liked it! With each position shift, you'll move to a different closed box position that's related to a movable major chord shape. When you've got a flow going with this song, try lifting out your favorite two-measure phrases to use as licks in other songs.

"The Famous Ballymote"

Named after a town in County Sligo, Ireland, with a castle built around 1300, the tribute tune in Tab 12-21 (Audio Track 128) is likely of more recent origin. This open-position arrangement in the key of D is a great way to experience the power of single-string technique when applied to Irish music. "The Famous Ballymote" is often played *fast* by Irish musicians (and I mean *fast!*). There's no need for you to worry about speed right now as you work out the fingering — just enjoy the ride! My thanks to banjo great Tony Furtado for this arrangement.

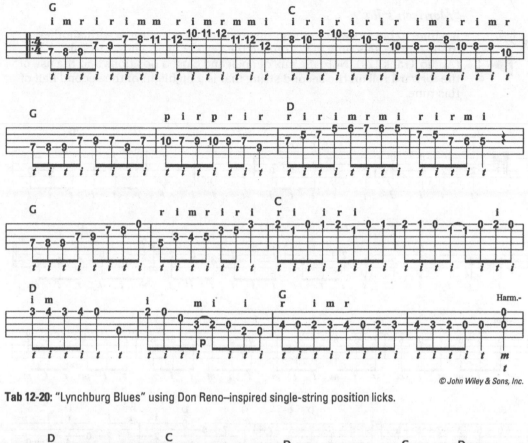

© John Wiley & Sons, Inc.

Tab 12-20: "Lynchburg Blues" using Don Reno–inspired single-string position licks.

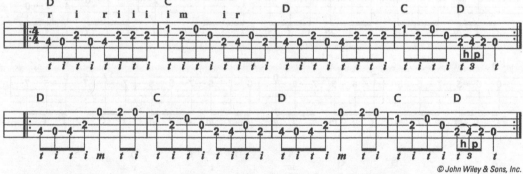

© John Wiley & Sons, Inc.

Tab 12-21: "The Famous Ballymote," an Irish tune played in open position in the key of D.

"Morrison's Jig"

It's time to bid farewell to these single-stringing adventures with another Irish favorite, this time in 6/8 time in the key of Em, as shown in Tab 12-22 (Audio Track 129). Note the mix of open and closed positions and the use of the forward roll on the second string that is a highlight of the second half of this tune.

Tab 12-22: "Morrison's Jig," an Irish tune using open and closed positions in E minor.

Part V
Keeping Your Banjo in Top Shape

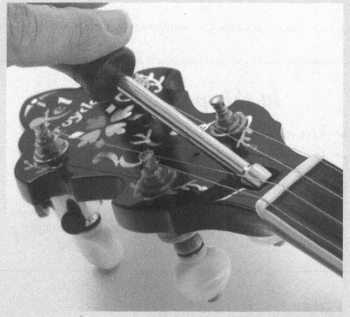

Photograph by Anne Hamersky

In this part . . .

- Keep your banjo in top shape with simple adjustments.

- Discover how head tension, bridges, and tailpieces affect the sound of your banjo.

- Select strings that match your playing needs and the sound you want to hear from your banjo.

- Follow a step-by-step guide to make changing your strings quick and easy.

Chapter 13

Setup Essentials: Getting the Best Sound from Your Banjo

In This Chapter

▶ Choosing a bridge and installing it on your banjo

▶ Setting head tension to make your banjo sound its best

▶ Adjusting the tailpiece to finesse your sound

▶ Using the truss rod to adjust the neck bow

---

*I*f banjo players aren't playing their banjos, then they're talking about them, often obsessively, to one another and to anyone else who may remain within earshot! There's good reason for all this banjo talk, however, because the banjo is one of the most notoriously adjustable instruments in the world.

The more hooked you become on the five-string banjo, the more you'll want to know about the different parts that can affect the sound and playability of your instrument. Banjo players use the term *setup* to refer to the kinds of parts we select and how they can be adjusted to make our banjos sound their best.

In this chapter, you get acquainted with the easiest — and safest — ways that you can adjust your banjo. You'll soon be able to distinguish a truss rod from a tailpiece and you'll more than hold your own when the topics of head tightness, bridge height, or string action come up in any cocktail party conversation. I'm not saying that this chapter will turn you into a banjo setup geek, but it certainly will get you started. If you're ready to start tweaking, read on!

Setting Up for Great Tone

Your banjo setup will be determined by the banjo that you play and what kinds of sounds you want it to make. People often model their tastes on the choices of their musical heroes, but there is no one perfect way to set up any banjo. Your own preferences are certain to change over time as your tastes evolve and as new banjos and banjo parts are introduced. This is what makes banjo setup so much fun!

Some players prefer the bright, cracking banjo sound associated with old-school masters like Earl Scruggs or Ralph Stanley. Others love the darker, guitarlike tone produced by modern players such as Alison Brown, Béla Fleck, and Noam Pikelny. Many bluegrass banjo players, such as J. D. Crowe and Tony Trischka, go for something in between in their setup preferences.

It's important for you to understand how your setup choices will affect the sound of your banjo. Banjos have a *lot* of potentially moving parts! The bridge, head, and tailpiece can all be swapped out, moved around, or loosened and tightened, and it's with these components that you can begin your setup experiments.

In the following sections, I fill you in on these parts, show you how they contribute to the sound of your instrument, and tell you how adjusting them can change the sound of your banjo.

Choosing bridges

The *bridge* is the carved piece of wood that sits on top of the head that transmits the musical vibrations from the strings to the head and ultimately to the rest of your instrument. Bridges are made from different kinds of wood and are available in varying heights, sizes, and weights. Each of these factors affects how a bridge colors the sound of your banjo.

Banjo players will routinely try many kinds of bridges to hear the different sounds that various woods and weights can produce. Luckily, bridges are not very expensive (they range in price from $15 to $35), and it's easy to swap out one bridge for another on your banjo.

Selecting woods

The time-honored, traditional choice for a banjo bridge is one that's made from maple with an ebony strip glued to its top. You can also find bridges made from birch, koa, teak, and even more exotic woods. Each type of wood conveys a unique sound, but you'll need to experiment to determine exactly what that sound is on *your* banjo!

The density of the wood combined with its weight are crucial in regard to how a bridge will impact your banjo's sound. Generally speaking, a denser piece of wood, with a tighter grain that's visible to the eye, will give your banjo a brighter sound, while a heavier bridge will lend more bass tones.

A bridge that's too light or too dense can sound shrill, where a bridge that's too heavy or porous may make your banjo sound dull.

You'll want to replace your bridge with a new one that is the same height. A ⅝-inch bridge is standard on many bluegrass banjos, but some professional players prefer higher bridges to better match their picking-hand position. Keep in mind that if you install a taller or a lower bridge, your string action will also go up or down accordingly. Even just a slight variation in bridge height will result in noticeable changes to your string action and playability.

Swapping out bridges

Bridges are held firmly in place by the tension of the strings but are movable. To replace one bridge with another, just loosen your strings and slide the new bridge under the strings in front of the old one. Then remove the old bridge, slide the new bridge into place where the old bridge used to be, and bring your strings back in tune.

A handmade bridge will make a big improvement in the sound of your banjo, even if it's an entry-level, starter instrument. Check out your favorite online retailer for the widest choice in quality banjo bridges and try one on for size. You'll be surprised at how much better your banjo will sound! Figure 13-1 shows some of the many kinds of banjo bridges available today.

Figure 13-1:
Banjo bridge options range from the traditional to the exotic.

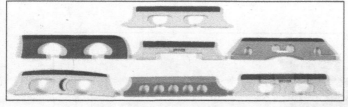

Photograph courtesy of Elderly Instruments

Knowing your head

The banjo has been called a drum on a stick, and there's no question that it's the head that's to blame for this moniker! The banjo head is literally a drum head that's attached firmly to the body of your banjo with brackets, nuts, and stretcher bands, just like an actual drum. More than any other banjo part, the head is responsible for the unique, percussive sound of this instrument that we love so much (and is so mystifying to much of the outside world). A banjo just isn't a banjo without a head!

Choosing banjo heads

It should come as no surprise that you have a wide choice of banjo heads. As with bridges, a thicker and heavier head lends more bass tones, while a lighter, thinner head can make your banjo sound brighter, but you'll really only know through experimentation which head works best on your instrument.

These days, heads contribute to your banjo fashion statement as well, with different color and design options available to complement your stage outfits. Check out Figure 13-2 to see some of the options available today.

Bluegrass banjo purists often stick to tried-and-true brand names such as Remo and Five-Star banjo heads, but smaller shops, such as Huber and American Made Banjo, also make banjo heads with coatings similar to those found on the classic banjo heads of the 1960s.

If you want to go fully retro, you can check out calfskin and goatskin heads to get closer to the sound of the early bluegrass banjo greats of the 1950s. Keep in mind that these organic heads are more expensive and sometimes require a lot of adjustment in response to temperature and humidity changes.

If you're ready to experiment with a different style or brand of banjo head, be sure your new head is the same size as the one you're replacing. Most bluegrass banjos come with 11-inch heads as standard equipment, but if you're in doubt, head to your nearest acoustic music retailer to ask for their advice. If they have a head in stock that you'd like to try, they most likely will install it for you as well. Ask if you can watch how it's done, and the next time, you can try yourself.

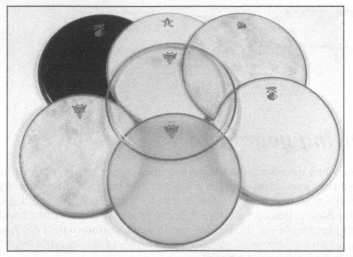

Figure 13-2: Banjo heads come in a variety of colors, designs, and thicknesses.

Photograph courtesy of Elderly Instruments

Adjusting head tension

Next to swapping out your bridge, the biggest change you can easily make in your banjo's tone is to tighten or loosen your head. If you're looking for a brighter banjo sound, you'll want to tighten your head, but if it's a darker tone with more bass you're seeking, you'll want to loosen it.

If you've just brought your banjo home from a big-box retailer or an online store that doesn't specialize in acoustic instruments, there's a good chance that no one has played your banjo since it left the factory half a world away (if at all). Under these conditions, it's likely that your head will need tightening.

TIP

To check the head tension, push your thumb against the head close to the bridge. If it bends significantly against the pressure of your thumb, it's a good idea to tighten your head. A properly adjusted head should provide a good amount of resistance, moving only slightly when tested by your thumb.

REMEMBER

If you're going to adjust your head, it's a great idea to know your banjo parts (see Figure 13-3). The head is stretched across the banjo tone ring by the tension hoop. Notches in the tension hoop support the top of the brackets, which hold the head in place and also control the amount of tension on the head. The other end of the brackets run through holes in the flange and stay attached to the flange via bracket nuts. The flange also provides a platform to keep the resonator attached to the banjo with resonator screws.

Figure 13-3: Many parts of the banjo pot are responsible for keeping your banjo head tight.

Head

Tension hoop

Side of head

Tone ring

Bracket

Resonator screw

Resonator

Photograph by Anne Hamersky

To adjust your head tension, you'll remove the resonator from your banjo and use a banjo wrench to tighten or loosen the bracket nuts (see Figure 13-4). Tightening these nuts applies more force to the tension hoop, literally tightening the banjo head down along the side of the tone ring.

The key to properly tightening or loosening the head is to make very gradual adjustments, moving the wrench no more than an eighth of a turn in the same direction for each bracket nut. Turn each bracket clockwise to tighten the head and counterclockwise to loosen it. Small adjustments in head tension either way will still make big differences in tone that you can hear when you reattach the resonator and play your banjo. As in most other aspects of banjo setup, players usually try to find a middle ground in regard to head tension.

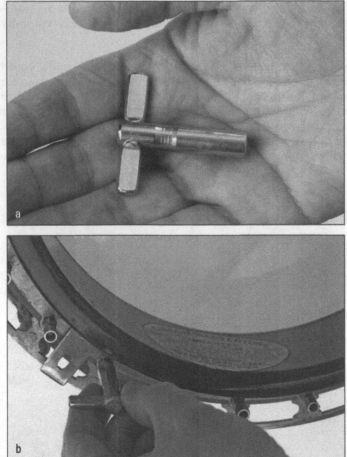

Figure 13-4:
Using a banjo bracket wrench to adjust the head tension on your banjo.

Photographs by Anne Hamersky

Tinkering with the tailpiece

The job of the tailpiece is to keep the strings secure at the opposite end of the banjo from your peghead. Most bluegrass banjos have adjustable tailpieces that control the downward pressure exerted by the tailpiece on the strings and set the angles at which the strings meet the bridge. These adjustments don't change the sound of your banjo to the same degree that a new bridge or a different head tension will, but it's still worthwhile to consider the more subtle effect your tailpiece exerts on your banjo's tone and volume.

REMEMBER

The vertical placement of the tailpiece changes the various overtones that you hear from your instrument. *Overtones* are the frequencies that are present above the primary pitch; it's the distribution of those various frequencies that defines the tone of any musical instrument. If you adjust the tailpiece down toward the banjo head, you'll hear a clearer sound that's also probably a bit thinner because there are now fewer overtones present. For an open, fuller tone, players will set the tailpiece up and farther away from the banjo head. This creates more overtones at the risk of your banjo sounding muddy. As in the other aspects of banjo setup discussed in this chapter, moderation is key — a tailpiece that's set not too high and not too low usually results in the best tone.

Tailpiece options

Several styles of tailpieces are available, and they differ mostly in the ways they can be adjusted. Presto-style tailpieces pay tribute to the tailpieces found on prized pre–World War II Gibson banjos. In their current manifestation, they're lightweight, inexpensive, and functional, but they can only be adjusted up or down in relation to the banjo head. At the other end of the spectrum, Fults handcrafted tailpieces can be adjusted not only up and down in relation to the banjo head but in and out in relation to its distance from the bridge. The Price straightline tailpiece guides your strings off the tailpiece parallel to one another, instead of at the angle of most other tailpieces. Take a look at your tailpiece options in Figure 13-5.

Figure 13-5:
Tailpiece choices have a subtle but measurable effect on banjo tone.

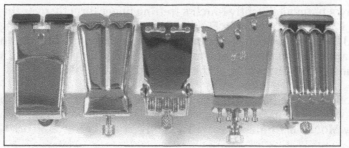

Photograph courtesy of Elderly Instruments

Adjusting the tailpiece

For Presto-style tailpieces, you adjust the tailpiece by tightening or loosening the bracket nut that holds the tailpiece to the flange, raising or lowering the entire tailpiece. Other tailpieces have one or more screw adjustments that more easily change the angle at which the tailpiece extends over the banjo head and provide more setup options.

Perfecting Your Banjo's Playability

While swapping out and tweaking parts can make your banjo sound better, there are other adjustments you can do that will make your banjo easier to play. In this section, you become familiar with two skills that will keep your banjo feeling great under your fingers. You'll set the bridge using *harmonics* to maintain perfectly tuned fretted notes all up and down the neck, and you'll set your banjo neck's *truss rod* to keep those notes buzz-free.

Setting the bridge

The position of the movable bridge on your banjo head determines whether your fretted notes will sound pitches correctly. Although you may have left the music store with a perfectly placed bridge, over time the bridge may shift a bit on your banjo head or fall over completely by accident. Also, if you're into trying out the latest in new bridge technology, you need to know how to install that new bridge properly.

Discovering harmonics

If you listen carefully when you pick a string, you'll hear not only the primary note but also an assortment of higher-pitched notes called *harmonics*. Also called *chimes* by banjo players, you can use harmonics to determine the — precise placement of your bridge on the banjo head.

To play a harmonic, lightly touch a fretting finger directly over the first string at the 12th fret (as shown in Figure 13-6). When you pick the string, you should hear a clear, bell-like sound that's characteristic of harmonics. You'll also harmonics on the first through fourth strings at the 5th, 7th, and 12th frets and on the fifth string at the 10th, 12th, and 17th frets.

Harmonics can be banjo showstoppers and provide the primary musical points of interest in Earl Scruggs's tunes "Bugle Call Rag," "Reuben," and "Foggy Mountain Chimes," as well as Tony Trischka's "New York Chimes."

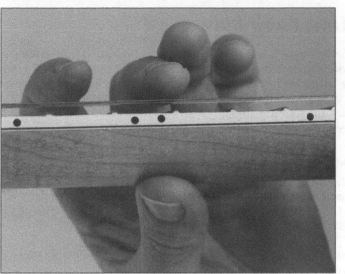

Figure 13-6:
Playing the
first-string,
12th-fret
harmonic.

Photograph by Anne Hamersky

Using harmonics to set the bridge

To set your bridge, you want to compare the pitch of the first-string, 12th-fret harmonic with the sound of this string when fretted at the same location. If the bridge is in its proper position, these two pitches should sound the same. If you can hear a difference in pitch, your bridge is likely out of position.

If the fretted note sounds lower than the harmonic, you'll want to move your bridge toward the neck (to shorten the length of the string). If the fretted note sounds higher than the harmonic, you'll need to move the bridge away from the neck (to increase the string length). In either case, only a very small adjustment of fractions of an inch should be required.

Try moving the bridge very slightly back and forth as many times as you need, comparing the harmonic with the fretted pitch until they sound the same. When you've done this for the first string, try the same procedure on the fourth string. When you've got both strings in tune, you've properly set the bridge! After moving the bridge, make sure that it's not leaning and that the bridge feet are in full contact with the banjo head.

You can now celebrate by lightly marking in pencil the position of your bridge on the head so that if you need to set it again or when you install a different bridge, you already have a great starting point.

Setting neck bow

A properly set neck has a slight amount of bow such that when you're fretting, your strings will ring clearly without any buzzes. However, with changes in your banjo neck over time and with variations in temperature and humidity (or if you fly with your banjo from one part of the country to another), you may find that the amount of bow in your banjo neck has changed, often literally overnight.

Determining neck bow

If you hear buzzing when you fret a string anywhere on your neck or if the string action on your banjo seems to have taken a sudden leap either up or down, there's a good chance that your neck has changed its position relative to the strings.

You can determine if you neck is properly set by following these steps (as shown in Figure 13-7):

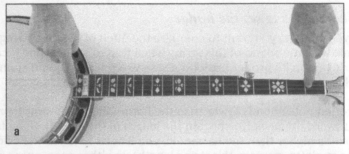

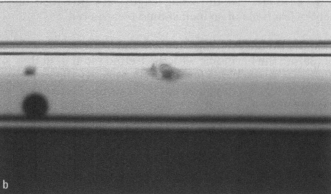

Figure 13-7: (a) Checking the neck bow using the third string as a reference point and (b) the desired clearance of the third string at the seventh fret.

Photographs by Anne Hamersky

✔ **Fret your third string at the highest and lowest frets *at the same time*.** When you do this, you've created a straight edge with the string itself. You'll now use this string to measure the amount of bow in your neck.

✔ **Check the amount of clearance between the third string and the banjo fingerboard at the seventh fret.** You'll need to look across your fingerboard to do this. It can help to hold the banjo against a light-colored background, or the white of a computer screen, to more clearly see the string's position relative to the fingerboard.

If your neck has a proper bow, you should see just a bit of space between the string and the neck. However, if the string is in contact with the fret, your neck is probably bent too far inward. Conversely, if there is too large a space between the string and the fingerboard, your neck is bowed outward.

Locating the truss rod

You'll use your banjo's *truss rod* to bring your neck back to factory specs. The *truss rod* is a one- or two-piece adjustable metal rod that has been hiding all along right underneath your banjo fingerboard. The truss rod provides stability to the neck, keeping it in proper alignment against the tension exerted by the strings and environmental changes.

Using the truss rod to adjust the neck bow

One end of the truss rod is located underneath the cover on your banjo's peghead. This is called — you guessed it! — the truss-rod cover. Remove this cover, and you'll see the end of the truss rod peeking out at you.

You can change the bow in your neck by turning the nut that's at the end of the truss rod. For most banjos, you'll need a ¼-inch nut driver for this task, but some banjos require an Allen wrench. Check to see what's in your case — it's likely that your banjo came with the tool that's needed to make this adjustment.

You only need to make very slight adjustments to push or pull the neck back into proper alignment. On most banjos, you turn the nut no more than ¹⁄₁₆ to ⅛ of a turn clockwise to flatten the neck and the same amount counter-clockwise to add bow. After each adjustment, play your banjo to determine if you're moving the truss rod in the right direction to make the changes you want (see Figure 13-8).

Figure 13-8:
Using a
nut driver
to make a
truss-rod
adjustment.

Photograph by Anne Hamersky

Adjusting your neck bow with the truss rod is a lot like checking the oil in your car. If you know how to do it, it's easy, but it can seem like a huge challenge if you're unfamiliar with the steps you need to take. Find a banjo mentor or contact your local acoustic instrument repairman and ask them to show you the steps involved. After you've seen it done, you'll have no trouble at all keeping your neck in top shape!

Chapter 14

All Strings Considered: Choosing and Changing Strings

You're right in the middle of the best banjo solo you've taken in your entire life when, quite suddenly and without a moment's notice, you feel an unfamiliar change in pressure in your strings and hear a very loud cracking sound. You look down to find one less string attached to your instrument. That's right: You have a broken string!

Sooner or later, this startling event happens to every banjo player. When it's your turn to suffer this fate, you'll be right back in the middle of the jam session with all five strings attached and in tune in no time at all after you've read through this chapter. From selecting the strings that best match your playing, to safely removing old strings and effortlessly putting on brand-spanking-new ones, everything you need to know about strings is covered in the following pages.

All About Banjo Strings

Whether you're staring wide-eyed at the rows of string sets at your local music store or scrolling through the 50 or more varieties of strings available from your favorite online music source, you'll find a bewildering variety of string options available for bluegrass banjo these days. In this section, I tell you when it's time to say goodbye to your old strings and what to look for in a new set. You also assemble a few tools that will make the job of changing strings a lot easier.

Knowing when it's time for a change

Depending upon your climate, your body chemistry, how often you play and the type of strings you're using, strings can last a long time or, well, not so long. If your strings are exposed to moisture, whether it's from you or the air around you, they'll wear out more quickly than if both you and your instrument are maintained in drier conditions. If you're playing for many hours per day or if you strike the strings with a lot of force, you'll need to replace your strings at more frequent intervals.

Some professional players change their strings before each performance, but I know one or two musicians who haven't changed their strings in *years*. Many banjo players don't change their strings as often as they would like to because they don't have confidence completing this task. Although banjo strings are designed to last a long time, your instrument will be easier to tune, will sound better, and will be easier to play if you can muster up the courage to install a new set of strings at least every now and then.

If a single string breaks (and it will, sooner or later — trust me on this one!), it's probably time to change all five of them. A new string sounds brighter and feels slicker than an older string, and these differences will be noticeable enough that you'll be glad you replaced them all. An exception: If you experience a string breaking soon after you've put on a new set, it's fine just to replace the one string.

If the same string breaks frequently on your banjo, that's a sign of a potential problem in the bridge or the nut slots that deserves the attention of your local repairperson. (Turn to Chapter 2 if you need to get familiar with these parts.)

Here are other indicators that it's time to spring for new strings:

- ✔ **You're able to get the open strings in tune, but your banjo sounds slightly out of tune when fretting chords.** As a string wears out, it loses its ability to sound both open and fretted notes in good tune. For me, this is the primary indicator that it's time to change strings. Keep in mind that the same problem will occur if your bridge isn't properly positioned on your banjo head. Follow the setup recommendations in Chapter 13 to make sure that this isn't the source of your problem.

- ✔ **You're having difficulty shifting positions or sliding with your fretting hand.** As strings oxidize, they build up gunk that grinds your fretting hand to a halt as it attempts to deftly move up and down the neck. If you can *see* this buildup on your strings (or if your strings have turned black instead of silver), then by all means, it's time for a change!

✔ **You're experiencing slippage in any string as you tune it.** Occasionally, you'll try to tune a string up to its desired pitch and it suddenly loses tension, requiring you to start all over. This could be a sign that the end of the string is slipping through the tuning post's hole at the peghead. If you've already trimmed the excess at that end, the string likely isn't long enough to reinstall. Later in this chapter, I explain how to properly install a string so that this won't ever happen to you!

If you're playing up to one hour a day and your banjo is properly set up, a new set of strings should last one to three months or more. Luckily, strings are not expensive, so when you get comfortable changing them, you're likely to swap them out more often. Some players prefer the mellower sound of broken-in strings and will try to keep them on their banjos for as long as possible, until tuning difficulties force the issue. As you gain experience playing, you'll discover what interval works best for you and your banjo.

Finding the right strings

String shopping is a lot like buying a new pair of socks: You have a world of choices, but you can't really go wrong if you purchase something that fits. With socks, you have your choice of color, design, and fabric; with banjo strings, you choose what works for you based on what kind of steel is used to make the string, how the string attaches to your banjo's tailpiece, and the thicknesses of the strings (expressed as *string gauge*, which is a measurement of the string's diameter).

Strings are usually sold in sets, with all five strings grouped together in a package. If you're experimenting with different string gauges to match your playing preferences or if you need a couple of extra individual strings to have on hand when a string breaks, it's a good idea to purchase the individual strings you need. However, it's more economical to purchase an entire set and many retailers offer discounts if you buy three or more sets.

Picking on strings of steel

Bluegrass banjo players use either nickel-plated or stainless-steel strings and you'll no doubt want to try both kinds after reading this section!

Most players agree that stainless-steel strings sound brighter than nickel-plated strings (although both kinds of strings will sound bright to your ears when you first put them on your banjo). Modern physics has entered the world of banjo string manufacture: The American Made Banjo Company offers a stainless-steel variety that is exposed to extremely low temperatures of –300°F (–184°C), cryogenically treating them to last longer. (Banjo players love this kind of scientific stuff!)

Because the fourth string is the lowest in pitch of your five strings, this string is wrapped with nickel, stainless steel, bronze, or *monel* (a nickel alloy) to increase its diameter, as with the fourth string on a guitar. Bronze and stainless-steel fourth-string wraps produce a comparatively brighter tone compared to nickel or monel, which offers the darkest tone of these options.

Matching strings to tailpieces

It's important to match the strings you choose to your type of tailpiece. The *tailpiece* holds the strings at the pot end of your banjo, directing them to the bridge (see Chapter 13 to find out more about tailpieces). The majority of bluegrass banjos today use *loop-end strings,* which fit over the fingerlike extensions or hooks found on this style of tailpiece. A few older, entry-level banjos have small holes in the tailpiece that require *ball-end strings,* which, like most guitar strings, have a short brass cylinder at the end. Figure 14-1 shows the two types of strings.

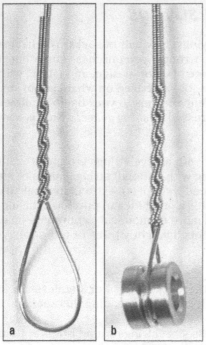

Figure 14-1:
(a) Loop-end and (b) ball-end banjo strings.

a   b

Photographs courtesy of Elderly Instruments

Before you head down to the music store, make sure you know which type of string you need.

Knowing your string gauges

Just about any string set you purchase will do a good job in brightening up the sound of your banjo. Where the real choice begins (and the fun starts!) is in finding *string gauges* to match your playing style. Strings come in different thicknesses to match your banjo tuning: Lower-pitched strings, like your third and fourth strings, require thicker strings to maintain the tension they need to stay in tune, while higher-pitched strings, like your first and fifth strings, call for thinner string diameters.

With string gauges measured in increments of one-thousandth of an inch, you have several choices in gauges that will work for each of your banjo strings. There will be a noticeable difference in the sound and playability of your banjo based on variations as small as one-half of one-thousandth of an inch. (I told you that banjo players like to think scientifically.) Banjo players love to experiment with different string gauges. Don't be surprised if your preferences change over time.

String sets come in extra-light, light, custom-light, medium-light, almost-medium, medium, heavy, and even stage and studio varieties, all based on ever so slightly different combinations of string gauges packaged together. As you compare strings in various sets, keep in mind that a set with heavier-gauge strings (with larger numbers) will lend a darker tone to your banjo and will also have a stiffer feel under your fingers. Changing to heavier-gauge strings may raise the action, requiring a truss rod adjustment (which I explain in Chapter 14). Lighter-gauge strings will give your banjo a brighter sound and are easier to play but can sometimes cause buzzing. Figure 14-2 shows a couple of typical string set packages.

Figure 14-2:
Strings sets differ according to the string gauges used.

Photograph courtesy of Elderly Instruments

Many bluegrass banjo players choose string gauges that today's manufacturers would group into a medium-light set. If you ask a banjo player what strings she uses, she's likely to quickly rattle off a list of five numbers. My own choices these days on my main banjo for traditional bluegrass playing are 10, 11, 13, 20, and 10. What does this mean? My first string is ten-thousandths of an inch, my second string eleven-thousandths, and so on. Your fifth string will almost always be the same gauge as your first string. On another instrument that I use for more progressive playing, my string choices are 10, 12, 14, 22, and 10 because I like the darker, smokier sound that the slightly heavier gauges lend to this particular instrument. Obviously, these are very small differences in string diameters that nevertheless *do* make a difference. Amazing, isn't it?

Luckily, string sets are not expensive — prices range from $3 to $8 per set. If you play with a softer attack in your picking hand or if you want to bring a brighter sound to your banjo, experiment first with a light or medium-light set. If you play with a lot of volume or you're looking for a banjo sound with more bass, go for a medium-light or medium set. Breaking in a new set of strings can take about a week, so give any new combination a bit of time before deciding if it's working for you and your playing style. You'll quickly figure out what works best for you after trying a few different sets.

Using accessories to help make the change

As you get ready to change your strings, you'll want to have on hand just a few tools that will make the job go more smoothly (as shown in Figure 14-3):

- ✔ **A sharp pencil:** You'll use this to lubricate the notches in the nut and bridge with graphite after removing your old string.

- ✔ **String cutters:** If you have a pair of wire cutters already around the house, these will do the job just fine. Combination string-changing and peghead-winder tools are small and light enough to store in a case and are the way to go if you're playing banjo outside your home.

- ✔ **Neck headstand:** Many players change strings with their banjos lying across a table. A neck headstand is a very useful tool that supports the banjo neck and keeps your instrument stable, reducing your overall string-changing stress level tremendously.

- ✔ **Electronic tuner:** Those new strings need to get in tune, and an electronic tuner that attaches to the peghead of your banjo is just the ticket for this job.

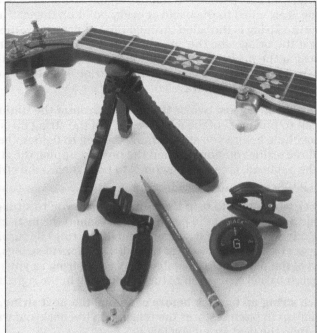

Figure 14-3:
A pencil, string cutter, neck headstand, and tuner — useful tools for changing strings.

Photograph by Anne Hamersky

You Can Do It! Your Complete Guide to String Changing

You've got your new strings at the ready, your tools are nearby and you've finally gathered up the courage to change those crusty old strings. Relax! Banjo players from all over the world have been painlessly changing their strings for over a hundred years, and you'll become a member of this elite club after you follow this guide.

Watch Video Clip 37 for even more positive reinforcement as I take you through the process of replacing the first string on my banjo.

Your string-changing checklist

Before you get started, keep in mind these general guidelines:

✔ **Change strings one a time.** Your bridge will stay in place on the head and it will be easier to tune each new string if you change strings one at a time.

✔ **Match what you see.** Before you remove an old string, take note of how that string is attached to the banjo at every point on the instrument. Note how the string is threaded through the tailpiece, how the string attaches at the bridge and the nut, and how it's wrapped around the tuning post at the peghead. (Use your phone to take pictures to help you remember!) Then when you install the new string, simply re-create the pathway that the old string traveled.

✔ **Wrap the new string just two or three times around the tuning post.** You'll want to pull most of the excess length of the string through the tuning-post hole before you start turning the peg to tighten the string. Two or three string rotations around the post, wrapping the string down toward the peghead, are usually enough to hold secure the string as it's raised to pitch.

✔ **Remember which way to turn the tuning pegs.** If you're sitting with your banjo and looking at the peghead from behind the instrument, you raise the pitches of your first, second, and fifth strings by turning these tuning pegs counterclockwise. For the third and fourth strings, a clockwise turn of the pegs raises the pitch. Play each string as you're bringing it up to pitch to make sure you're turning the peg in the right direction.

✔ **Tune each string up to pitch before changing the next string.** Tuning each string up to pitch restores the tension on the neck and will make it easier to tune the next string you install.

Changing your banjo strings

Here's a step-by-step guide to changing the first string on your banjo (see Video Clip 37). You'll change the other strings in exactly the same way, except you'll turn the third- and fourth-string pegs clockwise to tighten the new strings to bring them up to the desired pitch.

Step 1: Taking off the old string and selecting the new one

As you remove the old string, take note of how it's attached to the tailpiece and the tuning peg at the opposite ends of your banjo.

Many string sets come packaged in plastic envelopes with each string in a paper sleeve. You can use the plastic envelope as a receptacle for the old strings along with the clipped ends of the new strings. Wrap the old string into a small hoop and place it inside the plastic envelope to safely dispose of them.

Now check to see which string in your set is designated as the first string. It should be the string with the lowest number, and there should be two of these strings in your set: one for the first string and the other for the fifth. If the paper sleeve containing the string doesn't give you this information, check the outside packaging for the string gauge that corresponds to the first string (and remember, this can be a different gauge according to your choice of string set).

Step 2: Putting your pencil to use

Move your pencil through the loop end to expand it, providing a bigger area for the string to grab the tailpiece. Now gently mark the grooves in your bridge and tailpiece with the pencil, leaving a trace of graphite behind to allow the string to smoothly glide across both surfaces. Check out Figure 14-4 to see how it's done.

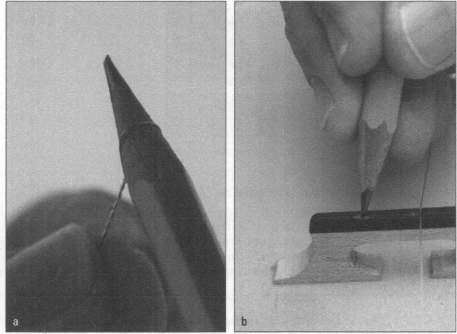

Figure 14-4: Using a pencil to (a) prepare the new string and (b) lubricate the bridge slot.

Photographs by Anne Hamersky

Step 3: Attaching the new string to the tailpiece

Tailpiece end first! Wrap the loop end around the corresponding tailpiece hook and thread the string through the tailpiece, pointing it toward the bridge. For your first string, you'll use the tailpiece extension that's to the far right. Different kinds of tailpieces grab and guide the strings in slightly different ways. Check out Figure 14-5 to see how the tailpiece gets the job done.

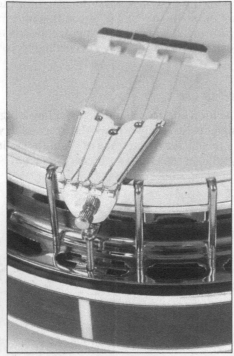

Photograph courtesy of Elderly Instruments

Figure 14-5:
Attaching
loop-end
strings
to the
tailpiece.

Step 4: Setting and guiding the string through the post

Before attaching the new string to the tuning peg, turn the peg by twisting the tuning-peg knob located on the other side of your peghead until the post hole is positioned parallel to the direction of your banjo strings. This will make it easier to move the string through the post. Now, pull the string through the post hole, leaving just enough slack to wrap it around the post two or three times (see Figure 14-6).

Step 5: Bending the string end to prevent it from moving back through the post

It's now time to get in on a couple of the string-changing secrets used by the pros! Where the string emerges on the other side of the tuning-post hole, create a bend that will guide the excess string toward the center of the peg-head. This crease will help prevent the string from slipping back through the post hole as it's brought up to pitch (see Figure 14-7).

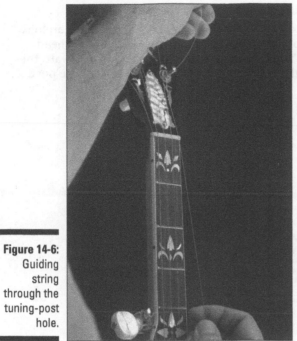

Photograph by Anne Hamersky

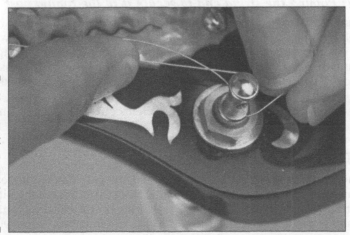

Photograph by Anne Hamersky

Step 6: Wrapping the string down toward the peghead

Grab the excess length of string and turn the first string peg counterclockwise to wind the string around the post from the center of the peghead (as shown in Figure 14-8). You'll want to guide the string down toward the surface of the peghead with each successive revolution around the post.

Figure 14-8: Guiding the string on the tuning post as you bring it up to pitch.

Photograph by Anne Hamersky

Step 7: Pinning the string end to secure it to the tuning post

You can take an extra step to help prevent the string from feeding back through the tuning-post hole. Grab the excess string and pull it toward the center of the peghead, and then move it back underneath and up against the post, underneath the string where it begins to wrap around the post. As you continue to tighten the string, this will pin the excess string against the post.

This requires a bit of sleight of hand but check out Video Clip 37 and Figure 14-9 to see how it's done and try it yourself!

Step 8: Tuning the string to pitch

It's time to attach your tuner to the peghead and get your brand-new first string in tune. As you turn the peg counterclockwise to raise the pitch of the first string, take a quick look to see if the string is still attached to the tailpiece and is positioned in the correct bridge and nut slots. When your string is tuned to a D note, you can break in the new string by pushing gently down to stretch it out just a bit. You'll probably need to bring it up to pitch once again, but this slick move will prevent additional retuning later, when you're making great music on your shiny new set of strings!

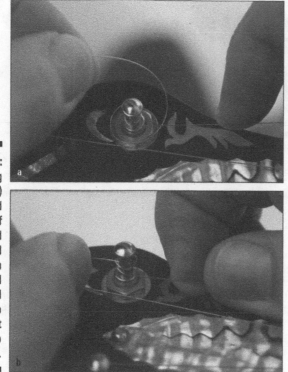

Figure 14-9:
Pulling
string (a)
toward
center of
peghead
and
underneath
wrapped
string and
(b) up
against
the post to
secure it.

Photographs by Anne Hamersky

The special case of the fifth string

Most banjos are equipped with a geared fifth-string tuning peg, like you'll find on the other four strings of your instrument. When attaching a new fifth string, you'll need to wrap it around the tuning post from the fingerboard side of the instrument, in the same way that your third and fourth strings are wrapped from the inside of the tuning pegs. You can still crease and secure the excess string in the same way as you did for the other strings.

Note that this string has its own nut and that you'll move the tuner in a counterclockwise direction to bring the fifth string up to a G pitch. Figure 14-10 gives you an idea of what your new fifth string should look like when it's attached properly.

When your new string is tuned to pitch, remove the excess string by cutting it close to the tuning post. These string ends are sharp, so take care to bend the small amount of excess fifth string out of the way of your fretting hand using either a small pliers or the ends of your string cutter.

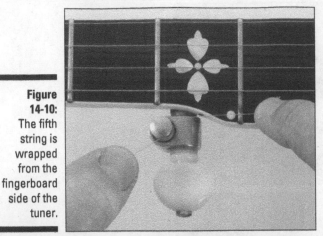

Figure
14-10:
The fifth
string is
wrapped
from the
fingerboard
side of the
tuner.

Photograph by Anne Hamersky

And now you're done. Congratulations! Changing your strings successfully for the first time is a huge accomplishment. Pat yourself on the back, put on your fingerpicks, and get back to playing more music, with an even bigger smile on your face.

Part VI
The Part of Tens

Find ten chord progressions to jam instrumentals you need to know in an article at www.dummies.com/extras/bluegrassbanjo.

In this part . . .

✔ Get acquainted with the most influential banjo players in bluegrass music and discover their contributions to the development of bluegrass banjo style.

✔ Practice the right way with helpful tips and suggestions to keep you on track.

Chapter 15

Ten (Or So) Groundbreaking Bluegrass Banjo Players

In This Chapter

▶ Meeting bluegrass banjo pathfinders

▶ Getting to know today's influential players

▶ Discovering important recordings

This chapter brings together a collection of some of the most important banjo players of all time, known for their musical innovation and influence and for forging new paths that have helped thousands discover and develop a passion for the world's greatest instrument.

From bluegrass banjo's first-generation masters to today's genre-busting stylists and master teachers, it's worth spending time getting to know these important musicians and their music. You'll become a better banjo player by opening your mind and ears to their amazing contributions.

Earl Scruggs (1924–2012)

Earl Scruggs was just 21 years old when the world first heard his revolutionary three-finger picking technique in 1945. Since that time, Earl's playing has come to define bluegrass banjo style. While others before him played the banjo using the thumb, index finger, and middle finger, Earl perfected this approach to create a vast landscape of techniques that not only redefined the musical potential of the instrument but set a standard for bluegrass banjo that is still observed today. He's still the best! All the other banjo players on this list ultimately base their own innovations on the foundation that Earl Scruggs laid many years ago.

Foggy Mountain Banjo is the classic instrumental album recorded by Earl Scruggs with his guitar-playing partner, Lester Flatt, and is worth seeking out. *The Essential Earl Scruggs* provides a comprehensive overview of his career, from his early days in Bill Monroe's band to performing with his sons in the Earl Scruggs Revue. Earl also makes important contributions to the historically significant *Will the Circle Be Unbroken* project recorded with the Nitty Gritty Dirt Band, Maybelle Carter, Roy Acuff, and many others.

Don Reno (1927–1984)

Down in South Carolina, Don Reno was developing his own three-finger approach to playing the banjo at the same time Earl Scruggs was honing his skills up in North Carolina. At the height of his professional career in the 1950s and early 1960s, Don's jazzy, guitar-influenced banjo style introduced single-string scales, chordal licks, and other sophisticated playing techniques that continue to inspire and influence today's top players.

Check out Don's 1950s recordings on the King label with guitarist Red Smiley to sample his many unique compositions and absorb his flashy, no-holds-barred approach to the banjo. Don was also a very snappy dresser and amiable band leader and showman. You won't regret heading online to find videos of his entertaining and virtuosic early television performances.

J. D. Crowe (1937–)

J. D. Crowe is the most influential bluegrass banjo player of the last four decades and is largely responsible for moving the banjo and bluegrass music as a whole into the modern era. Using Earl Scruggs as a starting point, J. D. incorporates folk, country, and early rock-'n'-roll influences to create a rhythmically precise, bluesy, and driving banjo style with some memorable classic licks. His recordings with his band the New South and as part of the all-star lineup of the Bluegrass Album Band series have set the modern standard for the way that bluegrass banjo is supposed to be played.

Veronica "Roni" Stoneman (1938–)

Along with her siblings Patsy and Donna, Roni Stoneman opened doors for women in bluegrass and country music as a member of the Stoneman Family and later as a cast member of the popular television program *Hee Haw*. She was the first woman to play bluegrass-style banjo on LP (*American Banjo:*

Three-Finger and Scruggs Style in 1957) and achieved crossover success with the Stoneman Family through their syndicated TV show. The group was awarded the Country Music Vocal Group of the Year award in 1967. Roni is still actively performing today. The best way to experience her hard-driving bluegrass banjo style is to catch a live show.

Bill Keith (1939–)

Bill Keith is largely responsible for creating and popularizing the melodic style of playing the banjo, an alternative to the Scruggs technique that enables you to play scales using conventional roll-based picking techniques. Melodic style (see Chapter 11) vastly expands the musical possibilities of three-finger-style banjo, opening the door to playing everything from note-for-note versions of fiddle tunes to a Bach invention or a Dizzy Gillespie jazz standard (Keith plays all three!). His dedication to music theory has inspired thousands of players to step outside their bluegrass comfort zones to embrace the banjo as an instrument that's capable of playing all kinds of music. Bill is also the inventor of the Keith "D" tuning pegs, which allow you to precisely change a string's pitch as a song is being played.

Tony Trischka (1949–)

Tony Trischka is the modern banjo player's banjo player. He's in his element whether he's playing a hard-driving traditional Scruggs-oriented original composition or exploring deep improvisational space at the outer edges of the banjo solar system. Tony is one of the banjo's most gifted composers, and he's a stellar instructor and author as well. His boundless curiosity and enthusiastic sense of exploration have influenced all banjo players in his wake. His recent recording, *Great Big World,* reveals all the various aspects of his musical genius.

Murphy Henry (1952–)

Known equally for her writing, teaching, and playing, Murphy is the author of the classic study *Pretty Good for a Girl: Women in Bluegrass,* and is the co-creator of the Murphy Method, a way of teaching that has helped thousands of adult learners to play bluegrass banjo without using tablature. She is a tireless spokesperson for women in bluegrass and a rock-solid, hard-driving Scruggs banjo stylist who is now hosting women's banjo camps with daughter Casey in northern Virginia.

Béla Fleck (1958–)

Béla Fleck continues to break down musical barriers and establish new connections with every project he undertakes. The most celebrated banjo player in the world today, Béla has expanded our idea of what's possible on the banjo by making the instrument right at home in the jazz, classical, and rock worlds. In the process, he has inspired thousands to take up the instrument.

None of this would have happened if Béla hadn't brought an awe-inspiring technical facility and stunning musicality to all that he plays. Whether he's playing with jazz great Marcus Roberts, a symphony orchestra, or his wife, Abigail Washburn, his music always inspires and surprises.

Alison Brown (1962–)

Alison Brown is the consummate modern bluegrass banjo stylist. Her original music combines Irish, folk, Latin, and jazz influences performed with warmth and lyricism. Alison also certainly knows her bluegrass, as her recent recording, *The Company You Keep,* proves. She also owns her own record label, Compass Records, which has become an important player in the modern acoustic music industry. Catch her live on the road with the Alison Brown Quartet, featuring piano, bass, and drums.

Jens Kruger (1962–)

The future of bluegrass banjo goes international with the phenomenal Swiss musician Jens Kruger. Performing with his brother Uwe and bassist Joel Landsberg as the Kruger Brothers, Jens's musicality and emotional expression have connected strongly with audiences all over the world. Jens combines complete technical mastery with a strong musicality to play banjo music that both moves and amazes, which can be a rare thing these days! Lately, Jens has composed long-form compositions for the Kruger Brothers and a string quartet or orchestra. It's worth traveling a considerable distance to experience one of these performances.

Kristin Scott Benson (1976–)

A four-time International Bluegrass Music Association Banjo Player of the Year award winner (2008–2011), Kristin is one of today's top mainstream bluegrass banjo masters. One of the first female instrumentalists to be featured in nationally touring bands, these days Kristin can be heard with bluegrass powerhouses the Grasscals. Check out her recording *Second Season* to discover her exciting mix of traditional and contemporary banjo sounds and techniques.

Noam Pikelny (1981–)

Noam gained national attention as a member of the Punch Brothers, the band led by mandolin player extraordinaire Chris Thile, but you'll also find him out on the road leading his own ensembles and sharing stages with fiddler Stuart Duncan and vocalist Aiofe O'Donovan. Noam reflects the taste and sensibility of a new generation of banjo players who naturally look more to Béla Fleck, Tony Trischka, and Radiohead for inspiration than to Earl Scruggs or Don Reno. Noam is in the midst of raising the bar even higher on what can be technically and musically accomplished on the banjo. It'll be exciting to see what future directions his music will take! A recent recording, *Noam Pikelny Plays Kenny Baker Plays Bill Monroe,* brought him accolades and acceptance from the mainstream bluegrass community, which is good for both Noam and bluegrass music!

Chapter 16

Ten Strategies to Make You a Better Player (Right Now!)

*T*here never seems to be enough time to play banjo! When you do finally get the chance to sit down with your instrument, you want to be sure that you're making the very best use of your effort by practicing those things that will transport your playing to the next level as quickly as possible.

You'll play more if you're feeling good about what you're practicing. The tips in this chapter will help you maximize your practice sessions and point you in the right direction to reach all the destination points on your musical journey. As you read through these recommendations, think about how you can put them to good use the very next time you reach for your banjo.

Sweat the Details

Bluegrass banjo is a demanding musical art form characterized by precision and speed. Whether you're a beginner or a more experienced player, it's essential to discover and adopt great picking- and fretting-hand positions and playing techniques to bring out the best in your playing. Chapter 4 presents a complete guide to getting both hands in shape and ready to play.

The secret to playing fast is to first sound great playing slowly. You want to have every roll note and fretting technique in place before gradually increasing speed in your practice. Don't cut corners in this regard: If you need to play something *really* slowly in order to play it correctly, that's okay! You want to spend your practice time playing things well, and slow practice allows you to reinforce the fundamentals of playing accurately, with good rhythm and great tone. This is always practice time well spent!

Take It Step by Step

It's tempting to want to tackle some of the most challenging songs as performed by your banjo heroes. But you'll become a better player more quickly by trying out songs and arrangements that match your current ability level. Better yet, work on tunes and techniques that are just beyond what you're capable of comfortably playing right now. If you're a new player, stick to easier tunes and arrangements, and add a few new licks and techniques with each new song you play.

For most adult learners with busy lives who are picking up an instrument for the first time, it can take two to four years to play a handful of songs well and to feel comfortable playing with other musicians in medium-speed jam sessions. View your progress on the banjo as a long-range project, and you'll be able to set realistic goals that you can actually achieve. If you take it slow and steady, you'll become a better player before you know it.

Find a Good Teacher

There are more ways than ever to access banjo information these days, but nothing replaces a great one-on-one instructor to help guide your development as a banjo player. A good teacher will direct you to the right things to work on at the right time and help you chart a course through the sea of instructional materials that are out there so that you can choose the materials that best match your interest and ability level.

Begin your search for a teacher by contacting your local music store or a regional store that specializes in bluegrass music. In addition, many nationally known banjo players offer one-on-one online lessons via Skype. Subscription-based online video lessons are an affordable option that allows you to access a large body of materials that you can study at your own pace. (You can check out my online lessons at www.pegheadnation.com.)

Play with Others

You'll progress much more quickly in your banjo playing — and have an absolute blast doing it — if you can play with other musicians as much as possible. Bluegrass festivals and music camps are designed to bring together musicians of all experience levels to enjoy music making. But don't forget to also seek out the year-round jams that are taking place right in your own backyard at local music stores, coffeehouses, and churches.

Becoming a virtuoso banjo player can take a lifetime, but you can start playing with others by mastering just a few basic techniques. If you can pick a few roll patterns and change chords without stopping, you're ready to find a jam session! Bluegrass musicians almost always welcome new players to the fold. Soon you'll be picking up new songs by ear as you get familiar with the techniques that banjo players use to sound great in a bluegrass band.

Use the Metronome

Understanding how roll patterns and other techniques fit into the timing of songs is essential to good banjo playing, especially when playing with others. The best musicians in the world keep a metronome close at hand to ensure that they're playing in good rhythm when practicing.

For most musicians, the trickiest aspect of using the metronome is figuring out how to get started. Before you begin, you need to decide how many roll notes will equal one metronome click. Most banjo players choose to play two roll notes for each click when first learning a song, setting the metronome at a speed that's slow enough to play the song well.

When you're in the groove, you can use the metronome to help you gradually increase speed and to reveal problem areas that need your attention. When you make the metronome your constant practice companion, you'll dramatically improve your playing ability.

Flow with Your Rolls

In a bluegrass band or jam session, playing with good rhythm is everyone's responsibility. For banjo players, this means keeping an uninterrupted stream of steady roll notes emanating from your picking hand, no matter what moves your fretting hand may have up its sleeve.

Playing without stopping can be a big hurdle for beginners, which is why isolating this skill in practice sessions is important. Our brains just naturally want to pause, even if just for a moment, each time we move to a new chord or need to play a slide, hammer-on, or pull-off. When this happens to you, shift your attention to your picking hand and keep those roll patterns cooking, even if the fretting hand stumbles a bit at first. When the fretting fingers get the message, both hands will come together, and you'll discover that you've raised your playing yet another notch!

Listen, Watch, and Learn

You can put in practice time even when the banjo isn't in your hands. Spend as much time as you can listening and watching your favorite players, and analyze what you're seeing and hearing. The banjo has a unique role in the bluegrass band. As you observe others play, note the different techniques that are used to accompany singers and other instrumentalists (and then visit Chapters 9 and 10 to start creating your own great backup). As you actively listen, you're internalizing what the banjo is supposed to sound like, and in the process, you're understanding more about bluegrass banjo style.

As you watch others play, take in as many fine details as you can. Look at hand positions, body posture, strap placement, and how the hands pick and fret the strings. Check out the player's tone, volume, and rhythmic feel. If you're aspiring to play on stage, take note of how great players use microphones and sound systems to enhance their sound. These days, some banjo players, like Noam Pikelny, Tony Trischka, and yours truly, sport some pretty outrageous socks, too, so watch out for the more subtle aspects of your favorite banjo player's fashion statements.

If you have a long commute, make daily listening to great recordings a part of your rush-hour routine. Don't ignore the classic recordings of the first generation of bluegrass performers (like Bill Monroe, Flatt & Scruggs, Jim & Jesse, the Stanley Brothers, the Osborne Brothers, and Jimmy Martin). Their songs are the ones you'll encounter most often in jam sessions.

Use Your Ear More Than Tablature

When bluegrass musicians come together to play, they leave their music stands at home. Banjo tablature is designed to convey an amazing amount of detailed information, but when it's time to make music with others, you have to set the tab aside and rely on your ear to react musically to what's happening around you.

Some players reach a stage in their development where they have to actively disengage from their dependence upon tab to gain more confidence playing with others. Better to keep tab in its place from the very beginning by using it sparingly.

Each time you begin to work on a new song, find a good recording and get the sound of the tune in your head before investigating the tab. You can then use the tab to work out and remember the fine details. When you get the info you need from the printed page, it's best to take your eyes away and let your ears take over once again.

Make the online audio tracks and video clips your first destination as you work through the songs in *Bluegrass Banjo For Dummies,* and you'll be playing the tunes in this book sooner than you ever thought possible.

Practice Using Looping Techniques

One of the most efficient ways to make quick progress on the banjo is to repeat small phrases and licks over and over again until you're playing them well. When you practice this way without interrupting the rhythm, you're practicing using looping techniques.

Looping techniques allow you to play faster and memorize pieces more quickly. When you break down a song into its constituent licks and phrases, you're also gaining insight into how melodies are assembled in bluegrass banjo style and how licks can be used in different songs. Looping prepares you for creating your own solos as you internalize the licks and phrases you encounter when you practice in this way.

Track Your Progress

It's gratifying to listen to a recording you made of your playing six months ago and realize how much better you sound today. Keeping a record of what you play can help focus your practice efforts and allow you to feel good about all that you've accomplished on the banjo.

Many players jot down brief notes after each practice session, with metronome settings, commenting on what went well and what needs more work. Others keep a master list of the tunes they know so they'll have something ready to suggest at the next jam session. Dare to record yourself as often as you can stand it (with the metronome!). Listen critically, but don't beat up on yourself. Use what you hear to set new goals and get back to playing more banjo!

Part VII
Appendixes

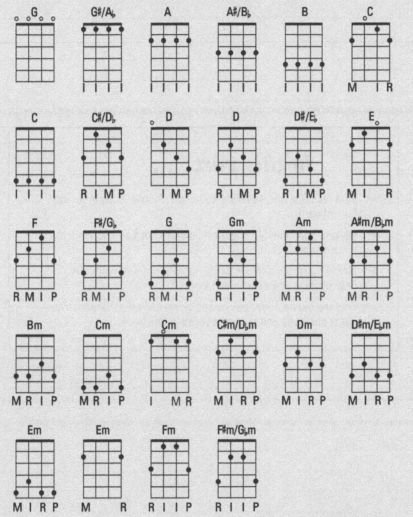

web extras

For Dummies can help you get started with lots of subjects. Visit www.dummies.com to learn more and do more with *For Dummies*.

In this part . . .

✔ Find major, minor, seventh, and ninth chords on your banjo fingerboard.

✔ Understand movable major and minor chord positions up the neck on your banjo.

✔ Name the notes on your banjo fingerboard and work out first-position scales in seven keys.

✔ Find the online audio tracks and video clips that demonstrate the techniques and songs covered in this book.

Appendix A

A Guide to Chords, Notes, and Major Scales

- -

Chords and chord progressions provide the basic framework for the music you create on the five-string banjo. Major and minor chords are what you use to play most bluegrass songs. Other kinds of chords — such as seventh, ninth, and diminished chords — are used frequently in blues and jazz styles and can also add spice to your bluegrass playing. The good news is that all the chords you need can be found in more than one place on your banjo fingerboard, within easy reach of wherever your fretting fingers may find themselves.

In addition to knowing your chords, getting acquainted with the names of the notes on each string will come in handy as you advance as a banjo player. As you create your own versions of songs, you'll most often use major scales, in various keys to play melodies.

A practical way to utilize the resources in this section is to gradually get comfortable with new chords and scales as you need them to play new songs. Be patient with your progress in this regard — you'll be training your ears in addition to your fingers!

Finding Chords

Figure A-1 presents the major and minor chords in all keys on the lower five frets of your banjo (sometimes called the *first position*). A few of these are *open*-position chords with one or more unfretted strings, but most are *closed*- or *movable*-position chords, which require you to fret all four strings.

The advantage of a movable-position chord is that you can play different chords by shifting the position up or down as needed. (Of course, the disadvantage is that you have to use three or four fingers to fret these kinds of chords!) The location of each chord corresponds to the order of the note names:

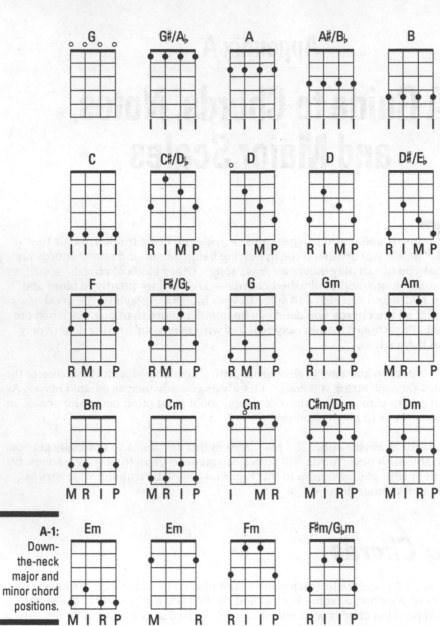

A-1: Down-the-neck major and minor chord positions.

G / G♯ or A♭ / A / A♯ or B♭ / B / C / C♭ or D♭ / D / D♭ or E♭ / E / F / F♯ or G♭

Line 4 of Figure A-1 provides chord diagrams for five different minor chords, all of which use the same fretted position. The second chord on this line is a C-minor chord that uses the same position as the B-minor chord that precedes it but is fretted one fret higher. If you look at the order of note names above, you see that B and C are next to one another, one fret apart on your banjo fingerboard.

Figure A-2 shows you sixth and ninth chord positions for G. These chords are commonly used in jazz and swing styles. Because all these chords are movable positions, you can locate any other sixth or ninth chord by moving up or down your fretboard the necessary number of frets. For instance, a C6 chord would be five frets higher than a G6 chord and a D6 chord, seven frets higher.

Figure A-3 is a movable chord chart showing you the distance between the different positions for the G, C, and D major, minor, and diminished chords. These chords are used frequently when playing up-the-neck backup (see Chapter 10).

Finding Notes

From from your open strings all the way up to the 22nd fret, there's a musical note name to match every note you can pick on your banjo. Figures A-4 through A-8 map out the notes you'll find along each of your five banjo strings in G tuning. Most players don't actively think of these individual note names in the middle of playing a song. But knowing your way around the fingerboard will help you to more quickly locate melody notes when you need them, as well as more easily combine notes to make chords.

Don't try to memorize the note names all at once. As you fret chords up the neck as part of your practice, every now and then, name the notes that make up each chord. Before long, the names and locations of these notes will become second nature.

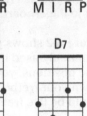
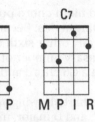

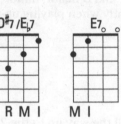

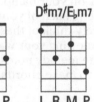
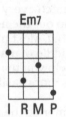

A-2: Sixth and ninth movable-chord positions for G.

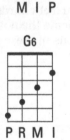
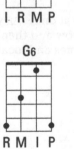

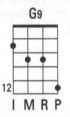

F-shape: ●
D-shape: ■
Barre-shape: ◆
□ = not necessarily fretted, but may be

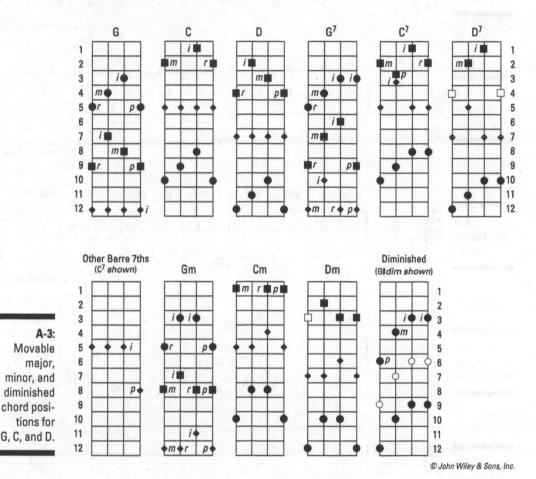

A-3:
Movable major, minor, and diminished chord positions for G, C, and D.

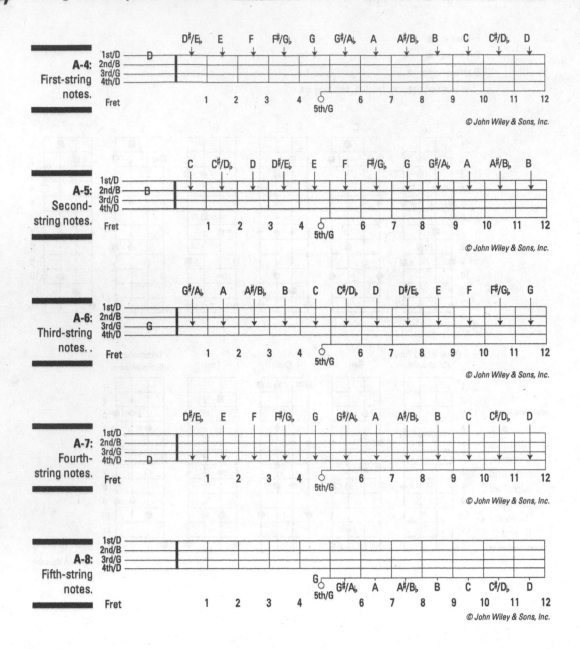

A-4: First-string notes.

A-5: Second-string notes.

A-6: Third-string notes.

A-7: Fourth-string notes.

A-8: Fifth-string notes.

© John Wiley & Sons, Inc.

Finding Major Scales

Many bluegrass melodies are assembled from the notes of a major scale (for more on the major scale, visit Chapter 8). Whether you're playing Scruggs, melodic, or single-string bluegrass banjo, knowing the notes of the major scale in the keys that you'll commonly use will help you in all aspects of playing, from creating solos to improvising.

Figures A-9 through A-15 show the positions for the notes of major scales in the keys of G, A, B♭, C, D, E, and F in the first position on your banjo. The first note of the scale (called the _tonic_) is in bold with the major scale notes that are found both above and below the tonic shown in each chart.

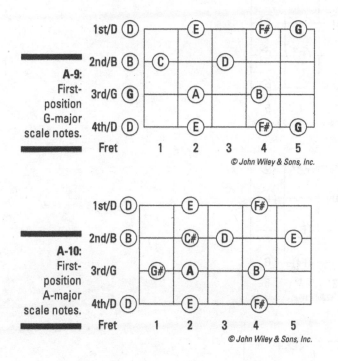

A-9:
First-position G-major scale notes.

© John Wiley & Sons, Inc.

A-10:
First-position A-major scale notes.

© John Wiley & Sons, Inc.

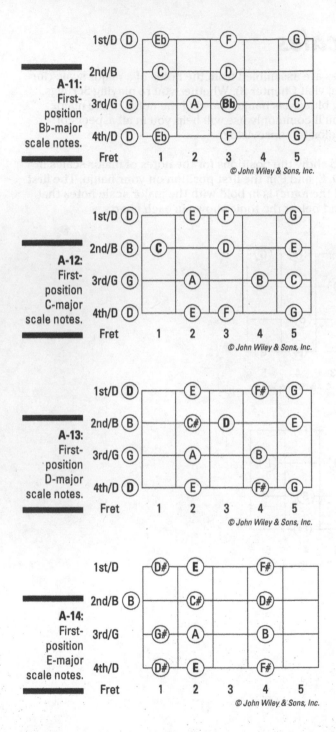

A-11: First-position Bb-major scale notes.

© John Wiley & Sons, Inc.

A-12: First-position C-major scale notes.

© John Wiley & Sons, Inc.

A-13: First-position D-major scale notes.

© John Wiley & Sons, Inc.

A-14: First-position E-major scale notes.

© John Wiley & Sons, Inc.

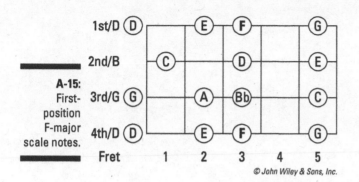

A-15: First-position F-major scale notes.

© John Wiley & Sons, Inc.

Appendix B

Audio Tracks and Video Clips

● ●

*Y*ou'll master the techniques, tunes, and licks in *Bluegrass Banjo For Dummies* much more quickly not only by consulting the banjo tablature but also by basing your understanding on seeing and hearing how each example is supposed to be played.

The Play This icon in the text directs you to the audio tracks and video clips that accompany this book. These examples cover everything from how to tune your banjo and change its strings, to hearing and seeing the most advanced playing techniques. You'll be glad to take the time to carefully explore these resources when you experience how they'll deepen your understanding and improve your playing.

If you've purchased the paper or e-book version of *Bluegrass Banjo For Dummies*, these audio tracks and video clips are available for you 24/7 at www.dummies.com/go/bluegrassbanjo. Best of all, you can download the audio tracks to your favorite digital device and take the music with you wherever you and your banjo may roam.

Listening to the Audio Tracks

Table B-1 is your complete guide to accessing the audio tracks that match every musical example in the book. Many of the songs have guitar accompaniment. Don't hesitate to try playing along with the tracks whenever you can.

Table B-1		Audio Tracks
Track Number	**Chapter**	**Description**
1	3	G-tuning reference notes
2	3	Tab rhythm exercise (Tab 3-2)
3	4	Strumming "This Land Is Your Land" chord progression (Tab 4-1)
4	4	Strumming "Wagon Wheel" chord progression (Tab 4-2)
5	4	Pinch patterns with G, C, D7, and Em chords (Tab 4-3)
6	4	"Will the Circle Be Unbroken" with pinch patterns (Tab 4-4)
7	4	"Long Journey Home" with pinch patterns (Tab 4-5)
8	5	Forward-reverse roll (Tab 5-1)
9	5	"Nine Pound Hammer" with forward-reverse roll (Tab 5-2)
10	5	"Little Maggie" with forward-reverse roll (Tab 5-3)
11	5	Alternating thumb roll (Tab 5-4)
12	5	"I'll Fly Away" with alternating thumb roll (Tab 5-5)
13	5	Forward rolls 1 and 2 (Tab 5-6), forward rolls 3 and 4 (Tab 5-7)
14	5	"Will the Circle Be Unbroken" with forward rolls (Tab 5-8)
15	5	Foggy Mountain rolls 1 and 2 (Tab 5-9)
16	5	"Long Journey Home" with Foggy Mountain rolls (Tab 5-10)
17	5	Roll demo: Lick roll (Tab 5-11), backward roll (Tab 5-12), middle leading/Osborne roll (Tab 5-13), index leading roll (Tab 5-14), Dixie Breakdown roll (Tab 5-15), and arpeggio roll (Tab 5-16)
18	5	Forward-reverse roll with variations (Tab 5-17)
19	5	Alternating thumb roll with variations (Tab 5-18)

Track Number	Chapter	Description
20	5	Forward roll with variations (Tab 5-19)
21	5	Foggy Mountain roll with variations (Tab 5-20)
22	5	Lick roll with variations (Tab 5-21)
23	5	"Nine Pound Hammer" with mixed roll patterns (Tab 5-22)
24	5	"Little Maggie" with mixed roll patterns (Tab 5-23)
25	6	Third-string slides, second to third fret (Tab 6-1), alternating thumb roll with third-string slides (Tab 6-2)
26	6	Third-string slides, second to fourth fret (Tab 6-3), forward roll with third-string slides (Tab 6-4), lick roll with third-string slides (Tab 6-5)
27	6	Fourth-string slides (Tab 6-6), forward roll with fourth-string slides (Tab 6-7), "Potatoes" intro with fourth-string slides (Tab 6-8)
28	6	First-string slides (Tab 6-9)
29	6	Third- and fourth-string hammer-ons (Tab 6-10)
30	6	Alternating thumb roll with third- and fourth-string hammer-ons (Tab 6-11), forward-reverse roll with third- and fourth-string hammer-ons (Tab 6-12)
31	6	Second- and third-string fretted hammer-ons (Tab 6-13), forward roll with second-string hammer-ons (Tab 6-14), Foggy Mountain roll with second-string hammer-ons (Tab 6-15)
32	6	First-, second-, and fourth-string pull-offs (Tab 6-16), alternating thumb roll with third- and fourth-string pull-offs (Tab 6-17)
33	6	Alternating thumb roll with third-string fretted pull-offs (Tab 6-18), forward-reverse roll with third-string slides and fretted pull-offs (Tab 6-19)

(Continued)

Table B-1 *(continued)*

Track Number	Chapter	Description
34	6	Second-string, tenth-fret choke demo (Tab 6-20), choke with Foggy Mountain roll (Tab 6-21)
35	6	Second-string tenth-fret bend and release chokes (Tab 6-22), pre-bend chokes (Tab 6-23), Foggy Mountain roll with chokes and pre-bend chokes (Tab 6-24)
36	7	Ten essential G licks (Tab 7-1)
37	7	Ten essential C licks (Tab 7-2)
38	7	Ten essential D licks (Tab 7-3)
39	7	Twelve essential fill-in licks (Tab 7-4)
40	7	"Banjo in the Hollow" with guitar accompaniment (Tab 7-5)
41	7	"Cripple Creek" (four versions) (Tabs 7-6, 7-7, 7-8, and 7-9)
42	7	"John Henry" with guitar accompaniment (Tab 7-10)
43	7	"John Hardy" with guitar accompaniment (Tab 7-11)
44	7	"Boil the Cabbage Down" with guitar accompaniment (Tab 7-12)
45	7	"Buffalo Gals" with guitar accompaniment (Tab 7-13)
46	7	"Train 45" with guitar accompaniment (Tab 7-14)
47	7	"Old Joe Clark" with guitar accompaniment (Tab 7-15)
48	7	"Cumberland Gap" with guitar accompaniment (Tab 7-16)
49	7	"Lonesome Road Blues" with guitar accompaniment (Tab 7-17)
50	7	"Reuben" with guitar accompaniment (Tab 7-18)
51	8	G-major scale (Tab 8-1)
52	8	"I'll Fly Away" basic melody with guitar accompaniment (Tab 8-2)

Track Number	Chapter	Description
53	8	"Long Journey Home" basic melody with guitar accompaniment (Tab 8-3)
54	8	"You Are My Sunshine" basic melody with guitar accompaniment (Tab 8-4)
55	8	"I'll Fly Away" using alternating thumb rolls with guitar accompaniment (Tab 8-14)
56	8	"Long Journey Home" using forward-reverse rolls with guitar accompaniment (Tab 8-15)
57	8	"You Are My Sunshine" using forward rolls with guitar accompaniment (Tab 8-16)
58	8	"I'll Fly Away" using fretting techniques with guitar accompaniment (Tab 8-17)
59	8	"Long Journey Home" using fretting techniques with guitar accompaniment (Tab 8-18)
60	8	"You Are My Sunshine" using fretting techniques with guitar accompaniment (Tab 8-19)
61	8	"Will the Circle Be Unbroken" solo with guitar accompaniment (Tab 8-20)
62	8	G modal scale (Tab 8-21)
63	8	"Man of Constant Sorrow" basic melody (Tab 8-22) and using forward rolls with guitar accompaniment (Tab 8-23)
64	8	"Cluck Old Hen" with guitar accompaniment (Tab 8-24)
65	8	Using licks to build a solo, version 1 (Tab 8-25) and version 2 (Tab 8-26) with guitar accompaniment
66	8	"Roll in My Sweet Baby's Arms" with guitar accompaniment (Tab 8-27)
67	8	Up-the-neck G fill-in lick (Tab 8-28) and bend lick (Tab 8-29), essential C and D licks (Tabs 8-30 and 8-31)
68	8	Up-the-neck solo using G, C, and D licks (Tab 8-32)

(Continued)

Table B-1 *(continued)*

Track Number	Chapter	Description
69	9	"Nine Pound Hammer" backup with alternating thumb rolls with guitar accompaniment (Tab 9-1)
70	9	"Will the Circle Be Unbroken" backup with forward-reverse rolls with guitar accompaniment (Tab 9-2)
71	9	Forward roll patterns for backup (Tab 9-3)
72	9	G fill-in licks (Tab 9-4)
73	9	"Roll in My Sweet Baby's Arms" forward roll backup with fill-in licks with guitar accompaniment (Tab 9-5)
74	9	"Blue Ridge Cabin Home" progression backup using two-measure forward rolls with guitar accompaniment (Tab 9-6)
75	9	Forward roll backup in the key of C with guitar accompaniment (Tab 9-7)
76	9	Forward roll backup using slides (Tab 9-8)
77	9	Forward roll G to C backup (Tab 9-9)
78	9	"Blue Ridge Cabin Home" progression backup mixing techniques with guitar accompaniment (Tab 9-10)
79	9	"Your Love Is Like a Flower" progression backup mixing techniques with guitar accompaniment (Tab 9-11)
80	9	"Sally Goodin'" backup with guitar accompaniment (Tab 9-12)
81	9	"Whiskey Before Breakfast" backup with guitar accompaniment (Tab 9-13)
82	10	G–C–D progression with F-shape vamping (Tab 10-1)
83	10	I–IV–V progressions in the keys of C and D with F-shape vamping (Tabs 10-2 and 10-3)
84	10	Vamping in the key of G using F and D chord shapes (Tab 10-4)
85	10	"Nine Pound Hammer" vamping using D- to F-shape transitions with guitar accompaniment (Tab 10-5)

Track Number	Chapter	Description
86	10	"Salty Dog Blues" vamping using F- and D-shape transitions with guitar accompaniment (Tab 10-6)
87	10	"In the Mood" backup pattern (Tab 10-7)
88	10	"Nine Pound Hammer" with "In the Mood" backup pattern with guitar accompaniment (Tab 10-8)
89	10	"Nine Pound Hammer" with "In the Mood" backup pattern using slides with guitar accompaniment (Tab 10-9)
90	10	"In the Mood" backup pattern with fourth-string slide (Tab 10-10)
91	10	"Blue Ridge Cabin Home" progression with "In the Mood" patterns with fretted fifth-string with guitar accompaniment (Tab 10-11)
92	10	Basic D-shape backup lick (Tab 10-12), Earl Scruggs's D-shape lick (Tab 10-13), J. D. Crowe's D-shape lick (Tab 10-14)
93	10	"Blue Ridge Cabin Home" progression backup with D-shape and "In the Mood" backup licks with guitar accompaniment (Tab 10-15)
94	10	"Blue Ridge Cabin Home" progression backup using advanced D-shape and "In the Mood" licks with guitar accompaniment (Tab 10-16)
95	10	"Six White Horses" licks (Tab 10-17)
96	10	"Salty Dog Blues," "Blue Ridge Cabin Home," and "Your Love Is Like a Flower" up-the-neck backup fill-in licks (Tabs 10-18, 10-19, and 10-20)
97	10	Two-finger backup licks (Tab 10-21)
98	10	"Bury Me Beneath the Weeping Willow" using two-finger backup licks with guitar accompaniment (Tab 10-22)
99	11	G-major scale using melodic techniques (Tab 11-2)

(Continued)

Table B-1 *(continued)*

Track Number	Chapter	Description
100	11	Expanded G-major scale (Tab 11-3) and with position shift (Tab 11-4)
101	11	Expanded G-major scale using fretted fifth string (Tabs 11-5 and 11-6)
102	11	G-major scale, two octaves (Tab 11-7)
103	11	Up-the-neck melodic lick (Tab 11-8) and cascading melodic lick (Tab 11-9)
104	11	"The Girl I Left Behind Me" with guitar accompaniment (Tab 11-10)
105	11	"Devil's Dream" with guitar accompaniment (Tab 11-11)
106	11	"Katy Hill" with guitar accompaniment (Tab 11-13)
107	11	"Cherokee Shuffle" with guitar accompaniment (Tab 11-14)
108	11	C-major scale using melodic techniques (Tab 11-15)
109	11	"Soldier's Joy" with guitar accompaniment (Tab 11-16)
110	11	"Billy in the Lowground" with guitar accompaniment (Tab 11-17)
111	11	D-major scale, two octaves (Tab 11-18)
112	11	"Angeline the Baker" with guitar accompaniment (Tab 11-19)
113	11	"St. Anne's Reel" with guitar accompaniment (Tab 11-20)
114	11	A Mixolydian scale (Tab 11-21)
115	11	"June Apple" with guitar accompaniment (Tab 11-22)
116	12	Basic single-string technique (Tabs 12-1 and 12-2)
117	12	Single-string crossover technique (Tabs 12-3, 12-4, and 12-5)
118	12	Single-string technique using middle finger (Tabs 12-6 and 12-7)

Track Number	Chapter	Description
119	12	Single-string technique in 6/8 time (Tabs 12-8 and 12-9)
120	12	G-major scale using open and closed positions (Tabs 12-10 and 12-11)
121	12	D-major scale using open and closed positions (Tabs 12-12 and 12-13)
122	12	G-major scales, middle- and index-finger positions (Tabs 12-14 and 12-15)
123	12	Modes in G major: Dorian (Tab 12-16a), Phrygian (Tab 12-16b), Lydian (Tab 12-16c), Mixolydian (Tab 12-16d), Aeolian (12-16e), and Locrian (Tab 12-16f)
124	12	"Sally Goodin'" with guitar accompaniment (Tab 12-17)
125	12	"Whiskey Before Breakfast" with guitar accompaniment (Tab 12-18)
126	12	"Blackberry Blossom" with guitar accompaniment (Tab 12-19)
127	12	"Lynchburg Blues" with guitar accompaniment (Tab 12-20)
128	12	"The Famous Ballymote" with guitar accompaniment (Tab 12-21)
129	12	"Morrison's Jig" with guitar accompaniment (Tab 12-22)

Watching the Video Clips

Table B-2 lists the video clips that accompany each chapter.

Table B-2		Video Clips
Clip Number	Chapter	Description
1	3	G tuning using relative tuning and an electronic tuner
2	4	Fretting and changing chords

(Continued)

Table B-2 *(continued)*

Clip Number	Chapter	Description
3	4	Fitting fingerpicks
4	4	Finding picking-hand position
5	4	Playing the pinch pattern (Tab 4-3)
6	5	Forward-reverse roll (Tab 5-1)
7	5	Alternating thumb roll (Tab 5-4)
8	6	Fretting-hand techniques: Slides (Tab 6-1)
9	6	Fretting-hand techniques: Hammer-ons (Tab 6-10)
10	6	Fretting-hand techniques: Pull-offs (Tab 6-16)
11	6	Fretting-hand techniques: Chokes (Tab 6-20)
12	7	Ten essential G licks (Tab 7-1)
13	7	Ten essential C licks (Tab 7-2)
14	7	Ten essential D licks (Tab 7-3)
15	7	Twelve essential fill-in licks (Tab 7-4)
16	7	"Banjo in the Hollow" (Tab 7-5)
17	7	"Cripple Creek" (four versions) (Tabs 7-6, 7-7, 7-8, and 7-9)
18	7	"Old Joe Clark" (Tab 7-15)
19	7	"Lonesome Road Blues" (Tab 7-17)
20	8	"I'll Fly Away" (Tab 8-17)
21	8	"Long Journey Home" (Tab 8-18)
22	8	"You Are My Sunshine" (Tab 8-19)
23	8	"Man of Constant Sorrow" basic melody and solo (Tab 8-23)
24	8	Up-the-neck solo using G, C, and D licks (Tab 8-32)
25	9	"Blue Ridge Cabin Home" progression down-the-neck backup (Tab 9-10)
26	10	Vamping techniques (Tab 10-1)
27	10	"Blue Ridge Cabin Home" progression up-the-neck backup (Tab 10-16)

Clip Number	Chapter	Description
28	10	Up-the-neck backup fill-in licks (Tabs 10-17, 10-18, 10-19, and 10-20)
29	11	Playing in melodic style (Tabs 11-2, 11-3, and 11-4)
30	11	G-major melodic-style scales using fretted fifth string (Tabs 11-5 and 11-6)
31	11	"Katy Hill" (Tab 11-13)
32	12	Single-string picking-hand exercises (Tabs 12-1 through 12-9)
33	12	Playing single-string scales (Tabs 12-10 through 12-15)
34	12	Playing G-major modes (Tab 12-16)
35	12	"Whiskey Before Breakfast" (Tab 12-18)
36	12	"Blackberry Blossom" (Tab 12-19)
37	14	Changing banjo strings

310   Bluegrass Banjo For Dummies

Index

About the Author

Although there are several well-known musicians with the name **Bill Evans,** it's a good thing for you that the author of this book is the internationally celebrated five-string banjo player. Bill decided to take up the five-string banjo in the 1970s as a teenager after watching Roy Clark play "Cripple Creek" on the TV show *Hee Haw* and he's never looked back. Forty-plus years later, he is one of the world's most beloved banjo players, known equally for his musicianship, performing, composing, teaching, and writing.

Bill has an inordinate amount of formal education for a five-string banjo player, with undergraduate and graduate degrees in anthropology and music from the University of Virginia and the University of California, Berkeley. However, Bill has never let his education get in the way of his music. He has performed and recorded with such bluegrass luminaries as J. D. Crowe, Tony Trischka, Noam Pikelny, Bill Keith, Alan Munde, David Grisman, The Infamous Stringdusters, Dan Crary, Peter Rowan, David Bromberg, Dry Branch Fire Squad, Fletcher Bright, and Hazel Dickens, among many others. He has also performed on *A Prairie Home Companion,* performed with the San Francisco Symphony, and toured Russia for the U.S. State Department.

Bill is a prolific recording artist with numerous solo, duo, and band releases. His recent number-one chart-topping CD, *In Good Company,* features 26 guest artists and was named to many "Best of the Year" critics' lists.

Bill is the author of *Banjo For Dummies.* He hosts six instructional DVDs for Homespun Music, AcuTab Publications, and the Murphy Method. He is also the author of *Parking Lot Picker's Songbook: Banjo Edition* and *Absolute Beginners: Banjo,* and he hosts his own banjo camps in Tennessee and California, in addition to teaching all over the world.

If that's not enough, Bill might have taught more five-string banjo players than just about anyone else in the universe. His students include many of today's top professional players, including Chris Pandolfi, Greg Liszt, Jayme Stone, Wes Corbett, Snap Jackson, and Erik Yates. Through his one-on-one lessons, group workshops, music camps, and Peghead Nation online banjo instruction, Bill has helped thousands of players and earned a reputation as a practical teacher whose methods are perfectly suited for the adult learner.

To find out more about Bill, visit www.billevansbanjo.com. Check out www.youtube.com/BillEvansBanjo for performance videos and more.

Dedication

Behind every banjo player should stand a family as supportive as mine! I dedicate this book to my wife, Kathy, and my children, Jesse and Corey. Thanks for accompanying me on this banjo journey for all these years!

Author's Acknowledgments

I would like to take this opportunity to thank just some of the many banjo players who have so generously helped me over many years of friendship and music making. These include Bob Zentz, Duff Porter, Ben Eldridge, Tony Trischka, Alan Munde, Bill Keith, Sonny Osborne, J. D. Crowe, John Hartford, Pete Wernick, Bob Carlin, Jody Stecher, and Ned Luberecki, among many others.

Thanks to Ann Jefferson, Ron Thomason, Larry Cohea, Cindy Sinclair, John Lawless, Don Nitchie, Murphy Henry, Ronnie Bales, Ken Perlman, Dix Bruce, and Happy Traum for their friendship, professional advice, moral support, and emergency banjo repair!

Thank you to Stan Werbin and Dave Machette at Elderly Instruments and to Anne Hamersky for providing most of the photos included in this book. Thanks also to Janet and Greg Deering and David Brandrowski of Deering Banjos for providing yet another fantastic cover shot and to Larry Marcus and Noam Pikelny for their photo contributions.

I am grateful to my Wiley team of Elizabeth Kuball, David Lutton, Kara Barnard, Paul Chen, Shelley Lea, Eric Hurst, and Lisa Holloway and to Carole Jelen at Waterside Productions, who all gracefully and patiently helped me through every stage of this project. A special thanks to Jim Nunally, who produced and played guitar on this book's accompanying audio tracks. Great work, as always, Jim!

Publisher's Acknowledgments

Assistant Editor: David Lutton

Project Editor: Elizabeth Kuball

Copy Editor: Elizabeth Kuball

Technical Editor: Kara Barnard

Art Coordinator: Alicia B. South

Project Coordinator: Patrick Redmond

Photographer: Anne Hamersky

Cover Image: © Chris Bryan/Deering Banjo Company